RETHINKING
COLLEGE
EDUCATION

RETHINKING
COLLEGE
EDUCATION

George Allan

University Press of Kansas

© 1997 by the University Press of Kansas
All rights reserved

Published by the University Press of Kansas (Lawrence, Kansas 66049),
which was organized by the Kansas Board of Regents and is operated and
funded by Emporia State University, Fort Hays State University, Kansas
State University, Pittsburg State University, the University of Kansas, and
Wichita State University

Library of Congress Cataloging-in-Publication Data

Allan, George, 1935–
    Rethinking college education / George Allan.
        p.   cm.
    Includes bibliographical references and index.
    ISBN 0-7006-0842-7 (alk. paper)
    1. Education, Higher—United States—Philosophy.   2. Education,
Higher—Aims and objectives—United States.   3. Educational change—
United States.   I. Title.
√LB2322.2.A45   1997
    378.73—dc21   97-11680

British Library Cataloguing in Publication Data is available.

Printed in the United States of America

10 9 8 7 6 5 4 3 2 1

To Marie Baker—
friend, secretary, office manager, counselor,
font of knowledge, morale booster, de facto dean

A university is not a machine for achieving a particular purpose or producing a particular result; it is a manner of human activity. . . . The pursuit of learning is not a race in which the competitors jockey for the best place, it is not even an argument or a symposium; it is a conversation. And the peculiar virtue of a university . . . [is that] it imparts something without having expressly to teach it; and what it imparts in this way is at least the manners of the conversation.

—*Michael Oakeshott*

Contents

Acknowledgments   xi

Introduction   1

1. The College as Faithful Community   13

2. The College as Guild of Inquirers   43

3. The College as Resource Center   77

4. The Essence of a College   109

5. The Playfulness of a College   147

6. The Standards of a College   187

Index   223

Acknowledgments

I would like to thank the following people for their willingness to think with me about the nature of a college education. Dickinson faculty and administration colleagues: Marge Fitzpatrick, Peggy Garrett, GailAnn Rickert, Phil Grier, Gisela Roethke, Cyril Dwiggins, Cheri Quinn, Joan Bechtel, Dan Bechtel, Steve MacDonald, Susan Nichols, Peter Balcziunas, and Lee Fritschler. Colleagues and friends elsewhere: John Ramsay, John Lachs, Don Sherburne, James Allan, Malcolm Evans, Bob Gowin, Pete A. Y. Gunter, Joan Mazur, and Sally Fellows. Teachers and students at Wilmette Junior High School, Wilmette, Illinois, and its principal, Christine Golden. I would also like to thank Nancy Scott, acquisitions editor at the University Press of Kansas, for her timely interest and help.

A long time ago I published an article on "The Neglected Focus in American Education: The Conversation of a College" (*Soundings: An Interdisciplinary Journal* 66 [1983]: 109–30). It offers the critique of essential purposes that is central to this book and provides the basics of the threefold typology of purpose-defined institutions so important to my argument. It is a grandparent of this book, about as similar and as different from its descendant as most grandparents are from their grandchildren. I am grateful to *Soundings* for its permission to use the ideas from that article and on occasion to use phrases and sentences verbatim.

The epigraph for this book is taken from Michael Oakeshott's essay "The Idea of a University," first published by *The Listener* in 1950. His essay is included in *The Voice of Liberal Learning: Michael Oakeshott on Education,* edited by Timothy Fuller (New Haven, Conn.: Yale University Press, 1989), pp. 95–104. The quotes are from pages 96, 98, and 99.

Introduction

This is a book about education. In reading it, I hope that you will come to agree with me that some features of learning are essential to becoming properly educated, but that these features are too often overlooked in contemporary America.

This is a book about human communities. We can agree, I hope, that an important part of education takes place within socially sanctioned institutional structures. In America these are called schools, including at the most sophisticated levels of education our colleges and universities. I will be arguing that we should be far less interested in *what* these structures are than in *how* they are structured. Why educational features of our schools that should not be overlooked have in fact been overlooked is because we tend to look at the "what" rather than the "how" of things. My goal is to shift your attention from the nouns and verbs of education to the adverbs.

This is a book about metaphysics. Societies such as our own, in addition to sanctioning institutional structures, also foment conceptual structures: frameworks for shaping experience meaningfully. Institutional structures, indeed, are expressions of conceptual structures. Our schools are pictures of how we think. Our sense of self and society and world, and the beliefs and practices that express that sense, are functions of the worldview that emerges from the cultural traditions within which we live from birth to death. The conceptual structures of American culture are why the institutional structures of our colleges and universities overlook important features of how students should be educated.

This is a book about reform. I want us to look at what has been overlooked. I want Americans to reform how they teach students. Therefore I want us to alter how our schools structure learning, which means that I think our cultural point of view should shift. I would like to begin by nudging your cultural point of view, enough so that you become convinced that America is not educating its students properly.

1

But I cannot lay my case before you as though it were a lawyer's brief, presenting some carefully developed contentions and the reasons in support of them. Because what is at issue are not matters of social policy and institutional programs. I do not want to create yet one more special commission white paper, one more task force report. You already know what any such study will recommend: higher standards, better facilities, more fully integrated courses of study, more interactive pedagogies, clearer assessment tools, more competent and productive teachers and faculty, and leaner administrations. Helpful as these studies may be, they all presuppose their frames of reference. They all take for granted the moral, cognitive, and affective footings for the edifice they hope to repaint, repair, remodel, or replace. But these presuppositions are what are at issue. It is not the programs and policies of our schools, colleges, and universities that need rethinking and reworking, but their assumptions about the nature of the world, about how people become persons within that world, and about why they do.

So, finally, this is a book about indirection. We never think we have any presuppositions, for presuppositions are what we can see in others but not in ourselves. Consequently, this book will need to find a way to show what it cannot always tell: that we, individually and as a society, have certain presuppositions, that they are inadequate, and that they need to change.

These are tough times for America's academic institutions, as you well know. The providers of education in the United States, from day-care centers to elderhostel programs, are under attack for failing in one degree or another to do their job. You have probably had occasion yourself to voice such criticisms, perhaps to engage in some action aimed at convincing teachers, school administrators, or public officials that a certain educational situation is intolerable and needs immediate attention.

The growing disparity between the cost of education and the ability—or the willingness—of taxpayers, parents, and philanthropists to pay for it has sharpened the point on these criticisms. You are hardly unreasonable to insist on getting something of obvious value in return for expending so many hard-earned dollars. You want a good return on your investment, especially when your current funds are tight, your sources of income increasingly at risk, and the items on your list of needs far more than you can hope to satisfy.

The pinch is pandemic. Your family budget is a poor match for almost all private school, college, or university tuitions, and for more and more public ones as well. The financial aid resources of governments are dwindling because the political climate you helped create has demonized taxation as an instrument for achieving communal values. Educational institutions, with a few exceptions, have been unable to make up the difference through their own resources, because their own fund-raising efforts increase income only marginally while the cost of educational materials—books and periodicals, libraries and cybernetic networks, scientific equipment and artistic supplies, high tech classrooms and student support services—grows considerably faster than the overall inflation rate.

So you and the communities to which you belong struggle to determine their priorities. You are worried about the quality of your neighborhood grade school but don't think you can afford the time and money necessary to switch your children into a magnet school, religious school, or private academy. You wonder whether a traditional college education has any worthwhile purpose, whether it is any longer a relevant way for your children or for you to acquire the practical skills needed in order to get a good job and live satisfying and productive lives. You go over your budget for charities, paring back on gifts that seem not to deliver what they have promised or that allow too much of their income to be spent on overhead. You vote for politicians who promise to reduce your taxes by hard-nosed strategies of retrenchment at the local, state, or national level that are akin to what you are doing to your home budget. The impact on education of these parsimonious decisions has been immediate and in some cases immediately devastating. You have not merely sharpened the point of your criticisms but barbed them as well.

In response, schools, colleges, and universities have been busy of late rethinking and rearticulating what they take to be their essential purpose, then reshaping their academic curricula and nonclassroom environments accordingly. Institutions of every sort do long-range planning, and our nation's educational institutions are no exception. The usual framework for a "strategic plan" is a decade. First, information is compiled on what the school, college, or university has done over the past five years, what has been happening in the wider educational and societal environments, and what have been the dynamics of the interaction between the institution and these environments. The institution has confronted a myriad of problems during the last half decade or so. Some it has addressed, others it has finessed. A few problems have been allowed to fester without anyone paying them much attention. Opportunities have presented themselves, and some have been exploited wonderfully while others have been ignored. Most attempts to capitalize on an opportunity have fallen short of success or have taken some unexpected turn.

With this historical and contextual information in hand, long-range planners then analyze these experiences and shape them into interpretations that reveal trends. These are extrapolated into five-year projections. When done across the whole range of factors from admissions to alumni affairs, from physical plant to graduate programs, from playgrounds to coliseums, from cleaning people to chancellors, the resulting matrix of past and anticipated practices permits—or rather requires—relevant decision-makers to construct alternative possible courses of action and to commit the institution to one of them. Such plans of action can be as precise as the formulas of a management by objectives statement, a response to state-mandated standards document, or an outcomes analysis report, replete with explicitly stated goals, objectives, and implementation strategies. Or they can be no more than a vaguely perceived and vaguely expressed sense of direction, a lot of pious aspiration seasoned with a tablespoon of presumed good luck.

Strategic planning in the last few years, however, has taken on an urgency it did not have for half a century. This urgency is because of the growing intensity of the negative criticisms voiced by you and your neighbors, criticisms not just voiced but translated into shrinking resources. Planning becomes very important if a perspicacious plan of action, astutely carried out, can make the difference between survival and bankruptcy. Sometimes even the mere appearance of such planning can make the difference by reassuring parents, taxing authorities, and benefactors that the institution is stable, well-run, and knows what it is doing. This supposition is why school, college, and university planning of late has involved a reexamination of charters, mission statements, and other expressions of the institution's primary purpose. With survival at stake, nothing can be merely presumed. Perhaps the school's founding aims will need to be changed; perhaps by returning to its originating dreams the college can renew and deepen its sense of purpose. Whatever the result of any such reconsideration of first principles, the fact that planning now always encompasses serious and systematic foundational considerations is ample proof that what is at issue is a matter of institutional life or death.

Although responses of this sort to your criticisms are going on at the primary and secondary school levels in almost every community throughout the United States, and in all three thousand or more of the institutions composing the American higher education industry, they are occurring with exceptional poignancy among the private liberal arts colleges. These colleges, after all, have prided themselves on being the paradigms for American education. If they are in trouble, can the other citadels of learning be far behind? There are some who argue that the liberal arts are out-of-date and deserve to die in the demise of the millennium that has for so long nurtured them. But for others, myself included, without its paradigms higher education in America will lose its way. As Amherst goes, or for that matter as Morningside College goes, so goes the nation.

Partly for this reason, my perspective in this book will have its standpoint in that mode of education called the liberal arts and in that mode of its institutional expression called the college. Since for nearly all of my career I have been associated with Dickinson College, a private, four-year undergraduate liberal arts institution, my examples and intuitions are inevitably going to be biased by this biographical fact. The other reason for my standpoint, not surprisingly, is that no one's knowledge anymore is sufficient to encompass adequately the motley of important things that go on in America at all the elementary schools, secondary schools, community colleges, four-year colleges, comprehensive colleges, general universities, and research universities, some private and some public, educating students, from the metropolitan or county area, the region, or the nation, late adolescents or working adults or senior citizens, men and women with all kinds of cultural heritages, economic resources, sexual orientations, and religious beliefs, full-time or part-time, residential or commuting.

So as a reminder of the standpoint from which I generalize, and for the sake of orthographical efficiency, I will usually let the word "college" serve as a synecdoche for everything from the Omaha public school system to Grinnell College, from Central Oregon Community College to Harvard University. In doing so, I am obviously claiming that there is something fundamentally similar about the conditions for education at these otherwise very different institutions. What is similar is an often overlooked feature essential to education, a feature pushed even further into obscurity by the current frenetic effort of educational institutions to define their purposes more clearly.

Colleges need to have clearly stated goals by means of which they are guided in conceiving, implementing, and evaluating their academic programs and support activities. These goals, if they are genuine, will point toward real anticipated results. The success of the college's goals can therefore be assessed by looking at what has actually resulted from actions undertaken under the aegis of those goals. There is a lot of good sense to this. As colleges find themselves forced by the grim circumstance of dwindling resources to change what wares they offer, and for whom, how, when, and even where they ply their trade, a recourse to statements of institutional purpose and achievement is the better part of wisdom. Where budgets must be trimmed, programs cut, and faculty or staff let go, it is best that the reason be some sense of institutional priority as defined by its fundamental educational purposes and a clear-eyed sense of what sort of education it in fact provides. The alternative to judgments based on well-honed institutional purposes is the age-old practice of jockeying for power, which in a time of abundance fosters the politics of accommodation but in times of scarcity descends to the brutish, nasty stratagems of that all too familiar Hobbesian war of each against all.

The importance of a college fully understanding what it is doing is driven home by another source as well: students and their ever-insistent parents. Having discovered their rights as consumers, prospective freshmen want explicit assurance that their tuition dollars are buying something worth the price. Everywhere across the nation, majors are increasingly selected with employment opportunities in mind. Engineering and management majors flourish, and literature professors find themselves transformed into instructors of business English or tutors in social welfare Spanish. The success rate for placement in first jobs, medical school, law school, or corporate boardrooms is taken to be as important as SAT or ACT averages in judging a college's quality. Catalogues boast of their career placement offices as loudly as they once bragged about the number of their Rhodes scholars.

These efforts, sadly enough, have only tended to exacerbate the problem. You are not impressed, and so the place you give to education in your hierarchy of importances continues its steady descent. I think that the reason for your growing disaffection has to do with the growing emphasis on college purposes. Your skepticism about education is not a result of the colleges failing to state their purposes and outcomes clearly enough or to carry out effectively their long-range plans. The problem is that the colleges think their purposes are essential to what they are and do, that clarity in the definition of institutional purpose and effectiveness in the realization of that purpose are the most important items on their agendas. Unfortunately, this assumption is a radically truncated way to understand the nature of education. It is at best a half-truth and, therefore, when taken as the whole, pernicious. What the process of education is all about, and thus what the place of educational institutions is within American society, cannot be understood solely in terms of purposes. The educational process cannot be reduced to talk of missions, goals, objectives, and learning outcomes.

So I want to change how you view education. I would like to see education slide back up the scale of things that are important for you and for the communities to which you belong, until it is right up near the top. That is its proper place, I would argue, and this book is my effort to convince you that I am right. What I want to convince you of is this: that a college essentially serves no purpose, and that colleges betray their stewardship of that essence by attempting to argue otherwise.

It is okay for a college to have a purpose, but whatever that purpose might happen to be is not essential to the education a college provides. What is essential to a college is intrinsic to it, something without which it could no longer function as a college. Because purposes are necessarily extrinsic, they can change, and with changing circumstances they in response should also change. A college's purposes can be altered without sacrificing what is essential to it as a college. But, in contrast, if a college thinks its purposes are essential, and so if students, instructors, administrators, and benefactors forget what is really essential about what they are doing, then the results will be exactly what we are currently witnessing. The college, having lost its vital center, will begin a slow descent that soon slips into dysfunction, gives way to systemic corruption, and eventuates in the death of the education the college had thought it was providing.

If you will agree to come with me, I am going to begin this book by taking you on a journey through three different educational worlds. Each is exemplified by actual learning environments, and the three of them can even be arranged plausibly in historical sequence with respect to the period of their greatest ascendency. Each educational world has framed the lives of real people, providing in the most fundamental way possible their sense of meaning, their sense of who they are and why. But although I will touch on concrete realities, my three educational worlds are abstract. They are models of worlds, designed to emphasize certain features of actual schools, colleges, and universities, but with the jagged edges smoothed out and the warts burned off. The feature I want to emphasize in each of these three educational models is the relation between a purpose and its metaphysical presuppositions. Each approach to education centers around a particular sense of institutional mission, and each does so because it has a particular view concerning the nature of things. I want in each case to spotlight that relationship.

The first model is of what I call a Faithful Community; the second, a Guild of Inquirers; the third, a Resource Center. For reasons that will eventually become clear, I will associate these models with premodern, modern, and postmodern ways of understanding. But it would be misleading to tie these different ways of understanding to particular periods of history, since all three are alive and well in American higher education here at the end of the twentieth century. In describing a cluster of beliefs, attitudes, and practices as premodern, I mean that its roots lie in an understanding of things that predates the Enlightenment. By modern, I mean the fundamental beliefs, attitudes, and practices that predominate in European cultures since the seventeenth century. And when I refer to another cluster as postmodern, I mean that its roots lie in an understanding that has rejected Enlightenment beliefs, attitudes, and practices. All three of these ways of life flourish in our contemporary world, often without those who compose them being able to articulate their premises, without many even being aware that their world differs in fundamental ways from those of their friends and neighbors.

Frederick Rudolph, one of the best historians of American higher education, in a 1992 essay for his class's fiftieth reunion and the college's two hundredth, characterized Williams College in terms of three "cultures," each dominant for an era in the college's history. He associates his trio of cultures—the Christian college, the gentleman's college, and the consumer's college—with premodern, modern, and postmodern sensibilities. But I see Rudolph's gentleman's college as merely a secular extension of the Christian college, both of which are definitely premodern. They are both, in their slightly different ways, what I call Faithful Communities. What Rudolph calls the consumer's college is akin to my model of the Resource Center, and educational institutions of this ilk are postmodern in their outlook on life. So Rudolph finds no place for what I have called a Guild of Inquirers, although the reason may be because his highly critical stance toward liberal arts colleges like his alma mater obscures his view of the degree to which they have at times reflected the essentially modernist commitments he favors and to which he associates the research university.

Bruce Kimball, in his important book *Orators and Philosophers,* offers an alternative typology of educational models in the form of a dipolar contrast between the "oratorical" and "philosophical" educational traditions in Western civilization. His distinction squares nicely with the difference between premodern and modern sensibilities. Ivan Illich's *In the Vineyard of the Text* echoes this distinction while exploring the difference between the understandings and technology that support a "monastic" reading of texts in contrast to a "scholastic" reading. Both Kimball and Illich mark the twelfth century as the point of transition to the scholastic world, although in the later chapters of his book Kimball is concerned with tracing the continuing struggle between the older and newer approaches to education, including the compromises that develop in the nineteenth and twentieth centuries, whereas Illich's interest is limited to what he thinks is the most crucial moment in that development, the shift away from a monastic approach to texts and the irreversible shift in worldviews that this change entailed. My first two models are in accord with these distinctions, even though by associating the Guild of Inquirers approach with the Enlightenment I focus upon a matured instance of modernism rather than upon its first flowering.

Even though I will adapt some of the historical distinctions made by Rudolph, Kimball, and Illich to my own typology, my emphasis is not historical. My models trace metaphysical differences rather than historical ones, and it would be quite possible, even appropriate, for me to propose that you consider a model for which there are few historical moments in which its world was predominant. As long as the model is coherent and consistent in the view of reality and the purposes for educational institutions it sketches, it is presumably capable of being instantiated in some actual college community in the form of charters and buildings, students and instructors. Such a rarely realized but nonetheless always realizable model might be thought of as a neglected ideal that I could propose should be given prominence. It would be a model sketched not to fill a slot in the logic of my typology but to invoke your belief in its importance, your conviction that it should guide needed educational reform, and your commitment to a course of action aimed at effecting that reform.

This is precisely what I will do, except that the fourth model of a college which I will propose differs from the other three in one important, transformative way. Faithful Communities, Guilds of Inquirers, and Resource Centers are all kinds of educational institutions determined by the ends they serve, the goals for the sake of which they were created as educational institutions. By emphasizing the dimension of institutional purpose in my first three models and by yoking purposes to worldviews, I hope not only to show you three approaches to education, and to make the strongest case possible for each one of them, but to convince you that all three are nonetheless fundamentally, essentially, inadequate. I hope to persuade you that these kinds of colleges are inadequate because they define themselves in terms of their purposes. The argument I cannot make in propositions but nonetheless hope to demonstrate is that the sorry state of most education in the United States results from the reduction of a college to the educational goals to which it is committed. If I am able to persuade you that this is so, then you will be interested in trying to understand the fourth model of education that I will eventually present. It will be the model of a college not defined by its purposes, an educational environment essentially without any purpose.

This notion of purposeless colleges may sound silly to you at the moment, but I am betting that your reaction will change by the time you have read through to the end of my book. Chapters 1, 2, and 3 display the three models of essentially purposive institutions. In order to make the strongest possible case for each model, I have written its chapter from within the perspective of the educational worldview exemplified and have tailored the style of the chapter (even including the method used for citing sources) to fit snugly around its contents. Chapter 4 shows why, despite their manifold virtues, these approaches are all deeply problematic ways to institutionalize education. This chapter and the next then explore my fourth model, that of an essentially purposeless college, one in which education has to do with learning the conditions for appropriate action independently of whatever purposes might motivate that action. I develop the notion of "moral practices" found in the work of Michael Oakeshott, and the similar notion of *phronēsis* in Aristotle, as a way to make this point. And I use "play" and "conversation" as root metaphors for getting at how the purposeless dimension of purposeful activity can best be learned.

In Chapter 5, I also return to the other three models and indicate how I think they can avoid the inadequacy to which they are prone by widening their institutional aims to make room for aimlessness. Chapter 6 explores these same ideas by means of "a quadrivial conversation" among the three purposeful and one purposeless educational models. The topic, selected with the oxymoronic mix of seriousness and playfulness appropriate to idle conversation, begins by considering whether or not educational standards can be devised for determining if students have learned anything in school. The topic eventually wanders off into a more general consideration of standards.

1
The College as Faithful Community

Be convinced that education and diligence are in the highest degree potent
to improve our nature, and associate yourself with the wisest of those who
are about you and send for the wisest men from abroad whenever this is
possible. And do not imagine that you can afford to be ignorant of any
one either of the famous poets or of the sages; rather you should listen to
the poets and learn from the sages and so equip your mind to judge those
who are inferior and to emulate those who are superior to yourself.
—*Isocrates, "To Nicoles" 12–13*

The American colonists, in founding their first colleges, spoke of them as
having a "mission." The heart and soul of a college lay in its sense of mission, its commitment to fulfilling the tasks with which society had charged
it. The faculty and overseers of a college had been sent on a mission and
were to be judged by how successfully they carried it out. The religious
overtones of the recurrent use of the word "mission" were not unintended.

The Puritans in particular had a clear sense of God's purpose for the
world and of the role they believed they were playing in its realization.
They had been sent on a divine mission to the New World. They had
trekked across the great Atlantic wilderness in order to found on its distant shores a model Christian community, a city set high on a hill for all
the world to see. By its light, first England would be led to Christ, the
gospel would then be spread throughout the earth, and, as a result, the
millennial rule of the Saints of the Most High would be ushered in. Unfortunately, the English were too preoccupied with their internal political
struggles to notice the New World beacon. Cromwell and the English Puritans, valuing the compromises necessary to gain political ascendency more
than the purity of soul necessary for a genuine covenantal relation with
God, indifferently turned their back on New England. Disconcerted but
resilient, the Puritans at Plymouth and Massachusetts Bay soon adjusted

their sense of purpose. They had been sent on a mission into the wilderness because God wanted them to build a godly commonwealth in the New World, not as an instrument for achieving some Old World purpose but as an end in itself.[1]

The world of the Puritans is purposeful through and through. The motion of the stars and the changing of the seasons are for the sake of their Creator, and people are born and die because of an end determined by Providence from before time began. If it should not be God's purpose that those He had sent to the New World be used as heralds of the thousand-year reign of the Saints, then most certainly there was some other purpose their arduous journey must be serving. They may have mistaken God's purpose for them but not that such a purpose existed. The contrary would be not only unthinkable but unimaginable. So it is not surprising that the New World settlers rebounded quickly from the failure of their original sense of mission by finding themselves a new mission. In a universe where to exist in any sense is to serve ends ordained by Providence, a question about the meaning of one's life is not ontological but moral. Not if there is a meaning, but how best to carry it out. The Puritan worry was not whether they swam in a sea of divine purpose, but whether in faithful obedience to that purpose they had caught the current rightly.

When the world is a function of the purpose for which it was fashioned, it is natural to think of human institutions as needing to be fashioned similarly. It would be unthinkable that a Puritan college not have a clearly understood educational purpose, a purpose fully conforming to and in some explicit way furthering God's purposes. The college, just like the church and the state, should be an instrument of the divine will. A college should be a microcosm of the macrocosm, mirroring the whole of which it is a part by conforming its finite and limited aims to the wider aims of society and ultimately to the transcendent aims of God. A college should not merely mirror those aims; it should arise from them.

The wider ends of church and state are what generate the need for educational institutions. Society's ends predefine what the purpose of its colleges must be, just as the wider ends of history predefine the ends of a particular society and the infinitely wide end of sacred history, that End

---

[1]The argument for a shift in Puritan purpose is developed famously in the eponymous first essay of Perry Miller's *Errand into the Wilderness* (Cambridge: Harvard University Press, 1956).

for which the whole creation groans, predefines all lesser ends. Nested deep within this layered hierarchy of purposes, the college has a clearly defined role to play. Its good serves wider goods that account for its existence, define its worth, and set its tasks.

This strong sense of purpose, this conviction that an institution's essential meaning lies solely in its mission, presumes a society that rests on a worldview to which all its citizens subscribe, a worldview defined by a religious vision of things and the institutionalization of that vision in an ecclesiastical tradition which if not theocratic is at least culturally omnipresent. A college is the place where society's youth complete their appropriation of that worldview, its definitions of what is important and what is worthwhile, and acquire the habits of mind, the skills, and the sensibility they need if they are to prepare themselves adequately to shoulder the religious, cultural, and civic responsibilities of adulthood.

This ideal of the college as a Faithful Community is one where instruction in basic beliefs and preparation for careers and public office go hand in hand. In the Puritan theocracies the blend was blatant, even the right to vote having as its prerequisite a religiosity confirmed through church membership and publicly declared covenants of faith. Only the sons of the Saints need attend college because only they have demonstrated the belief that is prerequisite for the proper uses of a liberal arts education.

The situation was more complicated in the middle colonies where the church was not established, where the land was filled with settlers who lacked the Puritan sense of Christian commonwealth.[2] The American frontier, moreover, was a wilderness where good Christian souls were too easily tempted away from the familiar protections of society, where they learned an independence and utilitarian proclivity at odds with the vision of organic community. The founding by the Presbyterians of colleges in the middle colonies illustrates how the ideal of the Faithful Community guided the colonists into cooperative educational endeavors even when they were not of one mind concerning the particulars of the faith and of its proper expression.

---

[2]For my historical information, I have relied on Howard Miller, *The Revolutionary College: American Presbyterian Higher Education 1707–1837* (New York: New York University Press, 1976), and Frederick Rudolph, *The American College and University: A History* (New York: Knopf, 1962). Also see my review of Miller's book: George Allan, "The Broken Vision," *John and Mary's Journal* 3 (1977): 37–44.

The Great Awakening of the 1740s had split American Presbyterians into two warring factions. The Old Light Presbyterians clung to a traditional understanding of the Church and its mission in the world, a tradition that emphasized obedience to both ecclesiastical and secular authority and that found in the creedal doctrines of the faith an appropriate test for orthodoxy and righteousness. In contrast, New Light Presbyterians found in the affections of the soul a foundation for spiritual renewal sorely missing in the formalism of older ways. They preached to the heart and saw in the fervor of anguished repentance and fresh resolve the proper signs of orthodoxy and true righteousness.

The Old Light Presbyterians responded to the challenge of religious diversity and indifference by making every effort they could to assure a stabilized social order. If the citizens in this new land were straying from the fold, it was because they lacked effective shepherds to instruct them in the behavior proper for a citizen in God's elect community. What was needed, therefore, was an educated clergy trained in the profundities of Calvinist doctrine, practiced in the skills of corporate leadership, able to teach their congregations the virtues of obedience and the responsibilities of duty and station. These proponents of order and learning quite naturally founded their own grammar school, the New London Academy in Delaware, and sought arrangements by which their sons might then continue their study at that citadel of Old Light tradition, Yale College in Congregationalist Connecticut.

Meantime the New Lighters were founding a college of their own. For the champions of virtue, the solution to a decay in Christian commonwealth lay in the reform of souls. The problem of social disorder was at its root a problem of selfishness, of narrow-spirited contentiousness. What society needed was a change in heart, the inculcation of a new moral attitude rooted in love, in fellow-feeling, in a preference for the common weal over one's individual desires. The College of New Jersey, later called Princeton, was founded in 1746 to nurture young men who would grow up to be public-spirited leaders, virtuous citizens whose hearts were attuned to the spiritual needs of those around them. For New Light enthusiasts, the role of education was not primarily a matter of what they called "head-knowledge"; book learning was worthwhile only because it served a higher end. Study and recitation were the ways to evoke first an understanding of right and wrong, and then through this understanding an appreciation of the virtues of civic duty.

Thus although education was as important to the New Lights as to the Old, they each saw it serving a different purpose. For the New Lights, education nurtured piety, and from pious men social order would emerge. For the Old Lights, education trained those able to shape a social order, in the center of which virtue would emerge.

Despite differing views on every one of the fundamental points of Church theology and polity, and despite the creation of separate synods and separate colleges, the Old Light and New Light Presbyterians refused to surrender their shared vision. They both labored on behalf of a single Christian commonwealth encompassing both England and America, responsible to God and responsive to His special calling of them as instruments of His redemptive purpose. If the seamless garment of the commonwealth was torn by their disputes, it was not rent asunder, and the two sides were able to weave it back anew when differences with the English throne threatened a far graver dismemberment of the common order.

It was good the Presbyterians reunited, because the danger turned out to involve more enemies than George III. In 1776 Pennsylvania approved a radical new constitution, egalitarian in its unicameral legislature and nonsectarian in its toleration of religious diversity. The College of Philadelphia, later to become the University of Pennsylvania, had been managed by Anglicans but nonetheless was considered a proper place to educate Presbyterian youth. Now it fell under the control of the new radical majority, men who rejected precisely those values assumed by Old and New Lights alike. For a political commonwealth to be legitimate it must be founded on Christian virtue, so that foundation must not for any reason be abandoned. One might dispute whether respect for authority or heartfelt love for others was the linchpin of society, whether stable order or moral reform was the key to its well-being. But for both factions it had always been clear that God suffered the survival of the colonies, indeed of the English peoples, only insofar as their affairs were informed by His will. And whatever else this meant, it surely meant that government must support and encourage a sense of virtue neither secular nor equivocal.

Dickinson College was chartered in 1783 in response to the dangerous developments in Philadelphia. Its mission was to help assure the vital presence of civic and religious virtue in the new Republic just emerging from the chaos of civil war. The community of English-speaking peoples had been shattered by the rebellion, but the fledgling American nation must nonetheless continue to be faithful to the mission of its Puritan forebears.

It could achieve this purpose as long as its colleges continued to inculcate sound moral principles in the youth who would soon assume the adult burdens of civic leadership.

Dickinson's founder, Benjamin Rush, had been a New Light champion during the prewar controversy, but the specter of radicalism led him to temper his focus on feeling with a growing appreciation for the importance of the legitimate orders of society. He could agree with the egalitarians in Philadelphia that artificial distinctions of class and rank were iniquitous, but he insisted that there are real distinctions of ability and temperament which define a proper station in life and which radicalism was ignoring. He agreed that there was no place for partisan religious resentments in the new nation, but he insisted that Presbyterian piety and learning were necessary precisely to discern the true nature of social harmony and to nurture the public-spirited commitments needed to bring it about. The College of Philadelphia, and radicals generally, threatened the commonwealth because they mistook the crucial role played by moral virtue in the nurturing of civic good. If the failure of Europe lay in its distortion of the social order through privilege, wealth, and false religion, the radicals were equally distorting social order by rejecting all distinctions rather than merely the false ones, by ignoring moral education rather than seeking to broaden its base.

Dickinson College had an important role to play, therefore. The charter of 1783 intones: "Whereas the happiness and prosperity of every community (under the direction and government of Divine Providence) depends much on the right education of the youth, who must succeed the aged in the important offices of society, and [whereas] the most exalted nations have acquired their preeminence by the virtuous principle and liberal knowledge instilled into the minds of the rising generation."[3] If young people are to be properly educated, the intimate connection between "virtuous principle" and "liberal knowledge" must be instilled in their minds. Only then will the American Republic acquire preeminence among the nations and secure for its citizens the happiness and material success that are the outward and visible signs that they are as a people fulfilling God's mission for them. Against the onslaughts of radicalism, Dickinson saw itself as a Faithful Community, serving as one of the bulwarks for society

---

[3] *The Dickinson College Charter and Bylaws* (Carlisle, Pa.: Dickinson College, 1966).

through the education in virtue it provided. The handful of liberal arts colleges, beginning with Harvard and increasing steadily in numbers as the New World settlements grew and a new United States was then born of their common covenant, needed to succeed in their educational mission. The fate of a nation hung in the balance.

The lineage of the Faithful Community can be traced back through the English college system and the New Humanism of the Renaissance to the Roman oratorical tradition identified with Cicero and Quintilian and beyond that to ancient Greece and Plato's chief rival, the rhetorician Isocrates.[4] In order more fully to appreciate what it is to live in a world shaped by the Puritans and their successors, in a world fundamentally grounded in purposes that create communities and delineate what individuals must do in order to live meaningful lives, let us examine three of the primary texts from that tradition. I have selected for our consideration these three texts: the speeches of Isocrates, the *Metalogicon* of John of Salisbury, and Cardinal Newman's *The Idea of a University.* Becoming intimately acquainted with an ancient heritage through a careful study of its authoritative texts is, as we shall see, the most appropriate mode for acquiring those invaluable treasures of virtuous principle and liberal knowledge that the Faithful Community claims to bestow.

Listen to how Isocrates[5] explains to the king of Cyprus why he should respect the ancient laws of his people. This argument, written about 370 B.C.E., was so crucial for Isocrates that he repeated it verbatim nearly twenty years later to his fellow citizens in Athens: "[Persuasion is] that power which of all the faculties that belong to the nature of man is the source of most of our blessing. For in the other powers which we possess we are in no respect superior to other living creatures; nay, we are inferior to many in swiftness and in strength and in other resources" ("Nicoles"

---

[4]Bruce A. Kimball, *Orators and Philosophers: A History of the Idea of Liberal Education* (New York: Teachers College Press, 1986).

[5]The most trustworthy extant manuscript source for the speeches of Isocrates is *Urbinus* Γ, from the late ninth or early tenth century. This source is the basis for the best critical edition of Isocrates, part ii of George Baiter and Hermann Sauppe, *Oratores Attici* (Zürich, 1839). The English translation I have utilized appears, along with an updated critical text of the Greek, in George Norlin, ed., *Isocrates,* 3 vols. (New York: G. P. Putnam's Sons, 1928). Citations, following normal practice, refer to lines of a particular speech as they appear in the Baiter and Sauppe. These line numbers are also indicated in the margins of the Greek text in Norlin.

5; "Antidosis" 253). Our stereotypes of what the Greeks thought to be the most distinctively human characteristic are so influenced by Plato's and Aristotle's celebration of reason that we may well be shocked at first by what Isocrates is asserting. What is fundamental about us humans, he says, is not our powers of reasoning at all. Nor is it our ability to make tools, nor our capacity for laughter, nor our propensity to play. What makes us special is that we can talk persuasively. Not *Homo faber* or *Homo ludens* or even *Homo sapiens*. We are *Homo oratiens*.

There must be an explanation for why we have this faculty of persuasive speech, of course. In a world where to be is to be for the sake of some end, we cannot simply note the distinctiveness of speech as a bare fact. We cannot just identify it as a quality humans happen to possess. Nor is it enough to argue that speech is not only a distinctive but also an essential aspect of our humanity. Speech cannot be understood as merely a marker, useful at best in a field guide for mammals as a good way to identify creatures of the human ilk, a good way to avoid confusing them with other featherless bipeds. Speech, Isocrates argues, is more than this. It sets us apart from the animals by the end for which it is the means: why we can speak is so that we might be able to interact with others. Speech is not mere vocalization, a means for aesthetic self-expression. We speak so that we can communicate with others.

If speaking in order to communicate with one another is at the heart of who we are, then humans are essentially communal beings. Because we communicate, we exist as human beings and not merely as animals. Isocrates rejects the claim that we are first of all human by virtue of being rational, and as an expression of that rationality we begin to speak. It is not that our rational capacities, our ability to think logically and to calculate, are the precondition for our speaking, as though first we had ideas and then found our voice in order to share those ideas with others. On the contrary, Isocrates insists that in communicating with one another we find ourselves human, and that our ability to reason, to imagine and to conceive of ideas, is an outgrowth of that ability.

Isocrates goes further, however. The mode of the communicative interactions central to our nature is neither imperative nor interrogative; we do not speak, most fundamentally, by commanding or questioning. Nor is our voice raised primarily to describe or to explain, neither to give an account of what we have experienced nor to account for why we had that experience. We speak, first of all, in order to persuade. The oddity of

Isocrates' choice is striking. Of all the human qualities for him to have selected as the one essential to a definition of what it is to be human, persuasion is a surprising candidate. It is somewhat plausible to have picked speech as the most important of the human faculties. In doing so Isocrates anticipates most twentieth-century Western philosophy where language has become the filter through which everything else must pass before it can be recognized as good, true, or beautiful. But why does he single out persuasion as the key form of linguistic expression?

Isocrates is explicit in indicating the reason for his choice. Since "there has been implanted in us the power to persuade each other and to make clear to each other whatever we desire, not only have we escaped the life of wild beasts, but we have come together and founded cities and made laws and invented arts; and, generally speaking, there is no institution devised by man which the power of speech has not helped us to establish" ("Nicoles" 6; "Antidosis" 254). We are already in community by virtue of our power to speak to one another, to interact verbally, but only when those exchanges are noncoercive do they result in lasting, historically viable communities. That we have desires and that our actions are motivated by the quest for their satisfaction are truisms. It is also a truism that we desire power, that we enjoy commanding others to obey our wishes, to minister to the satisfaction of our desires. But Isocrates brushes aside any hedonistic or utilitarian claim on behalf of the primacy of appetite and will. What makes us human is not our desirings nor our will to power, important though they be, for which speech is one of the means by which they are fulfilled. Quite the contrary, what makes us human is our ability to share our desirings with others, to explain to them that we are in need and what we think we need, to hear from them what they want and need, to forego imposing our desires but instead to work out a way for all of us to cooperate in fulfilling our varied purposes.

The way worked out, our agreement to cooperate, is more than a particular isolated event, however. It is not merely a fleeting arrangement that all too quickly will be superseded by new needs and new occasions for persuasion. What we have worked out in the exigencies of a given situation has a shape that is repeatable and if repeated often enough will become a habit. And from habits of cooperation eventually grow the customs, rituals, and laws of a society. A tradition or rite or statute is the form shared by a number of conventional activities, a common form abstracted from the differing contents of those varied actions and codified as wise sayings, rules of thumb, guidelines, regulations, principles. For a viable community to exist, people first have to be convinced that they should pay attention not only to their own needs but to the needs of others as well. Then they have to be persuaded that their needs can be met more effectively by cooperating than by acting separately. And finally, people have to be convinced that their common efforts have a form and direction valuable enough to set boundary conditions to their behavior generally. That rule-governed societies exist, and in doing so make possible an incredibly enhanced quality of life, is a tribute to the power of persuasive discourse.

Hence Isocrates immediately draws the ethical lesson: "For this it is [persuasion] which has laid down laws concerning things just and unjust, and things base and honourable. . . . Through this we educate the ignorant and appraise the wise; for the power to speak well is taken as the surest index of a sound understanding, and discourse which is true and lawful and just is the outward image of a good and faithful soul" ("Nicoles" 7; "Antidosis" 255). Having been persuaded to cooperate, and having found the fruits of cooperation sweet, we human beings come to value also the form which that cooperation takes. We then use these forms of cooperation both to guide and to assess our subsequent actions. And over time, advice becomes admonition, the helpful becomes the worthy. What we are pleased has been done becomes what we think should be done. To be unaware of these important forms of the actions of our ancestors seems to us gross ignorance, to ignore them inexcusable. And eventually the outward becomes the inward. A good person comes to be understood as someone able to articulate persuasively to his or her fellow citizens the value of the way of life they share. To be a good person in our society is to be faithful in word and deed to the good life that has been exemplified by our predecessors and distilled in the traditions and laws by which we interact. What once was done from shrewd self-interest comes to be done because that is what it is expected one would do for one's friends and neighbors.

On another occasion, while admonishing his fellow citizens for failing to appreciate their traditions, Isocrates explains why persuasive speech and virtue are so closely linked. More than any other society, Athens has honored eloquence because

> she saw that in other activities the fortunes of life are so capricious that in them often the wise fail and the foolish succeed, whereas beautiful and artistic speech is never allotted to ordinary men, but

is the work of an intelligent mind, and that it is in this respect that those who are accounted wise and ignorant present the strongest contrast; and she knew, furthermore, that whether men have been liberally educated from their earliest years is not to be determined by their courage or their wealth or such advantages, but is made manifest most of all by their speech, and that this has proved itself to be the surest sign of culture in every one of us, and that those who are skilled in speech are not only men of power in their own cities but are also held in honour in other states. ("Panegyricus" 48–49)

Our power to persuade others presumes they are free to accept or reject that of which we wish to persuade them. We can bend others to our will by the emotional power of our rhetoric just as much as by using force of arms to back up our edicts and commands. But neither physical threat nor verbal legerdemain is persuasion. Coercion effected with a tongue rather than a fist is still coercion: it is not essentially a linguistic act. Mere rhetoric attempts to take away our freedom rather than appealing to it.

Those who genuinely seek to persuade others, notes Isocrates, value the ability of their listeners to understand what is at issue. When they speak they expect others to understand their point fully enough to be able sensibly to weigh what is being proposed against its alternatives and then to be able for good reasons either to agree or to fail to agree with the persuader. Persuasive discourse depends on both speakers and listeners possessing those qualities of taste, intelligence, and sensitivity that are the sure sign of culture because they are its highest achievement. Athens, accordingly, which affirms itself as the most cultured of cities, the epitome of civilization, must likewise affirm that persuasive speech is the highest human faculty. It should therefore value its orators above all else. Its heroes should be those best able to persuade others by appealing to their understanding, common sense, and sound judgment.

Wealth or poverty, good health or ill, even courage or cowardliness, are matters of luck or fate, whereas the strength of character, the breadth of understanding, and the wisdom required to be a good orator, to be successful in persuading others to believe and to act in accord with what is best for their community, is the result of a sound education. Eloquence is both a consequence and a source of freedom, an example of the triumph of human purpose over the blind forces of chance and necessity. The power of persuasive speech is what makes us distinctively human because it both presumes our freedom and cultivates it. In learning how to speak well, we acquire an appreciation for the forms of persuasion necessary to create communities. We also develop the loyalty to those forms necessary for communities to continue and to flourish. When living in this way, we live as animals cannot: freely.

So Athens should be proud of her reputation as the educator of the world's best talkers: "And so far has our city distanced the rest of mankind in thought and in speech that her pupils have become the teachers of the rest of the world; and she has brought it about that the name 'Hellenes' suggests no longer a race but an intelligence, and that the title 'Hellenes' is applied rather to those who share our culture than to those who share a common blood" ("Panegyricus" 50). Athens, the exemplar in its own traditions of this ability to nurture great orators, has become the place where those from other cities and traditions know they must come in order truly to learn these qualities, from which they can then return home to improve their own communities.

And then Isocrates once again startles us. For, he says, in carrying out this educative role, Athens has transformed the very concept of community from one based on genealogy to one based on culture, from a unity that is inherited biologically to one that is acquired by training. The freedom implied by persuasive speech finds its highest expression in a society defined by that freedom. Athenians are not a tribe of kith and kin but a voluntary gathering of citizens.[6] "What can only be learned must therefore, obviously, be taught. Since the government of the state is handed on by the older men to the youth of the coming generation; and . . . since the succession goes on without end, it follows of necessity that as is the education of our youth so from generation to generation will be the fortune of the state" ("Antidosis" 174). A good society requires good citizens, good citizens are the products of a good educational system, a good education

---

[6]Socrates appeals to this notion of Athens when rejecting Crito's plea that he flee the city in order to avoid the death decreed by its unjust judicial system. He says that the city would say to him: "We brought you into the world, we raised you, we educated you. . . . Yet we proclaim if any man of the Athenians is dissatisfied with us, he may take his goods and go away wherever he pleases. . . . But we say that every man of you who remains here, seeing how we administer justice, and how we govern the state in other matters, has agreed, by the very fact of remaining here, to do whatsoever we tell him" (*Crito* 51d–e; F. J. Church translation, revised by Robert D. Cumming, in Plato, *Euthyphro, Apology, Crito* [New York: Macmillan, 1948]).

means preparing students to be good orators, and only those good at oratory, only those who have already demonstrated the quality of their persuasive skills, can teach it properly. Isocrates' syllogism is unrelenting: Athens will succeed or fail depending on its respect for traditional education and for the orators who transmit it to each new rising generation.

Isocrates, self-proclaimed as Athens's paradigmatic orator, its best and brightest citizen, then spells out the course of study he thinks most suitable for the youth of Athens and of all Hellas: "Certain of our ancestors, long before our time, seeing that many arts had been devised for other things, while none had been prescribed for the body and for the mind, invented and bequeathed to us two disciplines, physical training for the body, of which gymnastics is a part, and, for the mind, philosophy" ("Antidosis" 181). This is the familiar "sound mind in a sound body" argument, but with its authority traced back to our ancestors and an emphasis placed on discipline. Learning the ancient ways is the best form of education because it trains a new generation in the habits of mind and body that brought our ancestors success. These habits are therefore the conditions in turn for our success. Isocrates sketches the various sorts of "instruction, exercise, and other forms of discipline" that go into the training of athletes and then suggests that philosophy—by which he means the approach to creating orators that he is about to describe—should proceed in "parallel and complementary" fashion in the training of students' minds.

First, students need to be taught "all the forms of discourse in which the mind expresses itself. Then, when they [teachers] have made them familiar and thoroughly conversant with these lessons, they set them at exercises, habituate them to work, and require them to combine in practice the particular things which they have learned, in order that they may grasp them more firmly and bring their theories into closer touch with the occasions for applying them" ("Antidosis" 183–84). Students are to learn the "forms of discourse" in the sense not merely of rhetorical styles but of the disciplinary "theories" those styles are designed to express. For an orator to be able to speak effectively, to argue convincingly with respect to some public issue, he must be familiar with all of the characteristic kinds of knowledge and how these are typically communicated. Eloquence is not merely a matter of verbal acrobatics; it requires a profound grounding in the assumptions and underlying context out of which the various forms of persuasion arose as recurrent patterns for reaching mutually agreed upon solutions to real societal problems. Genuinely persuasive oratory requires showing the relationship between today's issues and the ways by which our ancestors, in addressing yesterday's issues, have provided us with the best resources for carrying out our present tasks.

Exercises that discipline the mind are important preparatory activities. Isocrates mentions, as examples, grammar and music at an early level of preparation, geometry and astronomy at an advanced level. These activities are not self-justifying, however, and if pursued exclusively can be debilitating. Because scientific studies are abstract and speculative, students who spend too much time at them will "allow their minds to be dried up by these barren subtleties." For instance, some scientists maintain that

> the sum of things is made up of infinite elements; Empedocles that it is made up of four, with strife and love operating among them; Ion, of not more than three; Alcmaeon, of only two; Parmenides and Melissus, of one; and Gorgias, of none of all. For I think that such curiosities of thought are on a par with jugglers' tricks which, though they do not profit anyone, yet attract great crowds of the empty-minded, and I hold that men who want to do some good in the world must banish utterly from their interests all vain speculations and all activities which have no bearing on our lives. ("Antidosis" 268–69)

Thus the only value of abstract speculation is as a warming up exercise for the more demanding task at which students must become adept: bringing their familiarity with the forms of discourse to bear on concrete contemporary problems. A student cannot simply deduce from abstract principles what the best course of action might be in a particular situation. Persuasion is an art, not a science. By adapting general theories to specific occasions, by trying out a judgment of what seems appropriate given their grasp of the issues at hand, students can eventually become skilled at making selective judgments. And when skilled in this art of choosing well, when rightly educated, students will be ready to take up the responsibilities of adulthood. "For since it is not in the nature of man to attain a science by the possession of what we can know positively what we should do or what we should say, in the next resort I hold that man to be wise who is able by his powers of conjecture to arrive generally at the best course, and I hold that man to be a philosopher who occupies himself with the studies from which he will most quickly gain that kind of insight" ("Antidosis" 271).

Thus the world of the Faithful Community as portrayed by one of its earliest advocates is thoroughly holistic. Isocrates rejects the sufficiency of specialized scientific knowledge for two reasons: its goal of absolute certainty is unattainable, and by the exclusive pursuit of such a goal one soon loses sight of the reason for seeking such knowledge in the first place. This is not to say that scientific knowledge is irrelevant, but that its value lies in its contribution to a more integrative understanding of things. Integration, not specialization, is what is required by the leaders responsible for mediating the varied needs of those who compose their community. Science must always be a handmaiden to the art of governance.

The practical skill required of a community's leaders is the ability to make good choices in the absence of complete or certain information, to do the right thing in a world where absolute knowledge is impossible and belief therefore the best we have to work with in making judgments concerning the things that really matter. Plato and Aristotle shared this view, but unlike Isocrates they also lay claim to higher truths, to the certain and absolute knowledge vouchsafed by reason to those with the ability and the leisure to find their way from the half-light of opinion into the presence of the bright sun of Truth. But if speech and not reason is the essence of our humanity, then Plato and Aristotle are claiming to be gods, denying the constraints of their humanity. Isocrates knows better: we are free to be together fully human, but we are not free not to be human.

We enter into a Faithful Community freely, but freedom is a capacity we learn. Our commonality is grounded not in our biology but in our freedom; yet that commonality is what makes us free. Hence a society, originating in the willingness of individuals to be persuaded to cooperate, survives only by nurturing a culture that fosters members able to persuade themselves and others to continue that cooperation. Because society requires a loyalty it cannot command, its values must be couched in institutions, customs, laws, and persons able to attract that loyalty by their word and example. The community arose by acts of individual will, by choices that need not have been made. There are no necessary truths that assure its value or its power to endure, only the success it has in convincing each new generation of the importance of its forms of discourse, of its traditional ways. Education, both the formal training of young people to be articulate advocates of an ancient way of life and the continuing reinforcement of those values for adults, is the slender thread that keeps civilization from straying into barbarism. No wonder Isocrates praised the orators and those who teach them as Athens's most precious possession.

In the centuries since Isocrates, the most obvious change in the oratorical worldview concerned the character of the founding, the nature of the original act of freedom upon which a community rests. Cicero, for instance, still sounds like Isocrates when declaiming on Roman origins, but he shifts the emphasis from the persuasive powers of his ancestors to the codified results of their efforts recorded in the "single little book" of the Twelve Tables. Virtue, empire, and dignity are linked because the Twelve Tables inculcate virtuous principle in the people governed by them, and virtuous people are successful in their ventures and so should receive from others the praise and respect for which their notable accomplishments make them worthy. Law rather than speech, product rather than process, is the focus of attention. But Isocrates' Roman disciples continue to insist that the source of conditions for individual virtue and social cohesion is ancestral tradition, and that it is the responsibility of the rhetorician to transmit that tradition to others and to incarnate it in his own paradigmatic words and deeds.

With the coming of Christianity, a further shift occurs: the originating human lawgivers are replaced by a divine lawgiver. God's laws are said to be timeless and perfect, unlike human laws that are contingent and parochial. But we still need to be taught them. We must write them in our hearts if we are ultimately to be good citizens in a heavenly commonwealth, and if in the meantime our earthly commonwealth is to succeed. Our loyalty is first to God and His purposes but secondarily to the worldly manifestation of those purposes—insofar, that is, as the kingdoms of this earth mirror in the forms of their institutions and customary ways the forms appropriate to the Kingdom of God. Insofar as our societal microcosms reflect as closely as possible the meaning of the macrocosm in which they are embedded, they deserve our devotion and loyalty. Our decision to commit ourselves to an earthly community is enabled by faith and sustained by grace, but it is nonetheless a genuine choice we make. Puritans are members of a religious Congregation and through it of a political Commonwealth only if, as a result of an explicit covenant experience, they have first aligned their wills with God's will.

This key difference between the pagan and religious versions of a Faithful Community is surprisingly unimportant educationally. John of Salisbury, secretary to Thomas Becket, completed a manuscript in 1159 that explicates and defends the liberal arts.[7] His *Metalogicon* never mentions Isocrates, but it draws constantly from those he had influenced. The distinctive feature of human beings for John, however, is twofold: no longer just speech but reason as well. Nature "has, among the various living creatures which she has brought forth, elevated man by the privilege of reason, and distinguished him by the faculty of speech. . . . Borne aloft, so to speak, on wings of reason and speech, he is thus enabled, by this felicitous shortcut, to outstrip all other beings, and to attain the crown of true happiness" (book 1, chap. 1).

Reason, although "the mother, nurse, and guardian of knowledge, as well as of virtue," is "feeble and maimed" if not linked intimately with speech. This is so because "all things lack something when isolated" and hence any skill or strategy, any insight or glimpse of truth, which a solitary individual might acquire will be improved by being shared. And speech is what makes sharing possible. We are imperfect creatures, but by mutually supporting one another we can do together what we could not accomplish separately. "Speechless wisdom" cannot lead us to happiness, for happiness is impossible "apart from mutual association." But neither is "eloquence unenlightened by reason" a viable guide, since it is blind and so cannot discern its goal. Rather,

> it is this delightful and fruitful copulation of reason and speech which has given birth to so many outstanding cities, has made friends and allies of so many kingdoms, and has unified and knit together in bonds of love so many peoples. . . . Deprived of their gift of speech, men would degenerate to the condition of brute animals, and cities would seem like corrals for livestock, rather than communities composed of human beings united by a common bond for

---

[7]The earliest extant manuscript is in the library of Corpus Christi College, Cambridge University: "Johannis Sareberiensis Metalogicon." Known as the *Cantuariensis* or "C" codex, it is the original copy presented to Becket. The first printed edition is by Hadrian Beys (Paris, 1610); the definitive critical edition is that of Clement C. J. Webb, *Metalogicon Libri IIII* (Oxford: Clarendon Press, 1929). The first complete English translation, from which my quotations are taken, is by Daniel D. McGarry, *The Metalogicon of John of Salisbury* (Berkeley: University of California Press, 1962).

the purpose of living in society, serving one another, and cooperating as friends. (book 1, chap. 1)

Although John, unlike Isocrates, believes in an ultimate and transhistorical community, our earthly community is for the sake of an important end as well. "True happiness" is a quite temporal goal, but one that cannot be attained by individuals acting separately. Nor can it be achieved by people collected into groups by means other than "bonds of love" and for purposes other than "serving one another and cooperating as friends." In groups without the bonds of love and service, people are no better off than animals, their cities no more than sheep pens.

John reaffirms Isocrates' insistence that persuasion rather than force is the uniquely human faculty which makes civilization, that uniquely human of achievements, possible. Genuine community requires cooperation, and the necessary condition for cooperation is speech. Isocrates emphasizes the persuasive function of speech, its appeal to another's freedom, whereas John focuses on its supportive function, its capacity to create bonds of commonality. For both, we are fully human only when we are committed participants in a community, cooperating with others in the pursuit of common ends. The quality of a community is thus a function of the quality of the speaking that persuades people freely to bind themselves to one another.

But the "appropriate and effective" use of speech, eloquence, is not a gift of nature: "Not everyone who speaks, nor even one who says what he wants to in some fashion, is eloquent. He alone is eloquent who fittingly and efficaciously expresses himself as he intends" (book 1, chap. 7). Eloquence is a learned skill. There is an art to knowing how to convey precisely the meaning you intended, and to do so at the right time, in the right place, in the right way.

John characterizes an "art" as a shortcut: a technique devised to "expedite" our ability to do things "within our natural capabilities." When we do something again and again, we are able by use of our reason to see a general pattern in our actions and to improve upon that pattern, perfecting it. We then are guided by this perfected pattern in our subsequent actions. Thus persuasive speech is an art, for "the first disputation developed by chance, and the practice of disputing grew with repetition. Reason then perceived the form of disputation, the art of this activity. This art, on being cultivated, conferred a corresponding faculty" (book 1, chap. 11). Just as Isocrates had argued, so does John: civilized actions grow out of

the disciplining of more primitive behavior by discerning and then culti-
vating the forms of whichever actions succeed in realizing commonly
desired ends. The arts of civilization offer us a better way—a more efficient, more effective, and indeed more graceful way—to do what before
we had done poorly.

The function of education is to teach the arts needed by a civilized community. And first among those arts is eloquence, since without it there can
be no community. John acknowledges that the mechanical arts are important, for without food, clothing, and shelter we cannot live. But were such
arts the only ones available, we could not live as humans. For that higher
form of living, the liberal arts are also needed. They alone inform our judgments about how best we might together attain the happiness we seek. Furthermore, a distinction needs to be made within the liberal arts between
"logic" and "scientific knowledge." Scientific knowledge is an art composed of the practical skills, abstract principles, and specialized information we need in order to understand our world and be virtuous members
of our community. But knowledge of this sort presupposes another kind
of art, "the science of verbal expression and reasoning" (book 1, chap. 23).
This special art is called logic. The general skills needed to acquire, assess,
and apply knowledge, which logic teaches, are the arts of reasoning and
of eloquence and the art of grammar upon which they both rest.

John is arguing along a carefully constructed logical sortes. Happiness
is possible for individuals only where the society to which they belong is
good. A society can be good only if its citizens are virtuous. A person is
virtuous only if his or her actions are informed by appropriate knowledge.
Knowledge can be acquired only if a person knows how to learn. Learning is dependent on verbal expression and reasoning. The key to verbal
expression and reasoning is grammar. Hence only if we as students learn
our grammar, and learn it well, will our social interactions perfect our
lives in happiness.

Grammar, however, is not just a matter of syntax. "Speaking and writing correctly" includes, in addition to the rules in a given language for
constructing meaningful sentences and for properly pronouncing and
phrasing them, the ability to "understand everything that can be taught
in words" and the ability to "regulate our very voice so that it is suited to
all persons and matters" (book 1, chap. 21). To know how language
works means to be able to understand and interpret a text, whether by
reading it for oneself or hearing it read by another. It also means to be

able to communicate a text to others, perhaps by taking pen to parchment but more typically by explicating it orally.

Those who know their grammar well are able, like the orators of old, to teach others, to prepare them by a study of the appropriate authors for the responsibilities of adulthood and civic leadership. Although this mode of teaching was beginning to change decisively during John's lifetime, the experience of learning grammar and the other liberal arts was little changed in the twelfth century from what it had been for Cicero. John provides an engaging portrait of his own teacher, Bernard of Chartes, who taught grammar to his students in a rigorous manner but one "commensurate with their powers of assimilation." Bernard emphasized "diction" because of "the employment of metaphors, whereby speech is transferred to some beyond-the-ordinary meaning for sufficient reason," and insisted (by "exhortation" and if necessary by "flogging") that his students not only learn the rules for good diction and be exposed to properly spoken language, but that they "imitate what they were hearing." So Bernard brought his students into the presence of great texts authored by the Greek and Roman

> poets and orators who were to serve as models for the boys in their introductory exercises in imitating prose and poetry. Pointing out how the diction of the authors was so skillfully connected, and what they had to say was so elegantly concluded, he would admonish his students to follow their example. And if, to embellish his work, someone had sewed on a patch of cloth filched from an external source, Bernard, on discovering this, would rebuke him for his plagiary, but would generally refrain from punishing him. After he had reproved the student, if an unsuitable theme had invited this, he would, with modest indulgence, bid the boy to rise to real imitation of the [classical authors], and would bring about that he who had imitated his predecessors would come to be deserving of imitation by his successors. (book 1, chap. 24)

The monastic teacher reads from one of the great texts while his students listen.[8] The parchment he holds in his hands is a prized possession,

---

[8]Ivan Illich paints a wonderful picture of this way of teaching in his account of the early twelfth-century context within which Hugh of St. Victor taught and for which he composed his famous book; *In the Vineyard of the Text: A Commentary to Hugh's Didascalicon* (Chicago: University of Chicago Press, 1993).

perhaps the only copy of the text available in that region. Its letters fill each sheet in unbroken sequence, the pages often ornamented with designs and occasional figures that reinforce the meaning of the text. In order to convey the meanings locked up in the manuscript, the teacher must gather up the letters into Latin words and speak them for the students to repeat and to copy onto their wax tablets. The teacher thus gives sense to the endless flow of letters by searching out their hidden structure and incarnating it in spoken words and sentences. This sense, now made present among the group, is explicated as the teacher pauses in his reading to comment, to elaborate, to make connections to other texts, and to invite his students to restate in their own words what has been said and meant.

From text to text, over the years, the students and their teacher proceed, until the truths sleeping in those texts have been awakened and they, by their lively action, have awakened the minds of the students. Until, as John of Salisbury so wonderfully puts it, the students have learned by imitating their predecessors the skills that will make them worthy of being imitated by their successors. Then the students will be ready, the familiar voices of the ancients now whispering in their ears, to set aside their schooling and to take up their responsibilities as leaders in their community.

Education is thus triply a community activity. It takes place as teachers and students together appropriate the understanding incarnate in texts long honored by the community. By this means it inculcates in young people the beliefs and arts they need if they are to contribute productively to the good of the community. And, as a result, it assures the continuation of the community across the generations. Thus John is true to the basic argument first propounded by Isocrates: that the well-being of a society depends on well-educated citizens, people loyal to the ideal ends upon which that society was founded, and skilled in the art of realizing those ends in history. The Faithful Community is intentional, its meaning and hence its justification found in an end that each new generation must be taught to love and to embody.

This worldview is essentially unchanged when Cardinal Newman in the mid-nineteenth century published his *Idea of a University*.[9] The institution

---

[9] John Henry Newman, *Discourses on the Scope and Nature of University Education: Addressed to the Catholics of Dublin* (1852); combined with *Lectures and Essays on University Subjects* (1859) and published in 1873 as *The Idea of a University Defined and Illustrated* (London: Basil Montagu Pickering). My references are to the annotated and corrected text of the ninth edition of 1889, edited by I. T. Ker (Oxford: Clarendon Press, 1976).

he wishes established in Dublin is for the education of Roman Catholic children. But its purpose is not to do what only the Church should do, which is to inculcate religious beliefs. A university, Newman insists, "is a place of *teaching* universal *knowledge*. This implies that its object is, on the one hand, intellectual, not moral; and, on the other, that it is the diffusion and extension of knowledge rather than the advancement. If its object were scientific and philosophical discovery, I do not see why a University should have students; if religious training, I do not see how it can be the seat of literature and science" (p. 5). If religious training has no place in a university, neither does research. Faculty wishing to pursue original scholarship should do so under the aegis of the many literary and scientific academies created for just that purpose, such as the Royal Society or the Antiquarian Society. Universities are where students go to acquire knowledge and the general skills needed for further learning and for work. They are places for teaching; their mission is educational.

Nonetheless, a university "cannot fulfil its object duly, such as I have described it, without the Church's assistance; or, to use the theological term, the Church is necessary for its *integrity*. Not that its main characters are changed by this incorporation: it still has the office of intellectual education; but the Church steadies it in the performance of that office" (p. 5). Newman's statement is somewhat disingenuous, however. As he soon makes quite clear, the Church "steadies" the university by providing it with its essential purpose. What will give "integrity" to the various activities of the new university, its programs of literary and scientific study, will be the end those programs serve. The objective of education is not literary and scientific knowledge as such, but rather "some benefit or other, to accrue, by means of literature and science" (p. 6). This new university, to be founded by Catholics, needs to develop in the children who attend it "certain habits, moral or intellectual": those conducive "to their spiritual welfare and their religious influence and usefulness" (p. 7).

But the education of spiritually mature and intellectually capable people—virtuous citizens—is no more the primary end of a university education than is the learning and discipline that fosters such people. The moral and intellectual habits students are to acquire while studying at the university are taught "with the object of training them to fill their respective posts in life better, and of making them more intelligent, capable, active members of society" (p. 7). The primary end of education is the good of the community, a community which for Newman is a Christian commonwealth.

An education proper for Christians in a Christian commonwealth will lead students to be aware of and then embrace fundamental truths; those who are poorly educated will be cut off from such foundations. But this does not mean that professors are to teach those truths as a body of conclusions to be memorized dutifully and repeated on command. What is to be taught is a way of learning, a discipline of mind that once acquired gives students the capacity to distinguish truth from error. Let a student "once gain this habit of method, of starting from fixed points, of making his ground good as he goes, of distinguishing what he knows from what he does not know, and I conceive he will be gradually initiated into the largest and truest philosophical views, and will feel nothing but impatience and disgust at the random theories and imposing sophistries and dashing paradoxes, which carry away half-formed and superficial intellects" (p. 13).

Furthermore, for any community to be well-run, and in particular a Christian community, its leaders must be well-educated. Hence the Pope and Prelates, as leaders of the Catholic Church, must be themselves educated appropriately and must see to it "that their people should be taught a wisdom, safe from the excesses and vagaries of individuals, embodied in institutions which have stood the trial and received the sanction of ages, and administered by men who have no need to be anonymous, as being supported by their consistency with their predecessors and with each other" (p. 15).

The Church, for Newman, is a community extending over time. Both it and its members may have an origin and destination that lie outside of time, but in the time between those times, penultimately, it has the characteristics of any community. Its people need to be wise enough to adhere to institutional structures and patterns of action that have stood the test of time. They need to be loyal to a way of life they find modeled for them by the great leaders and authors from the past of which they are heirs. And so they need an educational system able to inculcate that loyalty by teaching each new generation ideas, methods, and a sensibility firmly rooted in the commitments by which the community was originated.

The American liberal arts colleges, founded by religious communities both Protestant and Catholic, echo Newman, John of Salisbury, and Isocrates. Some of these religious communities had been political entities as well: the Puritans in Massachusetts and Connecticut, the Catholics in Maryland. But the sectarian pluralism in the middle colonies became an increasingly characteristic arrangement, and with the disestablishment in the U.S. Constitution of all ecclesiastical authority the idea of a Christian commonwealth changed radically. America was henceforth to understand itself as a single nation "steadied" by a number of different Christian communities rather than merely by one. The nation was not to be Christian, but Christians were to provide through their privately supported religious schools and colleges the moral education necessary for social stability.

Narrow-spirited contentiousness grew rampant, however, in the absence of the political repression of religious diversity. The ancient vision of a single godly commonwealth was soon overwhelmed by sectarian divisiveness. By the early nineteenth century, the denominational voluntary society—the religious sect—had usurped the nation of virtuous citizens as the ideological fulcrum for action. Sectarian loyalty was best achieved through presenting the faithful with a distinctive profile of their group's special insights into truth and virtue and then making invidious comparisons with other groups. The political commonwealth was seen as no more than a marketplace within which competing religious commonwealths struggled for survival. The denominational sect, and not the nation, was henceforth to be the locus for saving grace and communal fulfillment.

The multitude of denominational schools in existence by that time began to redefine their responsibilities, drawing their students from partisan rather than national sources. Moral education was exhibited in strict obedience to the beliefs and practices of the sect. The aim of education was the nurture of good denominationalists rather than good citizens. Jeremiah Atwater, for instance, Dickinson's president in the early 1800s, waged incessant war against the enemies of Presbyterian purity. He chastised the local tavern owners as purveyors of wantonness and expelled from campus the distinguished scientist Thomas Cooper whose atheism was proven by the very secularism of his learning. Under such a narrowed vision, however, the soul withers. Dickinson College closed its doors in 1816, reopened after a few years at the initiative of local citizens, but in 1831 once more surrendered to its own divisiveness and insolvency. A similar fate was in store for many of the other Presbyterian colleges. Even Princeton fell into an enfeebled decline from which it did not emerge until after the Civil War.

The *Niles Register,* announcing that Dickinson College had closed, suggested that the cause was "too much sectarianism, and too little true piety." If so, regeneration was available through the ministration of the Methodists who in the 1820s and 1830s had become a new force in society, confident in their sense of true piety and of their mission to redeem the nation. In so many ways, they were a fresh incarnation of New Side beliefs in the importance of a properly attuned heart. Also like their Presbyterian predecessors, but more belatedly and less surely, they came to acknowledge the importance of a proper education in Christian virtue. Although the Methodists had for a long time felt no need whatsoever to train their clergy—Drew Seminary was not founded until 1867—they soon saw the appropriateness for having colleges to educate their laity. Wesleyan in Connecticut was founded in 1831, and two years later Dickinson was purchased from a desperate Presbyterian board to serve as Wesleyan's more southerly counterpart.

Under its first Methodist president, John Price Durban, Dickinson prospered both financially and spiritually. Avowedly sectarian, it nonetheless admitted students of any Protestant faith and provided them a stern, pious, and properly classical education. Virtue was still the primary purpose of education, the president's culminating course in Moral Philosophy still required. But it was now possible for piety to be conceived apart from public responsibilities. A college must both teach virtue and prepare students for citizenship, but the two were not necessarily connected. So Dickinson began to graduate young men, and ultimately young women as well, whose individual conduct was scrupulously upright but who did not readily see the relevance of private virtue to public practice. Under the Presbyterian aegis, virtuous citizens had given way to virtuous denominationalists; now sectarian virtue was being replaced by individual virtue. God's salvation was for persons but seemingly no longer for a people.

Many American colleges have retained this sense of themselves as rooted in a specific sectarian religious tradition. They tend to have a clearly articulated mission statement and a campus leadership dedicated to its accomplishment. Such colleges are well prepared to weather the storms buffeting higher education at the end of the twentieth century. The distinctiveness of the religious college is salient and readily publicized. Its financial and student clientele are self-identified and their needs explicitly addressed. Some of the sectarian movements that founded utopian communities in nineteenth-century America survive today with strongly thriving educational extensions: the Mennonites with their Goshen College, the Mormons with their Brigham Young University. Some Roman Catholic schools remain that hold to a similarly explicit sense of mission. The most expansive versions of this model are those created by the Protestant fundamentalists:

Bob Jones University, where laxity in physical fitness is taken as a sign of moral weakness; Wheaton College in Illinois, where ignorance and religious ignorance are so fully intertwined that proof of "a vital Christian experience" is one of the admissions criteria.

Other colleges have been unwilling to pay a sectarian price for continuing their religious commitment. Not wanting to abandon their sense of civic responsibility, their mission to educate young people with a broad vision rooted in loyalty to their nation and its traditions, they settled for a generalized ethical humanism as the foundation necessary to be a well-educated citizen. The divestiture of their sectarian affiliation was rarely dramatic, however, or even overt. It was more a matter of gradually increasing neglect that eventually transformed an explicitly denominational connection into a vague affirmation of the college's religious heritage.

Newman dismissed the ideal of an "English Gentleman" as too "narrow or fantastic" an educational goal (p. 6). "The manners and habits of gentlemen" are best acquired in the home and through foreign travel. Although valuable, these virtues are hardly sufficient for the strength of character required of those who were expected to be tomorrow's leaders. Similarly, Frederick Rudolph mocks the "gentleman's college" that schools like Williams had become by the close of the nineteenth century: "There young men could practice the conversational arts fueled by their courses . . . ; there they learned how to hold their liquor, express ideals appropriate to their age, and swagger a bit in the knowledge that the world was their oyster and it eagerly awaited their arrival."[10]

Nonetheless, the "Christian gentleman" became the ideal for a large number of the liberal arts colleges in the United States by the turn of the century. Fifty years later, typically, the adjective "Christian" had been dropped, not only to accommodate the increasing number of Jews, Moslems, and even Buddhists in a religiously pluralistic redefinition of institutional purpose but also to appeal to the increasingly secular character of public life.

A sense of mission couched in a humanistic rather than religious sensibility harkens back to Isocrates. The appeal to tradition as a source of the virtue and understanding needed for the realization of the common good rings true in many modern ears. For instance, Dickinson, in the fol-

---

[10]Frederick Rudolph, "Williams at Two Hundred," in *The Fiftieth Reunion* (Williamstown, Mass.: Williams College, Class of 1942 Yearbook, 1992), p. 200.

lowing quote from a recent catalogue, parses its college seal in a way that, although idiosyncratic in its details, is typical of an Isocratic interpretation of how and why one is faithful to a community:

> The ideas and goals expressed by the founders of Dickinson in their design of a College seal and the choice of a College motto provide an appropriate symbol for the education we strive to provide our students. The Dickinson College seal contains three items—a book of scriptures, a telescope, and a liberty cap.
>
> The telescope symbolizes learning. Students who graduate from Dickinson have been introduced to the world's intellectual and cultural heritage, have befriended its great minds, learned its methods of problem solving, become acquainted with its artistic and societal achievements.
>
> The liberty cap symbolizes the ideals of political freedom and responsibility. After graduation students will have the duties of citizenship to bear and opportunities for leadership to realize, challenges for which a Dickinson education should be a useful preparation.
>
> The book of scriptures symbolizes moral commitment and faith. Neither past or future learning nor past or future leadership roles will be worthy of students unless they have acquired a sense of right and wrong and have a mature commitment to high standards of personal and social justice.
>
> The College motto, inscribed within the seal, summarizes these symbols in a phrase: *Pietate et doctrina tuta libertas;* liberty is made safe by virtue and learning.[11]

The catalogue appeals to the ideals of the college's founders, the purposes by which they persuaded one another to cooperate in creating and supporting an educational institution on the edge of a wilderness. Students are promised instruction in a cultural heritage that will prepare them to be good citizens and effective leaders. They are told that the key to this preparation lies in the moral compass the college will provide them for finding their way. Their success and their nation's are said to be dependent on the knowledge and virtue they will acquire during their college years. Cardinal Newman and John of Salisbury would gainsay the tepid

---

[11]*1995–96 Bulletin: Dickinson College,* Annual Catalogue, vol. 85, p. 12.

manner in which the moral compass is described but otherwise would agree with the analysis.

When a college is a Faithful Community, it understands itself as having been given marching orders to achieve, nurture, and defend a specific, definable state of affairs. Its mission is to be sent on a mission: to make the world, the world of its worldview, safe from the intrusions of moral weakness, ignorance, and false belief. All of the college's tangible resources and its programs of study are justified by reference to this defined mission. Persons responsible for the institution, its trustees and teachers and staff, are judged worthy or wanton, prepared or foolish, insofar as their efforts contribute to the advance of that mission. The definition of a good student is one who accepts the discipline of the community, is fundamentally shaped by it, and can function in harmony with its purpose even when no longer under its regulative power. The aim of a Faithful Community is to inculcate its ideals in the successive generations, to perpetuate a vision of what ought to be, and to insist that believers in that vision act incisively on behalf of its realization.

Bruce Kimball identifies seven characteristics key to the tradition of educational institutions modeled on the ideal of the Faithful Community. He recurs to these characteristics (although not always consistently) in summarizing each of the historical periods in its development.[12] Let me conflate and elaborate Kimball's summaries as follows:

First, the task of liberal education is to develop good citizens and leaders in a community by imparting to students the view of life and the world which is foundational for that community. Second, in order for this training to be accomplished, the values and standards that are needed for the development of good character and as guides for proper conduct must be clearly identified. Third, students are expected to commit themselves to these values and standards: they are expected to strive to become adults of good character who will conduct themselves as good citizens of the community should. Fourth, an identifiable body of classical texts, constituting the community's cultural heritage, written by its major political and literary authorities, provides students the best access to these values and standards. Fifth, this education is provided to an elite, to the relatively small group of young people capable of acquiring the qualities necessary for societal leadership. Sixth, people so educated are confident of the cen-

---

[12]Kimball, *Orators and Philosophers,* pp. 37–38, 53–55, 87–89, 111–12.

trality of what they have learned and the ultimate importance of the sort of persons they have become. And finally, this education is taken by everyone to be an end in itself: something of self-evident and intrinsic value.

But let the one who had the first word in this chapter also have the last word. Isocrates, writing as an old man of ninety-seven, portrays in the following way the ideal graduate of a college that has dedicated itself to educating people who will become faithful stewards of their community:

> Whom, then, do I call educated, since I exclude the arts and sciences and specialties? First, those who manage well the circumstances which they encounter day by day, and who possess a judgment which is accurate in meeting occasions as they arise and rarely misses the expedient course of action; next, those who are decent and honourable in their intercourse with all with whom they associate, tolerating easily and good-naturedly what is unpleasant or offensive in others and being themselves as agreeable and reasonable to their associates as it is possible to be; furthermore, those who hold their pleasures always under control and are not unduly overcome by their misfortunes, bearing up under them bravely and in a manner worthy of our common nature; finally, and most important of all, those who are not spoiled by successes and do not desert their true selves and become arrogant, but hold their ground steadfastly as intelligent men, not rejoicing in the good things which have come to them through chance rather than in those which through their own nature and intelligence are theirs from their birth. Those who have a character which is in accord, not with one of these things, but with all of them—these, I contend, are wise and complete men, possessed of all the virtues. ("Panathenaicus" 30–32)

2

The College as Guild of Inquirers

1. A CRITIQUE OF THE PAROCHIAL

A Faithful Community is necessarily parochial. The community is defined by a set of beliefs and practices that are products of its history. Histories are unique; they trace the adventures of certain people trying to fulfill their desires, striving to realize their hopes, amid contexts marked by natural and man-made contingencies. One is then asked to be faithful to this idiosyncratic artifact, valuing it because in being unique it is therefore special. This is an irrational way of thinking, the traditionalist mindset.

[1.1] Most groups are quite arbitrary in origin and purpose and quite ephemeral. Often they reject any such descriptions of themselves, however. Groups that are massive in scope, spread wide across the planet and with roots reaching deeply into the past—clans, tribes, city-states, nations, peoples—think themselves rescued from the contingencies of history because of their own power or that of some sponsoring divinity. The facts, of course, do not support their claims. Those who once put their faith in Ninnevah or Tyre had cast their lot with a community they thought would endure indefinitely, but those kingdoms have long since perished and even the names of their faithful have been forgotten. Nonetheless, those whose communities are still thriving tend to think of themselves as an exception to the rule. The children of Abraham may no longer outnumber the sands on the shore, but the faithful remnant still believes itself chosen by the lord of history for a special purpose to which, however obscure it might be, they should be faithful. The children of the Nazarene and the sons of the Prophet hold similar views, as do the citizens of the United States and the peoples of China. But the gods first lift up whom they would destroy.

All communities must perish. The faith of these people is to a community. Therefore the faith of these people will perish. Quod erat demonstrandum.

[1.2] The problem with faith is that it cannot know itself as faith. Believers must believe that the world their community creates around them is an objective world, a work of nature or of God but not a human artifact. They must believe that they do not merely believe but know with certainty, even if all they might know is that the Power making possible their belief is absolutely trustworthy. A community, in educating its young people, since its purpose is to lead them to have faith in that community's faith, to make its practices habitual and its beliefs self-evident, must teach them that its parochial worldview is not parochial at all but is rather the sole repository of objective truth about the actual world. Education must be, at bottom, a lie, even though it be a saving lie.

In Plato's *Republic,* Socrates argues that there may be times when, for the good of the community, a falsehood must be spoken as though it were the truth. The responsibility to tell this lie falls to those in power, for they alone understand fully the end served: "If we were right in saying that gods have no use for falsehood and it is useful to mankind only in the way of a medicine, obviously a medicine should be handled by no one but a physician. . . . If anyone, then, is to practice deception, either on the country's enemies or on its citizens, it must be the Rulers of the commonwealth, acting for its benefit" (Plato 1945: 78). The falsehood—the "convenient fiction"—which Socrates thinks necessary, the one he proposes that the state should teach its children, is a "single bold flight of invention, which we may induce the community in general, and if possible the Rulers themselves, to accept." The young citizens of the Republic are to be taught that they as a people have sprung from the earth, that they are autochthonous: "So now they must think of the land they dwell in as a mother and nurse, whom they must take thought for and defend against any attack, and of their fellow citizens as brothers born of the same soil" (Plato 1945: 106). "Such is the story," Socrates concludes. "Can you think of any device to make them believe it?" And Glaucon replies, "Not in the first generation; but their sons and descendants might believe it, and finally the rest of mankind."

Community cohesion requires shared beliefs, especially those showing the members of the society to have had a common origin, preferably an origin that resulted from an action of a god or was otherwise sanctioned by the nature of things. It is permitted to inculcate these beliefs in each rising generation by telling the children tales of how their community came to be, by spinning ethnogenic myths and passing them off as truth. In this way, by the time they are adults the citizens of the community will have the passionate loyalty, the absolute commitment, requisite for their collective survival. The good of the whole permits the Rulers to deceive their subjects. But the best situation of all is when the Rulers themselves come to believe their own stories, when conveniently the "big lie" has become for everyone the Truth.

[1.3] Obviously a Faithful Community cannot tolerate differences in matters of fundamental belief. Thus as the newly formed American Republic became more religiously pluralistic, its colleges had an increasingly difficult time making sense of their founding mission. We have seen that some responded by becoming sectarian, others by becoming secular. If the educational mission no longer could be to teach Puritan truths to young men preparing themselves for leadership roles in a Christian commonwealth, then one of two alternatives would have to be embraced. Either the college must be content to teach Puritan truths to Puritans, or Methodist truths to Methodists, redefining the aim of this education as nurturing graduates who would live morally upright lives and who, as a sign of God's favor, might also prosper materially. Or the college must find its purpose in teaching general truths to young people of various religious backgrounds, the better to prepare them for the secular offices of society and for successful careers in business and the professions.

This choice was not benign, however. It trapped the colleges in a genuine dilemma: a choice between two equally undesirable alternatives. The first option would narrow the scope of the college's mission and in doing so expose its world as just another worldview, as merely one set of beliefs alongside many other sets. Anglicans, Methodists, Congregationalists, and Quakers might each continue claiming that they had a corner on the truth, but without the backing of the powers of the state their fulminations against the heresies and falsehoods of the other sects would seem no more than squabbles, one congeries of prejudice and superstition vying against another. The lie at the root of each of them would be exposed for what it was. It might be emotionally fulfilling and pragmatically effective for those who believe it, but nonetheless it would be known that it was a lie.

The second option was no better. In watering down the distinctive beliefs they had been founded to inculcate, searching for a common denominator among the different truths, the college would be forced to trivialize its beliefs, to replace vivid, life-inspiring verities with insipid, uninspiring shibboleths. But this approach would be just another way to expose for public scrutiny the fact that the distinctive perspective of the college's sectarian world was only one among a host of possible perspectives, that what made it distinctive was precisely that about it which was not time-lessly true but only historically interesting.

[1.4] Colleges that have tried to find a way between the horns of this di-lemma—which includes most of the private American liberal arts colleges still in existence—have ended up impaled on both. They fail to speak the truth and they also trivialize, painting glowing portraits of campus commu-nity in words emptied of believable reference. Notoriously, all catalogue state-ments and presidential addresses tend to be interchangeable. They promise, all of them, academic "excellence" through the application of "critical intel-ligence" and "reflective synthesis" to the "best which has been thought and said in the world." They envision the college years as an "opportunity for personal growth," the development of a "well-rounded personality," and the acquisition of life-guiding "standards of values," all fostered within a "com-munity of scholars and learners" that is at the same time both supportive and stimulating (Rudolph 1962: passim). But none of these terms is ever clearly defined, and campus realities usually are far removed from even the most generous interpretation of what they might mean.

The 1783 motto for Dickinson College, expressed in the terse Latin appropriate to the traditionalist world of the Faithful Community, asserts that *pietate et doctrina tuta libertas*. But by the late twentieth century, with Dickinson struggling to appeal to students of whatever faith and to those of no faith, the powers that secure liberty have ceased to be trum-peted as "piety and doctrine." No longer is it by their faith in the certainty of God's mighty acts in history and their confidence that they have a role in the working out of His purposes that students see themselves laying the cornerstone of a nation free from tyranny. The preferred reading of the college motto, the translation as it usually appears in Dickinson's publi-cations, mumbles vaguely about "virtue and learning," and the liberty the students have in mind is their right as individuals to do as they please.

Embalmed in pious platitudes, the old ideals linger. Long past their perishing.

2. THE ESSENCE OF MODERNITY

The only way to avoid the bathetic consequences of this dilemma is to abandon the educational model underlying it. The Faithful Community must give way to a different understanding of education. The ontology of the natural order and the principles of natural knowledge disclosed by modern science provide that new understanding.

[2.1] If religious belief is a private matter, then it has no place in the public sphere. The Church must be prevented from exercising public political power as a way to effect private spiritual ends. Écrasez l'infâme! The disestablishment of religion, explicitly insulating the powers of the State from those of the Church, is justified once faith and morals are understood to be personal matters. If a person's attitudes and convictions are understood to be subjective, rooted in feeling and emotion, then they should not be taught in the public schools. They should be taught in the home, learned by a child at its mother's breast and father's knee, then given wider communal expression in the rituals and the catechism classes of the religious sect to which the child and its parents belong. Personal beliefs about God, salvation, and moral duty can be commonsensical or outlandish, life-centering or whimsical, but the public order will tolerate them all—just so long, that is, as they are expressed only behind the closed doors of a sanctuary or in meetings of groups clearly identified as voluntary. Society can even tolerate the public expression of those beliefs, as long as their purpose is only to persuade others to hold similar beliefs. Coercive power is reserved solely to the civil government acting solely for the sake of public ends.

[2.2] Modern Western civilization rests on this key distinction between the private and the public. Its ontological expression is the separation of mind and body, famously argued by Descartes as the difference between thinking substance that has no spatial extension and extended substance that cannot think (Descartes 1960). An instantiation of thinking substance, an individual human self, responds to the world around it, including its own body, both emotionally and rationally. Insofar as its feelings and attitudes and its needs and desires are in abeyance, the thinking self is likely to gain accurate knowledge of its world and to make choices that will permit it to fulfill its ends. But the self can easily become a prisoner of its emotions and, acting hastily or willfully, from ignorance or uncontrolled desire, bring harm upon itself and others.

A person's capacity to think is best exercised not when thinking about objects of perception but when thinking about thoughts, and in particular when contemplating those ideas and the relationships among them that the very process of thinking has brought to mind. Such ideas are not known by relying on the senses, memory, or imagination; they are known by reason alone. When these ideas are those necessary to the very process of thinking or those found to be necessary consequences of such ideas, they can be shown to be systematically related. Thinking of this sort is called reasoning. Logic and mathematics are its noblest achievements: the sciences of rational thought.

According to Descartes, the world external to the mind is composed primarily of bodies: spatial objects devoid of mind, hence devoid of rationality, feeling, need, and purpose. The world also contains other minds that like one's own are related to bodies, although since minds lack extension and hence spatial location, the mode of that relation is obscure. Natural science is a technique for thinking rationally about what these objects are and how they interact. If ideas derived from one's bodily sense organs are limited to ideas that can be clearly defined and clearly distinguished from other ideas, omitting whichever of them are unclear or are dependent on the subject's situation, then these ideas can also be taken as necessary. Although such ideas are not necessary for rational thinking, they are necessary insofar as it is true that there are bodies in motion interacting with other bodies in motion. To the system of mental ideas, the laws of logic and mathematics, Descartes is therefore able to add a system of natural laws that gives order to the ideas derived from bodies. The latter laws are the application of the former to the world of extended substance.

[2.3] The essence of modernity is the claim that only what science can rationally know is objective. The real world is the experienced world understood in terms of mathematically expressed relationships among mathematically describable relata. Indeed, the real world is composed of—not merely understood by means of—those relata and relationships. The scientist, however, is a mind, and minds are realities of which there cannot be objective knowledge because they are not extended substance and so are not available for mathematical description. This fact poses a problem: how can what is not objectively knowable validate the claim that what it knows is objective?

This question is not easily answered. Descartes knows that he exists as thinking substance because even in thinking that he might not exist he is revealed as precisely the thinking substance of which he doubts. But beyond that bare truth of its existence, he can know nothing of his own mind except indirectly through its effects on material bodies. Moreover, since mind is the locus not only of reason but of feeling and will, of passion, memory, commitment, and imagination, a mind when thinking nonrationally can occlude the clear light of that reason by which objective knowledge of the external world is alone possible. It is therefore crucial that a way be found to assure scientists that when they are conducting their experiments and fashioning their theories they are doing science, that they are doing what is rationally validated and not simply indulging their prejudices.

[2.4] So the essence of science is its method. To do science is to be governed by a procedure designed to prevent a self from permitting nonrational considerations to intrude into its thinking, considerations traceable to its feelings, desires, and willfulness. Since a self most truly reflects its essence as thinking substance when its thinking is uninfluenced by its own body or by any other instances of extended substance, a method which constrains that self within the limits of reason is a method that divests it, for that moment, of all its nonessential, idiosyncratic qualities. Scientists, when they are doing science properly, are interchangeable; each is expressing fully the essence they all share as rational thinking machines. Their reasoning should therefore be replicable by any other scientist also proceeding properly.

The *Discourse on Method* is Descartes's most important work, because by elaborating a paradigm for rational inquiry he defines the essence of modern science and hence of modernity. The procedure he proposes is simplicity itself, but like all simple things it is easier to describe than to practice. Descartes says there are four rules to which one must adhere in order to reason scientifically, to pursue an inquiry that will lead to truth rather than falsehood:

> The first rule was never to accept anything as true unless . . . it presented itself so clearly and distinctly to my mind that there was no occasion to doubt it.
> The second was to divide each of the difficulties which I encountered into as many parts as possible. . . .
> The third was to think in an orderly fashion, beginning with the things which were simplest and easiest to understand, and gradually

and by degrees reaching toward more complex knowledge, even treating as though ordered materials which were not necessarily so.

The last was always to make enumerations so complete, and reviews so general, that I would be certain that nothing was left out. (1956: 12)

The famous "Cartesian doubt" of the first rule is a way to operationalize the warning against falling victim to one's own prejudices and preferences. Do not accept any idea until the light of reason has shown clearly that it contains no impurities, that it is transparently what it seems to be. It follows, according to the second rule, that anything complex will need to be broken down into its simpler components. What is experienced by the senses is extended substance, and whatever is extended is necessarily composed of parts into which it can be subdivided. Only by knowing the subdivisions can the whole dependent on them be known. This rule of analysis also applies to ideas, since the validity of reasoning from one idea to another is established by showing the logical dependence of complex theorems on simple premises.

The third rule reverses the process, except that now the building blocks are clearly and distinctly understood. The resulting structure, defining the relationship of subordinates to superordinates, of part to whole, should thus be as clear as the relata it organizes; whether or not the actual world is that clear, its reflection onto the map of knowledge should be. The last rule, which calls for detailed enumeration of the steps taken in the course of the inquiry, is not only a demand that the original investigators double-check their work but also the criterion for public validation of the investigation. The steps taken should be sufficient for another scientist to replicate the experiment.

The years since Descartes published his *Discourse* have seen numerous refinements in what the scientific method is thought to require, but Descartes's rules remain foundational.

[2.5] This understanding of how best to arrive at truth is not an invention of modern Western culture, even though it finds its fullest expression there. Its roots are in Plato, its stem is the distinctive work of the medieval Scholastics, and its first flowering is the Enlightenment. Bruce Kimball calls the educators who walk in this tradition "philosophers" (1986). The label is apt. Even though "orators" such as Isocrates always argued that they were the true philosophers, and even though Aristophanes was not alone in branding Socrates a sophist, the right to the title of philosopher belongs to the Socrates found in Plato's dialogues and to the tradition of thinkers defined by the work of Plato and his student Aristotle.

Plato's criticism of the orators is that they make truth and goodness a function either of their own desires or of the interests of a particular community. The argument in the *Republic* on behalf of ethnogenic lying is subject to precisely this critique. Therefore either we are to take Plato ironically when he approves substituting emotive meaning for rational truth as the source for communal unity, or this instance is one of a few places in his dialogues where Plato simply fails to live up to his own standards. Those standards are unambiguous. Man is not, as Protagoras had argued, the measure of all things; Thrasymachus is wrong in claiming that might makes right. The measure for determining whether something is right or true is independent of individual desires, societal interests, or even of beliefs as old as human memory.

In the *Gorgias,* Plato has Socrates repudiate traditionalists of the sort familiar to us from the defenders of the Faithful Community model of truth (Plato 1961). Socrates meets one of the great orators, a man named Callicles, who argues that "luxury and intemperance and license, when they have sufficient backing, are virtue and happiness, and all the rest is tinsel, the unnatural catch-words of mankind, mere nonsense and of no account" (Plato 1961: 274). Socrates chides Callicles for making such a cynical comment and proposes that all the renowned orators and sophists, and the politicians who are their pupils, share in this cynicism. They all play to the prejudices of their patrons in order to enhance their fame and fortune; they have no interest in doing what is right or saying what is true, especially if doing so might anger or embarrass those upon whom they are dependent for their positions as public figures. Socrates asks Callicles to name just one orator or sophist who has ever placed truth above self-interest. He cannot do so. It is better then, says Socrates, to be a philosopher even should that mean not entering public life. For the possession of truth and goodness, or at least the quest for them, is the only proper human end.

The orator uses speech rhetorically: to persuade others to agree with his point of view. The philosopher, in contrast, uses speech logically: to expose the falsehood and injustice that are paraded, through ignorance or deceit, as truth and goodness. The orator works horizontally, weaving ideas together into coherent systems of belief, weaving people together by means of those beliefs into effective communities. But the orator has no way to distinguish true from false belief or just from unjust communities. The philosopher, in contrast, concerned to make precisely those distinctions, works vertically, probing beneath the surface coherence of things and soaring above their limited context, seeking to determine whether what seems likely corresponds to what is actually true and good. The philosopher wants to know if apparently congenial companions exhibit true friendship in their interactions, if the society into which they were born and which means so much to them, although apparently a good place to live, is in fact truly just.

Plato provides a technical exposition of this move from the seeming to the real through his theory of universals. He wants to distinguish between the changing particulars of the world and the unchanging Forms that give them value, that give them shape and purpose. Plato's importance, however, lies not in his conclusions but in his method and its presuppositions. Plato is the first genuine philosopher because he recognizes that what appears to be real may not be, and he is committed unrelentingly to finding out what really is the case. What is foundational, with respect to what we might know for sure and with respect to how we might best live our lives, says Plato, transcends what is most immediately available. The familiar world of our commonsense experiences and habitual actions cannot be trusted. What is really real, what is truly or rightly the case, lies beyond the vicissitudes of time and space. What is timeless accounts for the recurrent qualities of what is temporal. The structures, trajectories, and purposes determining what come to be and perish: they neither come to be nor perish. Thus to know these transcendent realities, whether they be Plato's Forms or are better characterized in some other fashion, is to know all that one needs to know in order to understand what the world is like and why.

Plato's method is interrogatory: posing a question to a person, then systematically analyzing his response until the aspects of it that ring true have been noted and its inadequacies exposed. The person questioned is then invited to formulate a new response, one in which he will see more clearly where the truth lies now that his earlier unjustified confidence that he knew this truth has been stripped away. The interrogation proceeds until a response is made that leaves no room for further questioning. The quest for truth is iterative: put an initial idea into question, critique it until it has been stripped of its inconsistencies and confusions, attempt to reformulate the idea more adequately, and repeat this process as long as necessary.

[2.6] The Scholastics of the high middle ages are the inheritors of this mode of rational questioning, although their use of it is constrained by an envelope of special truths not available to criticism. They believed that the Truth of revealed religion is beyond the capacities of unaided human reason and so beyond questioning, beyond doubt. Within the envelope of faith, however, the search for understanding may proceed by the use of unfettered reason. Where its methods are competent instruments of inquiry, reason alone can secure genuine knowledge. It is inconceivable that such rational knowledge could ever contravene faith, because its truths, even if lesser than those of faith, are nonetheless still truths—and Truth is one.

Scholasticism formalized interrogation as the method for obtaining the truths available to reason. At first this approach meant no more than assembling the traditional authorities and working through their apparent differences to some sort of reconciliation. But this process was enough to shift the primary activity at the monastic schools from a mode of instruction in which the teacher leads pupils page by page through a traditional text to one requiring the instructor to organize selections from relevant texts in a manner that he thinks will most clearly exhibit their apparent or real disagreements. The scholar doing the organizing, not the texts from which he draws, becomes the focus of attention.

Libraries grew in importance once it was thought necessary for a monastery or university to possess copies of all the authoritative texts likely to be needed in undertaking these comparative analyses. This development meant finding ways to copy texts more quickly and more cheaply than before and devising a system for indexing those texts, in their whole and in their parts, with respect to the topics they treated. The structural sophistication of the scholar's work—the pattern of selected sources, their critique, and his conclusions—necessitated that his students analyze these materials carefully on their own. Merely hearing them through in linear fashion was insufficient. The structure of the reasoning needed to be seen, the links between premises and conclusions traversed backward as well as forward, with branching routes of argument followed out and their relevance to the main argument assayed. The scholar lectures or two scholars debate, and the students take notes; the scholar writes, and his book is spread in multiple copy as widely as possible.

This process is what Ivan Illich calls an intellectual revolution more important than printing: the shift from texts as sacred historical objects to "the bookish text." A text for the Scholastics is a replicable vehicle for conveying ideas that no longer are grounded in the particularities of the time and place of their first articulation. Ideas are no longer linked tangibly to specific manuscripts written by specific authors and preserved at specific places. The text is no longer a repository of tangible truths but an arbitrary location for abstract truths that have many other locations as well (Illich 1993: 93–124).

The result is somewhat paradoxical. On the one hand, truths are no longer fruits on a vine deeply rooted in a particular history of origin and destiny. They have become general characteristics detached from historical contingencies and parochial purposes. On the other hand, these truths are the work of specific individuals whose skill has led to their discovery. Truths require experts whose ability to select, weigh, and compile ideas makes it possible to determine confidently which of those ideas are actually true and which only apparently true. This yoking through a proper method of the particular subject as instrument of inquiry with objective universal truths as the outcome of inquiry is the signature of modernity. It is what Plato taught Scholasticism and what it in turn taught Descartes.

[2.7] The finest example of the Scholastic method is the work of Thomas Aquinas. Consider, for instance, how he argues against the claim that the existence of God is a self-evident truth (1945: 18–20). Thomas formulates the issue as a question: "Whether the existence of God is self-evident?" He then assembles what he thinks are the three strongest arguments in the traditional texts that answer this question positively. One is based on a point about natural knowledge made by John Damascene, another draws from what the Philosopher (Aristotle) says about the indemonstrability of first principles, and the third extrapolates from scripture. Against these arguments, Thomas sets one counterargument, based on scripture: since the fool has said in his heart that there is no God, the denial of the proposition "God exists" is thinkable; therefore the proposition is not self-evidently true.

Amid this swirl of contending views, Thomas develops his own position. He first distinguishes two senses of "self-evident"—"on the one hand, self-evident in itself, though not to us; on the other, self-evident in itself, and to us." Next he defines a self-evident proposition as one in which "the predicate is included in the essence of the subject." For example, in the proposition "Man is an animal" the predicate "animal" is part of the

essence of "Man." Were some creature not an animal it would follow necessarily that it was not a human being; or, to say the same thing obversely,
the fact that it was human would be sufficient to say as well that it was
an animal. So if a person knows what God's essential characteristics are,
for that person it would be self-evident that God exists. But for anyone
who does not know what the essence of God is, who does not know that
for God existence is a necessary attribute, for such a person it would not
be self-evident that God exists. Indeed, the very fact that Thomas intends
further on in his argument to prove that God necessarily exists demonstrates that the proposition is not a self-evident truth, for if it were self-
evident no proof would be required.

Thomas concludes by returning to the three initial arguments for self-
evidence, using his distinction between self-evidence "in itself" and "for
us" to show the extent to which each argument was correct and where it
slipped into confusion. Thus, for example, Damasene was correct in claiming that a knowledge of God is implanted in us by nature. This knowledge is of "a general and confused" sort, however. For instance, our
natural desire for happiness is implicitly a knowledge of God since God
is man's beatitude. But this "is not to know absolutely that God exists;
just as to know that something is approaching is not the same as to know
that Peter is approaching, even though it is Peter who is approaching; for
there are many who imagine that man's perfect good, which is happiness,
consists in riches, and others in pleasures, and others in something else."
To know something inchoately is not yet to know it clearly and distinctly
enough for one to know for certain what one knows.

What is striking about Thomas's style is the importance of logic. None
of the arguments in defense of self-evidence is simply an appeal to authority; each is a carefully reasoned extrapolation from an authoritative text.
The Aristotle text that Thomas uses, indeed, is from the *Posterior Analytics,* which is one of the Philosopher's treatises on logic. Thomas's own
view is grounded in an analysis of the logical form of propositions, combined with a crucial distinction and an erudite display of sequential reasoning that could easily be formulated as a syllogistical sortes. Thomas
the rational thinker, Thomas the expert in the theory of logical syntax and
syllogism, dominates the exposition. He is versed in the intellectual tradition and aware of the flurry of contradictory claims it encompasses. He
uses his analytic skill to cut through the morass of controversy to the
underlying truth of the matter and then uses that same skill synthetically

to reconcile the disputants, to show that their differences were only apparent, a result of their confusion and unclarity.

[2.8] Substitute for the traditional authorities the authority of those who have done relevant prior research on the topic in question, and Thomas's method of assemblage, assessment, and reconciliation is still normative today. In a typical report on research prepared for publication in a scientific journal, the authors first review what has been claimed by predecessors working on the same or similar topics. They then explicate their research method, formulate their own hypotheses, report the data they have been able to gather, and draw their own independent conclusions. In a closing discussion section, they reconcile these conclusions with those of their predecessors and indicate the agenda of unanswered questions still needing to be addressed.

3. THE KNOWLEDGE PARADIGM

The methods of Plato, Thomas, and Descartes underlie the scientific method as currently understood and practiced. I have argued that this method is the key to science, just as science is the key to modernity. Essentially interrogatory and rational, the use of the scientific method results in truths that are organized in pyramidal fashion. In order to become a modern person, to be able to make useful contributions to modern society, a student needs to learn not only how the scientific method works but also how the knowledge pyramid resulting from applications of that method is organized and how it can best be utilized. For to know the apex upon which all else depends is to know all else as well.

The knowledge paradigm is not easily described. I will attempt to do so by discussing three interrelated notions, each of them key tools—normative measures—for building a knowledge pyramid. First, the importance of a "syntax" of precise symbols permitting concisely expressed statements. Second, an "axiomatic" method for organizing statements into a rigorously deductive system. Third, a "semantics" for using the axiomatic system to describe, explain, and predict the events constituting our experience of the world (Von Mises 1956).

[3.1] A necessary condition for the organization of knowledge into a pyramidal system is that statements about facts be expressed with both precision and conciseness. There is a pleasing elegance to plain discourse shorn of obfuscating rhetoric, but its scientific value is that it is necessary to be precise and concise if the method of knowledge acquisition is to be successful. A system of knowledge is fundamentally vertical in its orientation, moving from a base in particular claims about the particulars of experience to general claims about the patterns recurrent in the ways those particulars interrelate. The challenge is to express the particulars with sufficient clarity and distinctness to reveal the pattern they contain, so that the vertical relationship becomes obvious.

To take a simple example, suppose that five automobiles leave at various times from a common location on some Saturday morning, travel to different locations, and arrive at their destinations at various times. One driver might report on the journey as follows: "I was driving the maroon '96 Ford Taurus; the one with the moon roof and the environmental license plate. I left late morning and drove at a moderate speed the whole way. The sun was shining brightly, so I needed my sunglasses, but traffic was light and fortunately I encountered no road construction or other delays. In no time at all, I had reached my destination and was able to enjoy a late lunch with an old friend at the cafe on the square." The other drivers would make similar reports, blending vague qualitative and quantitative information and with no clear sense of what facts to include or exclude.

It would be all but impossible to see any pattern in the stories told about these Saturday outings, no generalization that might lift the drivers' reports vertically up the knowledge pyramid, disclosing some sort of nontrivial law of which these events were a conforming instance. Suppose, however, that the drivers used precise measuring devices—clocks, odometers, and speedometers—and checked them regularly. Suppose we focused our attention on only this information about the trips, which we could easily express in concise numerical form:

	Ford	Honda	Buick	Toyota	Dodge
Time start	11:00 A.M.	11:10 A.M.	11:20 A.M.	11:30 A.M.	11:40 A.M.
Time end	1:10 P.M.	1:50 P.M.	12:50 P.M.	1:10 P.M.	12:50 P.M.
Speed	47 mph	65 mph	54 mph	60 mph	43 mph
Distance	104 miles	176 miles	81 miles	100 miles	49 miles

The value of a concise presentation of information is that it can be absorbed in a single glance. This permits relationships to appear that otherwise might go unnoticed. With respect to these particular data, unfortunately, no obvious pattern is revealed even after they have been so nicely compacted and displayed.

Massage the data a bit more, however, and a pattern emerges. Suppose we calculate the total elapsed time for each journey and use that information instead of start and stop times. Suppose we reorder the sequence of columns by speed from slowest to fastest and then convert the time quantities to a single unit of measure, minutes being the most convenient. The information now looks like this:

	Car 5	Car 1	Car 3	Car 4	Car 2
Speed: mpm	0.7	0.8	0.9	1.0	1.1
Time: minutes	70	130	90	100	160
Distance: miles	49	104	81	100	176

The speeds, when expressed in miles per minute and rounded to the nearest tenth, arrange themselves in a linear sequence of values that increases by one unit each column. But that pattern seems trivial, and the elapsed time and distance traveled correlate to it in no obvious way. Notice something else, however: for each column the figure in the distance row is the same as the product of the figures in the speed and time rows. So we have an important pattern after all: a relationship, $D = S \times T$, which is constant for all the five different journeys.

If we claim this result is a general pattern, applicable to any automobile moving at a uniform speed, we acquire a powerful tool for extending our knowledge. We no longer need to measure speed, distance, and elapsed time because given any two pieces of this information we can deduce the third. When we learn that a sixth vehicle made the same trip as the Toyota but in only half an hour, we can deduce its average speed. It must have been moving at over 200 mph because $D = 100$ miles, $T = 30$ minutes; so if $S = D/T$, then $S = 100/30 = 3\ 1/3$ mpm $= 200$ mph. As an interesting additional piece of information, we might then infer, but with less confidence, that this vehicle was an airplane rather than an automobile.

What should be clear from this example is how important it is for the scientific method that there be an interplay among three techniques: the disregard of certain data, the expression of the selected data in terms of precise quantities, and the visually compact presentation of the results of analyzing the data. By presenting information clearly and distinctly—precisely, concisely, and selectively—patterns that might otherwise go unobserved become visible. Because we chose to limit ourselves to the speeds, elapsed times, and distances of the five automobiles, and because we harmonized the way the data were calibrated and then arrayed them in a simple matrix, we saw (literally) that given any two of the variables the third could always be determined. Given the way the data were presented, it did not require a particularly subtle eye to make explicit a relationship until then only implicit in the information. (For an elaboration of this general point, see Tufte 1990.)

The $D = S \times T$ pattern is a general relational fact about our experience with these automobiles. It had been present in experience all along, but not until the observations of what was happening could be made more precise than the human eye can manage, and not until they could then be expressed in symbols more concise than any natural language permits, was it possible to be aware of that pattern as characterizing those particular experiences. Then, given the pattern, its scope could be tested by seeing if it correctly predicted our experience of other travel events. If so, the $S = D/T$ formula could be generalized. Eventually it would become clear that a pattern of relationships found among a few automobiles at a certain place on a certain Saturday was a pattern that relates time and distance to the velocity of any body whatsoever when its motion is uniform and unimpeded: the $v = d/t$ law found in any elementary physics text.

[3.2] At the heart of science, therefore, lies the methodological insistence that information about the world be represented in accord with Descartes's dictum: clearly and distinctly. The symbol systems of mathematics and logic are designed for just that purpose. The former can be used to represent numerically expressed statements; the latter, nonnumerical statements as well.

Suppose there were a language in which the only statements permitted are those expressed in the notations of mathematics and logic. Suppose further that each basic statement in this language (let us call them "protocol statements") is a claim that there exists some fact about the world. Then for every actual fact, there is a protocol statement that mirrors it, that represents it accurately; such statements are true. Those protocol statements that do not mirror the fact they claim to mirror are false. Suppose that every statement which is not a protocol statement can be shown to depend on one or more protocol statements, such that its truth or falsity is known given the truth or falsity of the protocol statements upon which it depends. Let us call these "derivative statements." Every statement in this language, therefore, must be either true or false; the task is to determine which.

The dream of such a language is at least as old as Leibniz: "If we had some exact *language* (like the one called *Adamitic* by some) or at least a kind of *truly philosophic writing,* in which the ideas were reduced to a kind of *alphabet of human thought,* then all that follows rationally from what is given could be found by a *kind of calculus,* just as arithmetical or geometrical problems are solved" (1965: 12). Ludwig Wittgenstein provided the framework for realizing Leibniz's dream when he laid out the conditions for a perfect language in his *Tractatus Logico-Philosophicus* (1922). The main-heading propositions of that book epitomize his claims (for our purposes a "significant proposition" is a "statement" and an "elementary proposition" is a "protocol statement"):

1. The world is everything that is the case. . . .
2. What is the case, the fact, is the existence of atomic facts. . . .
3. The logical picture of the facts is the thought. . . .
4. The thought is the significant proposition.
   4.001. The totality of propositions is the language. . . .
   4.06. Propositions can be true or false only by being pictures of reality. . . .
   4.1. A proposition presents the existence and non-existence of atomic facts.
   4.11. The totality of true propositions is the total natural science (or the totality of the natural sciences). . . .
5. Propositions are truth-functions of elementary propositions. . . .
   5.6. *The limits of my language* means the limits of my world. . . .

Wittgenstein noted that some statements do not assert anything in particular about the world because what they claim is compatible with any possible state of affairs whatsoever. Such statements are necessarily true. Wittgenstein called these statements "tautologies" because they are, in this sense, devoid of content. Tautologies are very important in logic and mathematics because of their role in linking derivative statements to protocol statements. So a perfect language would be composed of protocol statements, derivative statements, and tautologies. The subset of these statements that are true (exactly half of them!) would provide, when properly organized, an objective picture of the world. Our language would mirror the reality it describes.

[3.3] Thus the ideal science would use this ideal language to show, clearly and without any possibility for misunderstanding, how the statements of scientists, the conclusions at which they arrive by successive applications of the scientific method, fit together into a knowledge pyramid. At the base would be true protocol statements about atomic facts. The next higher layer up the pyramid would be composed of derivative statements that have only protocol statements as a necessary condition of their truth. At the next layer the derivative statements would have only those at the lower layers as the necessary condition of their truth, and so on until arriving at a layer that would have no higher layer for which it provided the necessary conditions.

The statements constituting the ideal knowledge pyramid are linked together in this tightly interdependent manner: every statement is a sufficient condition for a specifiable range of lower level statements and a necessary condition for at least one higher level statement. The pyramid can be called a "proof-tree" because the statements at the bottom thus follow deductively from those at the top. The truth of the apex statements is sufficient to establish the truth of all the other statements.

The paradigm in mathematics for deductive reasoning of this sort is found in Euclid's *Elements*. Euclid shows that it is possible to derive all the known facts concerning geometrical figures from a very few general statements. He identifies five "common notions" or axioms that he takes to be self-evident and therefore not in need of proof:

1. Things which are equal to the same thing are also equal to one another.
2. If equals be added to equals, the wholes are equal.
3. If equals be subtracted from equals, the remainders are equal.
4. Things which coincide with one another are equal to one another.
5. The whole is greater than the part. (1926: 155)

As Aristotle makes clear, every system must have some statements—he calls them "first principles"—that cannot be proved. In a hierarchy where some things depend on other things, there has to be at least one thing that does not depend on the others although they depend on it. Suppose that were not the case. Then whatever was used in proving the first principle either would (a) itself be unproved, and hence would be the real first principle, or (b) would need to have been already established by a proof using a first principle, which would be to have argued in a circle, to have presupposed what was to be proved. The only justification possible for a first principle, for the axioms of a system, has to be self-evidence, the impossibility of thinking that the denial of the principle could hold (Aristotle 1941: 112).

Euclid also asserted five "postulates," or principles particular to geometry, which are taken as true even though they are not self-evident. Euclid's postulates have to do with the existence of straight lines, circles, and right angles, plus the controversial postulate to the effect that parallel lines never meet. In the centuries since Euclid and Aristotle, the distinction between axioms and postulates has collapsed, because what is important to the deductive method is identifying the statements that are to be accepted without proof, no matter what their scope or degree of self-evidence.

[3.4] The Euclidean method of proof, if it could be extended beyond geometry to include every possible subject matter, would be the realization of Leibniz's universal calculus. One problem exists, however. Logic since Aristotle had been valued as an instrument of deduction, a way to show how truths could be disclosed that were implicit in already established truths, how truth could be preserved throughout a process of reasoning. But the rules of logic were seemingly ad hoc. They had no justification other than the fact that they worked.

A revolution in logical theory during the nineteenth century culminated in precisely what was needed: the organization of logic itself into a deductive system. Given an "alphabet" of precisely defined basic symbols, and given a "syntax" of rules for their combination into a vocabulary of symbol strings called "well-formed formulas," plus a few axioms and a rule or two for deriving new formulas from old ones, it could be shown that the laws of logic and the theorems of mathematics, from the Aristotelian syllogism to the theory of natural numbers, followed deductively (Kneale and Kneale, 1962: sections 5–10).

But the rules for manipulating formulas, like the axioms of the system, remained unproven. Why should they be trusted? Wittgenstein's answer was to take what happens when a rule is applied to any formula to create a new formula and define it truth-functionally. That is, the rule is defined by a little table that shows what happens to the truth or falsity of the component statements when they are aggregated into more complex statements or disaggregated into simpler statements. In this way, the axioms of a logical or mathematical system can be shown to be necessarily true, and any theorems derived by rules from the axioms can be shown to have preserved that truth and so also to be necessarily true.

For instance, all the other operators used in logical proofs can be defined in terms of these two: (a) denial, which converts the truth of a statement to falsity or vice versa, and (b) disjunction, which makes an either-or statement true if at least one of its components is true. These definitions are conveniently—concisely and precisely—stated in the following truth tables:

Negation [~]			Disjunction [v]		
p	~p		p	q	p v q
T	F		T	T	T
F	T		T	F	T
			F	T	T
			F	F	F

It may be more obvious that the negation operation preserves truth than that the disjunction operation does, but truth-functional definitions have no need to appeal to self-evidence. The operator only does what it is defined to do. A well-formed formula composed of basic symbols and operators can be determined to stand for a true or false statement depending solely on the truth and falsity of the statements represented by the basic symbols.

Two other key operators can then simply be defined in terms of negation and disjunction. Let the conjunction "p&q" be defined as "~(~p v ~q)": the conjunction of two assertions is true only if it is not the case that either one is false. And let the implication "p⊃q" be defined as "~p v q": one assertion implies a second only if either the first is false or the second is true.

Axioms can be generated that are true under any possible assignment of truth or falsity to the basic symbols. These axioms are necessarily true, and any well-formed formula deduced from them using rules defined truth-functionally is guaranteed to have preserved the initial necessity of the axioms. Only one rule of deduction is needed, and it can be defined in terms of negation and disjunction. The rule is this: given the statement "p" and the statement "if p then q," it is legitimate to assert "q." This is the rule the ancients called *modus ponens*. The statement "*modus ponens* is true" is necessarily true, as the following truth table indicates:

p	q	p⊃q	(p⊃q) & p	((p⊃q) & p)⊃q
T	T	T	T&T = T	T⊃T = T
F	T	T	T&F = F	F⊃T = T
T	F	F	F&T = F	F⊃F = T
F	F	T	T&F = F	F⊃F = T

The effort of symbolic logicians in the twentieth century has been to resolve various technical problems concerning the formalization of a logic sufficiently powerful to generate a complete knowledge pyramid, to devise a single function that could replace negation and disjunction, and to avoid the paradoxes that result when trying to design a logical system that accounts for itself. Although the problems are immense and some of them seemingly intractable, the ideal remains: to create a language with a perfect syntax, to make by means of it well-formed formulas, and to devise a method for deriving new well-formed formulas from established ones that is absolutely guaranteed to preserve truth.

[3.5] A syntax, unfortunately, says nothing about the world until it has been given a "semantics": until its symbols are given a meaning. To speak of the truth or falsity of a well-formed formula, indeed, is already to have moved beyond syntax into interpretation, into semantics. At the syntactical level, "T" and "F" are just marks, and the same goes for "p" and "q." In the expression "p v q" the symbols "p" and "q" could be understood as referring to statements of fact such as "Socrates is mortal" or "snow is white," but they could just as easily be taken as referring to electrical circuits, or to the gods and goddesses in the Greek pantheon. The operator "v" could be interpreted as logical disjunction, but it might be read as a symbol for mechanical divergence or sexual attraction. The logical-mathematical system needs to be given an interpretation in which its symbols are used to express statements about the world. The math needs to be applied to physics; some of the well-formed formulas need to be read as protocol statements about worldly facts.

Until recently it was thought that the symbols in Euclid's *Elements* referred to features of the actual world, about which they therefore expressed necessary truths. It was thought that physical space is Euclidean. Newton utilized Euclid's method to extend a system of truths about space to include truths about physical bodies as well. He posited three "axioms" or "laws of motion," from which he deduced all the theorems necessary to describe accurately the behavior of objects in motion, both earthly and celestial (1846).

Newton's laws are more like Euclid's postulates than like his axioms, however, for they are neither necessary truths nor self-evident. The first law, for instance, states that "every body perseveres in its state of rest, or of uniform motion in a right line, unless it is compelled to change that state by forces impressed thereon." This statement flies in the face of common sense, for if anything seems obvious it is that a body in motion, if not acted upon by any external force, will slow down and eventually come to rest. When someone quits pushing the cart, it soon comes to a stop. Its natural state is rest, and therefore if it is in motion there must be or there must have been some efficient cause that set it in motion.

But Newton, by moving deductively from his laws, can account for everything that we observe about the physical world and can predict future observations accurately. The power of his laws, even those that defy common sense, is due to the universal scope and unerring accuracy of the system for which they are first principles. Newton's laws are capstones of an axiomatic system interpreted as composed of statements about the world. They are at the top of a pyramid of explanatory abstractions, at the bottom of which are protocol statements confirmed and reconfirmed experimentally. As Newton comments just before beginning the deduction of the first proposition from his laws: "Hitherto I have laid down such principles as have been received by mathematicians and are confirmed by abundance of experiments." Whether self-evident or not, that they reside at the apex of a pyramid of well-established truths is why they command our belief.

[3.6] Any particular science can be defined by where its most general statements, its first principles, are located in the ideal pyramid of knowledge. The logical and mathematical sciences are at the apex because their statements are necessarily true. But, as we have already seen, tautologies tell us nothing in particular, nothing unique or even distinctive, about our world. For that we need sciences that are dependent on protocol statements.

Physics is at the most fundamental of the natural sciences because its first principles are about patterns that describe the essential characteristics of every physical fact. No matter how simple or compound the fact asserted, no matter how microcosmic or macrocosmic, it needs to be understood as analyzable into atomic facts concerning bodies that continue in uniform motion or remain at rest unless acted upon by other bodies external to them. Chemistry is subordinate to physics in the pyramid because it assumes certain key principles in physics while focusing upon a particular kind of physical structure, the atom, and upon the ways in which atoms interact to form and unform molecules. Biology is further subordinate because it presumes both physics and chemistry, limiting the scope of its investigations to systems of molecules that meet specified criteria for being organic and to systems of such systems. Anthropology restricts the scope of the biological to human organisms, including their evolutionary origins as well as the systems in which they function and those which they themselves have made. The first principles of economics locate it yet farther down the knowledge pyramid because it limits its attention to a particular feature of systems of human organisms. It is paralleled by political science, which has the same vertical range in the hierarchy but focuses upon a different feature of human systems.

Understood ideally, the knowledge pyramid encompasses the whole of the world—"everything that is the case," as Wittgenstein puts it, to the "limits of my language." The pyramid should reach to the limits of the universal calculus, which is, thereby, the limits of our—of *the*—world. But the ideal is only a goal. The established sciences have not yet been explored with a rigor sufficient to meet fully, in some cases even to meet in part, the criteria required by the ideal. John Dewey's exhortation to extend the method of natural science to the social sciences is still more dream than reality, and the humanities rarely manage to rise to a level where its statements are testable scientifically. So the hierarchy of disciplines takes on an invidious cast: from the "hard" sciences of which physics is primus inter pares to the "soft" sciences like economics or psychology, perhaps even including a cliometrical approach to history. Excluded from the tree of knowledge altogether are areas of endeavor hardly to be called disciplines, fields such as philosophy and poetry, which are matters of rhetoric rather than knowledge and so make no statements at all about the world, even though they sometimes claim to do so.

[3.7] The hard sciences, however, are now recognized not to be as sturdy as had once been thought. The development of non-Euclidean geometries made it clear that the Euclidean system does not necessarily apply to the actual world. Einstein's transformation of Newtonian physics, indeed, requires a geometry that rejects Euclid's fifth postulate, the one concerning parallel lines. Furthermore, it has been proven mathematically that no axiomatic system can be given an interpretation that includes every true protocol statement. Even more unnerving, the axiomatic method makes it clear that no law or theory about the world can ever be conclusively proven true. Recall the truth table for if-then statements. If we assume the truth of the theory-level statement that "if p is true then q must be true," we have to grant that it could be that "q" is true, but "p" is nonetheless false, since although the truth of "p" is sufficient to establish the truth of "q," the converse is not the case: the truth of "q" does not prove that "p" is true.

The more a scientific theory predicts what turns out actually to occur, the more confident we become about the truth of the theory. But that is only a psychological fact and does nothing to guarantee that the theory is true. We are increasingly willing to lean on the theory, to elevate it from tentative hypothesis to working theory to established law, but there is no way to tell if our experience is broad enough, the relevant factors identified fully enough, the processes consistent enough over time, to know for sure that the theory is true. The pyramid of knowledge rests on the certainty of the atomic facts described by the protocol statements at its base, but the laws of nature at its apex are only the most adequate ones currently available.

Begun in an act of Cartesian methodological doubt, the pyramid of scientific knowledge ends in a doubt required by that same methodology. But both these doubts are sources of energy rather than debilitating enigmas. They remind the scientist that the world is ever-changing, that human knowledge of it is finite, and hence that the knowledge pyramid must constantly change if it is to mirror reality as accurately as human skill can manage. The axiomatic method has not given us final truth, a way to find the universal and necessary laws of logic in the motion of physical bodies. But it has given us a way to approximate that final truth and perhaps to approach it asymptotically. Which is not a bad consolation prize.

4. THE EDUCATION PARADIGM

The job of education is to make scientists. To teach young people the scientific method. To teach them a way to acquire information and a way to solve problems using that information. To develop in young people the discipline of mind needed in order to be proficient at these tasks. To prepare young people for careers as experts in some specialized area of science so that they will be able to contribute to society, either by the new knowledge they add to the storehouse of already established objective truths about the world or by the application of old knowledge through technological invention for whatever individual and societal practical purposes seem opportune. The job of education is to apprentice young men and women into the guild of scientific inquirers.

[4.1] The traditional way of instructing apprentices is to provide them with the basic framework of truths by which the discipline to be learned is organized. Since the framework is a pyramidal hierarchy, a student should first learn the concepts at the apex, those upon which all the others depend. This process also involves acquiring the technical vocabulary in which these fundamental concepts are expressed and knowing some characteristic facts they govern. Further concepts then need to be introduced in the right order, so that an idea compounded from fundamental ideas will be studied only after the fundamental ones have been thoroughly mastered. An instructor usually has considerable discretion in selecting which facts to use to illustrate these ideas, since the fundamental concepts, precisely because they are fundamental, are relevant to a wide range of facts. Or the instructor might choose facts that have historical value: those, for instance, that originally stimulated the formulation of a basic concept.

A chemistry instructor might begin by explicating the general structure of an atom in order to convey principles of positive and negative valances and how chemical bonding works. The instructor might then introduce students to the simplest examples of an atom, those of hydrogen and helium, followed by more complex but crucial ones such as carbon, nitrogen, and oxygen. Next, by a kind of inductive generalization, the instructor might introduce the students to the whole periodic table, emphasizing the schematism, the fact that every atom known or possible has a specific location on the table. The class might then turn to an investigation of molecular bonds, utilizing hydrogen, carbon, oxygen, and nitrogen to demonstrate not only the variety of kinds of molecules that can be built up from the same kinds of atoms in different combination but also how those differences are systematic and hence, in some aspects at least, predictable.

In some such fashion, instructors in the various disciplines lead their apprentices on the long trek down a disciplinary pyramid from its apex. It is not necessary, of course, to learn all of the fundamental concepts before proceeding to intermediate ones. A student can be led down the hierarchy all the way to the base by considering only a limited region of the pyramid. Concepts at the same level of generalization, like simultaneous space-time events, are mutually independent. So whole regions of concepts can be ignored, or even if relevant they can be glossed over, in order to arrive sooner rather than later at a survey that runs from the top to the bottom of a science. The educational trajectory can then start down the hierarchy again, toward a new region of the base, as when in the discipline of biology a course in botany is followed by a course in ornithology. Or the trajectory could focus on a single general aspect of the hierarchy, as might happen in a course on ecology or paleontology.

These are the ways in which a traditional science lecture course is organized. Information acquired at various times and places by countless scientists, conducting their experiments under favorable or unfavorable circumstances, is formalized into an axiomatic system and these systemized results then taught to the student apprentices. The heuristic value of the systematization of knowledge is that it is easier to learn material when concepts are organized with respect to their importance and facts are seen not as strings of names and formulas requiring rote memorization but as the relata for general relationships, a content made comprehensible by the recurrent patterns it illustrates. The beauty of science is the way its pieces fit snugly together into a coherent whole. The student's appreciation of that unity is a powerful motivating force for being willing to persevere in the long journey required in order to gain mastery of very difficult material.

[4.2] A more process-oriented approach to science education argues that learning should begin with the particulars of observation and experiment, building up from them through a step-by-step sequence of increasingly sophisticated problem-solving situations to the general principles of which the initial observations are instances. Science is first of all a method; it is not a body of information but a technique. However much one might know about the results of scientific inquiry, knowing science means actually being able to do it.

For instance, a recent national initiative to improve science teaching, called Project Kaleidoscope, encourages faculty in the natural and mathematical sciences to emphasize hands-on interactive learning (PKAL 1992). One outcome of this approach has been an increase in the so-called "workshop" approach to introductory science courses, where lectures and labs are no longer distinct, where students begin with problematic situations and work collaboratively to design experiments that will sharpen their understanding of what is going on. Basic concepts that might prove relevant to that understanding are introduced as needed (Laws 1991).

The workshop approach mimics the "logic of discovery" rather than the "logic of justification" (Hanson 1958; Suppe 1977): it introduces students to scientific method by putting them in situations analogous to those in which professional scientists work when engaged in genuinely experimental research. The results of scientific inquiry must eventually be presented within the framework of a deduction pyramid, for only in this way can it be guaranteed that the scientists' findings are linked coherently with established truth. But the workshop advocates insist that apprentices should be taught the process by which these results are obtained, not simply the results, lest their zeal for doing science be nipped in the bud.

[4.3] Whether top down or bottom up, whether beginning with process or product, what is being learned is an integrated system of hierarchically arranged truths, with observations and protocol statements at one end and general theories and universal laws at the other. A modern curriculum should reflect this view of the world and of our knowledge about it. What is essential should be at the center of the curriculum. In elementary education, the course of study should be composed of nothing but requirements, since what is being taught are the concepts, facts, and coping skills relevant to daily life, those having to do with self-understanding, social manners, and work habits. The more advanced the study, however, the fewer the general requirements. For the learning trajectory grows ever more specialized as it moves up the knowledge pyramid. The pyramid begins with information that every citizen needs to master, moves through principles relevant only to an educated elite, proceeds on to principles requisite for one's chosen field of expertise, and ends finally with a study of principles only needed by those few scientists who, engaged in a carefully focused research specialty, are adding new truths to the storehouse of human understanding.

There is a possible confusion here that needs to be cleared up. As one moves toward the apex of the pyramid, the relevant knowledge becomes increasingly complex and those learned enough to understand it fewer and fewer. Yet what is being learned are principles of increasing generality, with a putative Unified Theory of Everything perched on the very top. What is narrow about first principles is their number and the number of people able to comprehend them. First principles should not be many, ideally only one, because the deduction model is a structure of dependency relationships: the dependency of the Many on the One.

The scope of common knowledge, in contrast, is quite limited. Although everyone needs to acquire these basic life skills and know these concepts and facts, they are superficial and parochial. Common knowledge is culture-bound, expressed in a language seriously burdened by the prejudices and happenstance of the peoples whose history it embodies. One's commonsense understanding of self, society, and nature is a poorly generalized vague expression of accrued trial-and-error experience, a stockpile of hard knocks and good fortune winnowed by the years into a fairly workable set of beliefs and practices. Science expands this crude base by replacing vague observations with clear and distinct ones, rules of thumb with laws of nature, the mere having of experiences with the reasoned practices of experimental inquiry. So although we all need to know that region of the knowledge base occupied by the common sense of our culture, it is only as we expand the base and move up into the higher reaches of the hierarchy it generates that our knowledge becomes more general. Education begins with the common, which is parochial, and moves toward the specialized, which is universal.

[4.4] The modern knowledge pyramid requires experts: sophisticates with respect to the specialized techniques, concepts, and information that accumulate within any of its specifiable regions. We speak of a group of such experts as composing an academic discipline, even though many work for businesses or governments rather than universities. But apprenticeship nowadays is conducted almost exclusively by educational institutions, and the universities are also where most basic research and theory development are carried on. Teachers in the colleges serving a Faithful Community were expected to be conversant with the intellectual heritage of that community and to inculcate it in their students for the long-term enhancement of the common weal it would assure. Professors in the modern university are masters in guilds, with an expertise that has a variety of uses, only one of which is to train apprentices.

The primary role of guild masters is to exercise their mastery, to contribute as only those with their expertise can to the body of knowledge for which the guild is responsible, and to keep themselves up-to-date in their field in order to do so. These tasks require working closely with other experts, which implies that those with similar expertise should be located, wherever feasible, in proximity to one another and that they should have ample opportunity to interact with whatever experts are not located nearby. The university system of academic departments built around disciplines and housed in a single building or complex of buildings is the obvious result, along with the geographic clusters of academic, commercial, and governmental interests found in such places as the Silicon Valleys of California, Texas, and Massachusetts and the University Triangle in North Carolina. Another example of the centripetal force of expertise is the practice of disciplines holding regular regional or international meetings for the exchange of information and the development of collaborative ventures.

This force is at the same time centrifugal, however, as the expertises increasingly narrow and the important meetings shift from disciplinary to subdisciplinary gatherings. As experts create more disciplinary and subdisciplinary pyramids within the overall knowledge pyramid, their expertise may leave them surprisingly ignorant of how their pyramid fits in with the other pyramids. Many are actually indifferent to the fundamental statements located at the apex of the overall knowledge pyramid, even though their own pyramid depends upon the continued viability of those statements.

[4.5] The history of higher education in the United States since the mid-nineteenth century can be viewed as the story of how the new science-based approach emerged, its struggle against the older collegiate model of education, and its eventual triumph (Rudolph 1962). The first battles were fought over the legitimacy of science as a subject for instruction, in part because a scientific attitude was thought to erode traditional values and in part because the practical consequence of offering science courses was that students needed, or at least wanted, to substitute them for some of the courses constituting the traditional required curriculum. Compromise came in the form of the "parallel course," a curriculum offered to young men unable or unwilling to learn Greek and Latin. Its graduates received only a diploma certifying achievement in the courses they had studied; the baccalaureate degree was reserved for those who had completed the "classical course." The traditionalist position was further compromised when this parallelism was replaced by an elective system and students awarded the baccalaureate for courses of study that as the years went by included increasingly fewer classical offerings. Indeed, the value in studying Greek or Latin, it was eventually claimed, resides more in the mental discipline it provides than in anything intrinsic.

The Board of Overseers for the new University of Virginia approved in 1824 a plan of education proposed by a commission headed by Thomas Jefferson. The faculty were to be grouped into ten schools:

Ancient languages
Modern languages
Pure mathematics
Applied mathematics (engineering)
Natural philosophy (physics, chemistry, mineralogy)
Natural history (botany, zoology)
Anatomy and medicine
Social studies (government, economics, history)
Law
Humanities (grammar, ethics, rhetoric, belles lettres, fine arts)

The prominence these groupings give to the sciences is striking, as also is the provision that the schools were to function independently, each with full control over its own professors, staff, and departments. Each school was to be located in an architecturally independent facility and was to be given a mandate to expand its program at its own initiative to whatever extent was warranted by the growth of knowledge in its area of learning, constrained only by the availability of funds. Students would be able to enroll in whichever school they chose and need attend only that school. There were to be no required courses or even class ranks. Students would study a subject until they had mastered it, were otherwise ready to move on to other subjects, or were prepared to leave the university for careers in business and government (Jefferson 1975: 332–46; Rudolph 1962: 125–26).

The Virginia Plan survived barely beyond its approval; as in so many things that Jefferson proposed, his was an idea ahead of its time. But with the Morrill Land-Grant Act of 1862, educational institutions in each of the states were created, or the purposes of old ones redirected, with a mandate to teach subjects of practical relevance, especially scientific courses in agriculture, mechanics, and the other useful arts. This new kind of university quickly flourished.

The more theoretically oriented Johns Hopkins University was founded in 1874 as a way to bring together a faculty of distinguished experts and to provide them with the resources requisite for their scholarly needs. Students were to be enrolled, initially at the graduate level but eventually at the undergraduate as well, only if they were sufficiently bright to contribute their ideas and energy to the perpetuation of a stimulating research environment. Johns Hopkins became a model for the non–land grant American universities to emulate, no matter how far short of the Hopkins standard most of them might fall, no matter how far afield they might extend the subjects deemed in need of a body of expert knowledge.

By the end of the twentieth century, the university model, the concept of an educational institution as a Guild of Inquirers, has obviously carried the day. All but a few of the liberal arts colleges have abandoned their commitment to serve a Faithful Community, portraying themselves instead as smaller, more intimate versions of the big universities. These colleges proclaim themselves blessed with a faculty of scholars more eager than their university colleagues to initiate young adults into the esoteric worlds of disciplinary research and thereby to lay the foundations of expertise they will need for productive careers. These colleges retain, and most of their university counterparts have acquired, an interest in the personal and moral development of students. But such old-fashioned concerns have been relegated to residential arrangements and extracurricular activities, a matter under the purview of student life professionals rather than the faculty.

5. SUMMARY

The mission of the academic Guild, the educational approach of the "philosophers" as opposed to the "orators," can be summarized in seven statements (based on Kimball 1986: 119–22; see also 228):

1. Human beings, because they are rational, are by nature equal.
2. The rational individual mind, not traditional authority, is the sole judge of truth.
3. The search for truth is an end in itself.
4. The search for truth must be free from externally imposed strictures.
5. The method for attaining truth begins with doubt: critical skepticism.
6. Different truth-claims should be tolerated because none are immune to doubt.
7. Morality is subjective: individual choice and personal growth are private matters.

The modern educational institution should be understood as composed of guilds of those expert in the scientific method. The guild masters and their apprentices treat this method as a treasure that transcends the particulars of any cultural heritage. They are protectors of a hierarchy of truths in which everything known is organized by a deductive model that represents iconically the objective world. A university's educational mission is, first, to add to that fund of truths and, second, to transmit that method and those truths to the rising generation.

This treasury of truths may rise to a sacred apex, as the Scholastics believed; or, as modern thinkers would have it, the ultimate principles may be quite secular. The university may be founded and sustained by clerics or by clerks. But the knowledge preserved, increased, and transmitted by a university should be the body of objective knowledge the guilds have determined is vital to the common end its members all serve.

REFERENCES

Aquinas, Thomas. 1945. *Summa Theologica,* part 1. In *Basic Writings of Saint Thomas Aquinas,* ed. Anton C. Pegis, vol. 1. New York: Random House.

Aristotle. 1941. *Posterior Analytics.* In *The Basic Works of Aristotle,* ed. Richard McKeon. New York: Random House.

Descartes. 1956. *Discourse on Method.* Indianapolis: Bobbs-Merrill.

_____. 1960. *Meditations on First Philosophy.* Indianapolis: Bobbs-Merrill.

Euclid. 1926. *The Thirteen Books of Euclid's Elements.* 3 vols. 2d ed. Cambridge: Cambridge University Press.

Hanson, Norwood Russell. 1958. *Patterns of Discovery: An Inquiry into the Conceptual Foundations of Science.* Cambridge: Cambridge University Press.

Illich, Ivan. 1993. *In the Vineyard of the Text: A Commentary to Hugh's Didas-calicon.* Chicago: University of Chicago Press.

Jefferson, Thomas. 1975. "Report of the Commissioners for the University of Virginia." In *The Portable Thomas Jefferson,* ed. Merrill D. Peterson. New York: Penguin Books.

Kimball, Bruce A. 1986. *Orators and Philosophers: A History of the Idea of Liberal Education.* New York: Teachers College Press.

Kneale, William, and Martha Kneale. 1962. *The Development of Logic.* Oxford: Clarendon Press.

Laws, Priscilla. 1991. "Calculus-Based Physics without Lectures." *Physics Today* 44.12 (December).

Leibniz, Gottfried Wilhelm von. 1965. "On the Universal Science: Characteristic XIV." In *Monadology and Other Philosophical Essays,* ed. Paul Schrecker. Indianapolis: Bobbs-Merrill.

Newton, Isaac. 1846. *Newton's Principia: The Mathematical Principles of Natural Philosophy.* Ed. Andre Motte. New York: Daniel Adee.

PKAL. 1992. *PKAL Report, Volume One. What Works: Building Natural Science Communities.* Washington D.C.: Project Kaleidoscope.

Plato. 1945. *Republic.* In *The Republic of Plato,* ed. Francis Cornford. New York: Oxford University Press.

——. 1961. *Gorgias.* In *The Collected Dialogues of Plato,* ed. Edith Hamilton and Huntington Cairns. Princeton: Princeton University Press.

Rudolph, Frederick. 1962. *The American College and University: A History.* New York: Alfred A. Knopf.

Suppe, Frederick. 1977. *The Structure of Scientific Theories.* 2d ed. Urbana: University of Illinois Press.

Tufte, Edward R. 1990. *Envisioning Information.* Cheshire, Conn.: Graphics Press.

Von Mises, Richard. 1956. *Positivism: A Study in Human Understanding.* New York: Braziller.

Wittgenstein, Ludwig. 1922. *Tractatus Logico-Philosophicus.* London: Routledge and Kegan Paul.

3

The College as Resource Center

I'm upset by all this talk about the importance of the liberal arts. The "liberal" here refers to freedom, of course. But freedom in what sense? You know the answer as well as I do: freedom from work. The liberal arts are in contrast to the servile arts. In ancient Greece, the menial tasks were done by artisans, slaves, and women, which freed a few wealthy men to spend their time talking politics and thinking abstract thoughts. Things you had to do with your hands, like digging in the earth or preparing a meal, were considered of less importance than things you did with your head and your tongue, like propounding a theory or extolling a virtue. And of course those distinctions made good sense, because what your servants do is obviously not as valuable as what you do.

I knew a young Hindu who had come from India to the United States soon after the Second World War in order to study agricultural engineering. He was from a wealthy high-caste family, but he had somehow gotten it into his mind, as a sort of noblesse oblige, that he should do something with his life that would be of benefit to his community and his newly independent nation. So he decided to learn about modern farming methods and was sent abroad at government expense to attend an appropriate American graduate program. Somehow he ended up at Iowa State in its "ag" engineering school. Everything went just fine, for he was an intelligent and diligent student, until he discovered that a requirement for one of his courses was that he construct a working model of some piece of agricultural machinery. The idea was that the task would help a student understand the design and purpose of the machine by becoming intimately familiar with its mechanisms as a result of building the parts to exacting tolerances and then assembling them so that they interacted properly.

My Hindu friend was unable to carry out this assignment not because he lacked sufficient manual dexterity, for he was an accomplished amateur watercolorist, but because he found the very idea of doing that sort of physical labor repugnant. He would try, but no sooner had he begun than his gorge would rise and he would become violently sick. The task he was being asked to perform was so beneath his station in life that it called into question his sense of self. To do what a menial does, to do as the lower castes do, is to become one of them, to be stained indelibly with the evidence of one's servility.

So going to a liberal arts college is really a form of conspicuous consumption. Having a big lawn proves you aren't so poor you need to use your land for raising crops to eat or sell; being liberally educated means you won't ever have to work for a living. Well, at least it means you won't have to work with your hands for a living. A liberal education means a white-collar instead of a blue-collar job. College presidents chatter on about educating tomorrow's leaders. But we know that's a code for educating those who will be in a position to make others do their work for them.

The liberal arts: its dirty secret is the class system it presupposes. It's a mark of class privilege parading around as an eternal verity. The value of a liberal education is that it locates you among the masters, the power brokers, the governing elite. Don't try to tell me then that a liberal education unlocks the door to great ideas and the enduring monuments of the human spirit when you know as well as I do that what it unlocks is the door to a well-paying job. Don't tell me that the liberal arts colleges scattered so thickly across the American landscape are there to help students develop their full potential as human beings. They're there to make it possible for the sons of privilege, and now even the daughters, to perpetuate their privilege. Not pretty, maybe. But effective. All I ask is that you be honest enough to call these colleges what they are: playgrounds for the leisure class.

❖ ❖ ❖ ❖ ❖

We were having a beer at the Faculty Club. I was just new to the college, with a fresh Ph.D. in philosophy and frothing over with stories about how my classes were going. My colleague was a jolly professor of German literature, listening with the bemused patience of someone soon to retire. I was being particularly enthusiastic about that morning's ethics class and my clever strategy for getting students to understand what Kant meant by the third formulation of the categorical imperative. The professor interrupted and asked somewhat incredulously: "There are freshman girls in that class, aren't there? Do you really think you can teach them Kant?" I nodded in the affirmative, and he exploded: "Well, it's my opinion that philosophy is wasted on women. Actually, it's wasted on most undergraduates. And Kant in particular: he's far too abstract and too profound a thinker for undergraduates ever to comprehend. Much less freshmen. Much less coeds. Maybe a few of your better majors, in a small senior seminar, but Kant for the masses? *Nie und nimmermehr!*" And he wandered off, shaking his head in perplexity.

I thought at the time that my colleague was merely displaying a bit of Germanic chauvinism with his Kantian idolatry, but it seems clear to me now that the real focus of his complaint was the women. He thought that undergraduates in a senior philosophy seminar on Kant might be up to the challenge, in part because they would have matured somewhat and as majors would already have at least a passing acquaintance with philosophical issues and ways of thinking. But the more important reason for the professor's toleration of the seminar was that he presumed our philosophy majors would all be men. Philosophy, like mathematics and math-dependent fields such as physics, deals with abstractions in a systematic fashion, and the female mind is unequipped for that. That a coed might enroll in such courses, or even major in such a field, would be a feat similar to a bear dancing: the wonder is not that it is done well, but that it is done at all.

We know that Aristotle thought this way about women. Like slaves and children, they lacked the rational capacities necessary for theoretical reflection and political discourse. The modern era was born with the repudiation of Aristotelian science, but we've found it hard to get past Aristotle's anthropology. For a long time it was argued that educating a woman would destroy her femininity. The fallback position was that education is fine as long as it is limited to practical subjects like home economics and nonintellectual skills like horseback riding or reading French novels. Eventually higher education was found acceptable, but only in women's colleges where the young ladies would not need to compete with men. When I was an undergraduate at Grinnell in the 1950s, we guys presumed, and our girlfriends tended to agree, that women went to college to get a MRS degree. The value of what they learned was that it permitted them to be interesting dinnertime conversation partners for their husbands. And even during my early teaching years at Dickinson, the college limited the number of women on campus to no more than a third of the student body on the grounds that an increase in alumnae would mean a decrease in gifts and bequests—since husbands rather than wives control the family's financial resources.

Feminists, scholars and activists alike, have demolished these creaky old arguments. My German literature colleague would be the laughing-stock of the Faculty Club were he to show up there today with his anti-quarian views intact. Indeed, the philosopher who is our Kant expert would probably respond to his remarks by throwing her glass of beer in his face. Besides, the proof is in the pudding, and more women than men are currently enrolled in American colleges and universities.

But old attitudes die slowly. Glass ceilings and all that. What a shock it'll be if we discover that most of Aristotle's lectures were actually writ-ten by his mistress.

❖   ❖   ❖   ❖   ❖

Elijah Muhammad provided the Black Muslims with a myth about racial differences. In the beginning, so the story goes, God created everyone with a little of his divinity in them, and because of this fact they were all black-skinned. But there came along a man who defied his creator, and God's punishment was to purge from him all traces of the divine, leaving the man white-skinned and godless. So whites are the devil, and their skin is the proof of it.

Turnabout is fair play. The Black Muslim demonization of whites was just the inverse of those stories about how Noah's son, Ham, found his drunken father naked and how he was condemned for this impiety. Noah's curse on Ham and his descendants, the Canaanites, was implacable: "Cursed be Canaan, slave of slaves shall he be to his brothers." And equally implacable has been its interpretation over the centuries, the swarthy Canaanites transmogrifying into Africans and the brothers to whom they were to be subjugated conveniently identified with whoever had sufficient power to enforce their interpretation. The black slaves shipped to America suffered from a special kind of original sin, it was argued. In Adam's fall we may have sinnèd all, but in Ham's further fall from grace his descendants had lost their freedom, which clearly meant that they had lost their humanity and probably even their access to God's redemptive love.

Henri Bergson defines a "closed society" as one that understands itself in terms of its enemies: we are those who are not them, the people whose unity is found in our struggle against the Other. Bergson says that this us/them mentality is a primitive instinct, deep-rooted and not easily dislodged. It certainly helps if the Enemy is easily distinguished from the People and if their evil and our good are intrinsic features of who we and they are. Demonizing others, and thereby dehumanizing them, is a very old and very serious game we humans play. It leads to lots of wars and persecutions, lots of subjugations and denigrations, lots of in-things and out-things. It's what communities of faith, both the religious and the secular kinds, are all about.

No wonder America's colonial colleges excluded unbelievers. No wonder it was such a problem later on for women to gain admission. Or for Jews, blacks, foreigners, communists, homosexuals—for whatever group happened at the time to constitute the Other. Societies are organized like onions. Those at the center look like, walk like, talk like, and think like the society's self-defined image of itself. Those at the concentric rings moving outward from the center vary in one or more dimension to some extent or other from the normative image, and those at the periphery of the society look or think strangely. There's not much difference, indeed, between those at the margins of our society and those who lie outside it. There's not much difference between deviance and otherness, between odd folks and enemies.

Our colleges have welcomed, even if reluctantly, those young people from the marginalized regions of American society who see higher education as their pathway to the center. Sports and entertainment are also pathways, of course, but a college degree has been considered the best passport out of the deviance of one's ethnic heritage into the national mainstream. The image of America as a melting pot permits, even requires, the constant influx of strangers with their strange ways. But that's on the condition that their presence as strangers be only temporary; they've got to be meltable. College is where you learn to speak plain, unaccented, grammatical English and to respond suavely when asked your views on aesthetic form in Maplethorpe's images. Those who in coming to college would wish to celebrate their ethnicity, to flaunt their deviance from the mainstream, are therefore a threat to the college's melting-pot mandate. Let them get their way, it's argued, and good-bye standards, good-bye objectivity, good-bye virtue, hello relevance and self-indulgence.

The problem with the liberal arts colleges is that they can't handle pluralism. They are closed societies when what we need are societies open to difference, able to see the virtue of cacophony and of disagreement even in fundamentals. The American college is a monocultural dinosaur that doesn't deserve to survive in the genuinely multicultural world struggling to emerge.

❖   ❖   ❖   ❖   ❖

The two of them are close friends, and when Arthur dies suddenly in his mid-twenties, poor Alfred is at his wits' end. He holds all these religious beliefs about how God loves us and that our souls are immortal and

> That men may rise on stepping-stones
> Of their dead selves to higher things

and that someday he too will be transformed and so once more be with his friend. But Alfred has scientific beliefs that are just as deeply held, and he knows full well the rhythms of Nature, knows that

> The woods decay, the woods decay and fall,
> The vapors weep their burthen to the ground,
> Man comes and tills the field and lies beneath,
> And after many a summer dies the swan.

Alfred knows that although he may cry out in rage over Arthur's early death and mutter darkly about the injustice of it all, although he can rationalize that

> 'Tis better to have loved and lost
> Than never to have loved at all

and although he can hope that he and Arthur will be reunited in eternity— and can even boast that it is such "mighty hopes that make us men"— Alfred knows that what his Sorrow tells him is the truth:

> "The stars," she whispers, "blindly run;
>   A web is woven across the sky
>   From out waste places comes a cry,
> And murmurs from the dying sun;

"And all the phantom, Nature, stands—
    With all the music in her tone,
    A hollow echo of my own,—
A hollow form with empty hands."

The dilemma tearing at Tennyson also tears at us. On the one hand, Nature, blind to the havoc it wreaks upon our lives, deaf to our cries for help. On the other hand, the Human Spirit, made to hope and dream, to love and yearn, to struggle, to succeed or fail. The one without purpose, the other purposeful; the one the real world we know but cannot love, the other the ideal world we treasure but cannot realize. Are we not a part both of Nature and of Spirit? Yet insofar as we are Nature, the atoms blindly run our lives and there is no room for Spirit. Yet insofar as we are Spirit, our lives have a worth and meaning that Nature cannot touch. How can these both be true?

This unanswerable question has also torn our colleges apart. For on one side of campus, or often on a newer separate campus, we find arrayed the departments and schools of science. In these pristine halls faculty extend our understanding of the laws of nature and students learn that the atoms run on blindly from an anomalous initial big bang to the inevitable loss of all thermodynamic differences. And arrayed on the other side, often on the older campus, we find the humanities. In their hallowed halls, faculty interpret profoundly important ancient texts and write wonderful poetry about the meaning of life and death. Scientists give tests with objective questions, and they expect the answers to be accurate to the second decimal place. Humanities essays have no right or wrong answers, although the faculty say that they can tell if the argument was poorly or effectively developed and if it made good use or not of the relevant texts.

Fractured knowledge, fractured selves. The first thing we did was bifurcate nature into minds and bodies, subjects and objects. Then we bifurcated education into humanistic and scientific realms, and some scholars even argued that each realm had its own distinctive way of knowing: analytic vs. intuitive, logical vs. hermeneutical. No wonder we find it difficult to think in holistic terms about anything, much less about ourselves. We have lost, it would seem, the very desire to be coherent. And if the only way we can see the world and ourselves is incoherently, squinting perplexedly through our cracked spectacles, then indeed we are lost.

Am I mad, that I should cherish that which bears but
    bitter fruit?
I will pluck it from my bosom, tho' my heart be at the root.

❖   ❖   ❖   ❖   ❖

If you were a Hexagon in Flatland, one of the lower nobility, and you
were approached by a Square lawyer, you wouldn't be able to identify his
professional standing immediately, and so you'd be uncertain how to greet
him. If the Square approaches with one of his sides perpendicular to your
line of vision, you'll see him as a straight line:

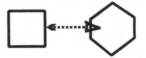

Although this could mean that the person was a Square, he could just as
well be a low-class Isosceles Triangle. Or since you have no way at a distance to distinguish a straight line from a curved line, the approaching
person could be one of your superiors from the Circle class. Or he could
turn out to be a she: a mere Line.

If you could manage to see the approaching person from a slightly different point of view, so that a couple of his sides were showing, and if you
also saw how right his angle was, you might be inclined to treat him as a
Square:

But because your information is still incomplete, it could turn out that he
was only half the man you'd thought, no more than a hard-working Right
Triangle. You'd have to move around and see him from all sides or from
every angle before you'd know for sure that he was a Square.

Given the two-dimensional restriction on your point of view, you Flat-landers have a lot of trouble determining the geometry of one another's social status. It would make sense for you to adopt some sort of color code. If all Squares were red and all Pentagons khaki, for instance, you could recognize who was who right off. But I have something even better than that for telling people apart. In strictest confidence, my friend, you should know that I'm from Spaceland, which means I have a perspective on your situation that you won't be able to make any sense of. But trust me when I say that I have no trouble distinguishing between the different classes of Flatlanders, because I can see each of you from all sides at once:

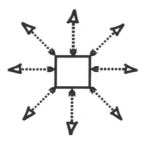

I can even see inside you; I can know your inner thoughts. It is necessary for you to move from one perspective to another and then to another, slowly building up a picture of the other person. You must acquire information sequentially before you can conclude that the approaching person is a lawyer, a four-sided, right-angled sort of guy. In contrast, I can see from all those perspectives simultaneously and so know in an instant what you can only come to know over time. Mine is a bird's-eye view, a God's-Eye view. I occupy the Eternal Now. I see *sub specie aeternitatis*. . . .

That's what the claim to have objective knowledge is: to see without occupying any perspective. It means seeing something freed from the limitations, the distortion, that a perspective necessarily introduces. An objective description of a fact is supposed to leave out the subject. The subjective point of view of the person who does the describing has got to be canceled out. It's necessary to do this canceling out because subjects, after all, are subjective—and what we're talking about is nonsubjective knowledge. Knowledge without a knower.

Well, balderdash. I can barely manage to imagine what knowledge without a knower might be. Like the Square and the Polygon might be able to imagine what it would be to see people from a location outside of their time and space. But neither they nor I can actually leap outside of our world. No way, José. I can't occupy a perspectiveless perspective, nor can you, nor can anyone. To know is always to know from a perspective. The subject's point of view is inherent to knowledge, and so our knowledge is always a function of historical contingencies, always shaped by where the subject stood when viewing what it claims to know. As William James says, "the trail of the human serpent is over everything."

If objective truth is perspectiveless, then it's an oxymoron. There can't be any such thing. There's only us, trying as best we can from within the limits of our Flatland points of view to build up a picture of things that we can use to make our way in the world, a bag of tricks that most of the time manages to keep us from thinking that Squares are Triangles or that the authority of Circles is anything more than a social convention.

❖   ❖   ❖   ❖   ❖

We have lived for the last four hundred years inside two "master narratives." They go something like this.

Once upon a time, our knowledge of the world and of ourselves was piecemeal and untrustworthy. We were dying in the trackless desert, buffeted by errant winds of ignorance and parched by the dry heat of our prejudice. Thank goodness we found a trickle of water in some wadi, mixed it with the rough earth of our perceptions and the straw of common sense, formed this mixture in accord with our dreams, and fired the results in furnaces of experimental testing. By this method we made solid bricks of objective fact, and with these facts started constructing a hovel of knowledge to secure us against the surrounding uncertainties. The construction is still going on, but our hovel has already become a house, its base widening to support an imposing pyramidal edifice that is nearly ready for the crowning pinnacle to be put in place. It's been slow in coming, but we're getting there. It won't be long before we'll be knowing fully ever after.

Once upon a time we were slaves in Egypt, forced to clear the swamps and build the pharaohs' pyramids. We hated having to do what others ordered us to do, but we did our work in silence and kept our resentment to ourselves. Over the years we grew in strength while the pharaohs grew soft; we became self-disciplined while our oppressors became lax. Until the morning dawned when we threw off the yoke of our enslavement, cast aside our tormentors, and thereafter built our own pyramids to house and celebrate our common aspirations. Some of us aren't really free yet, everyone doesn't have an equal chance at pursuing their own interests, and it's been particularly hard trying to treat everyone as brothers and sisters. But we are making progress; we're almost there. It won't be long before we'll be living happily ever after.

These two master narratives, the first one "speculative" and the second "emancipatory," are the stories Western civilization tells about the triumph of knowledge over superstition and the triumph of liberty over tyranny. They belong together, because—or so goes the story our parents told us and we in turn now tell our children—truth and freedom are indivisible. Only in a democracy are people free to pursue truth, and the free flow of information makes tyranny impossible. Education is the bulwark of genuine liberty, freedom the prerequisite for effective learning.

Unfortunately, neither of these master narratives is true. It's simply not the case that we have been approaching Truth by slow and measured step along an upward sloping avenue. Nor has our history been marked by the progressive spread of Liberty, of parliamentary democracy and economic justice. But that's good news, not bad. The trouble with master narratives is that they are made for us by our masters. They are stories concocted to legitimate the authority of those currently in positions of power: the scientific elite and the governing elite. Our colleges teach us loyalty to the Faithful Community, and so we pledge allegiance to the rich white male establishment. Our colleges teach us to love truth, and so we let the white-coated experts of the Guild of Inquirers set our priorities and define our worth. We permit our educational institutions to brainwash us into believing these things. We have swallowed a tale told to us about the truth of these two master tales. Swallowed it hook, line, and sinker.

So let's wise up and cut bait. Science has to operate on the basis of some general paradigms, stories about what counts as evidence and how it must be validated, just as government has to be conducted within a framework of political paradigms, stories about the limits and legitimacy of power. But these are just stories, not objective structures. And they can be changed if we want them changed.

The mere suggestion that a new approach is needed in science, however, the merest hint of the need for a new narrative, is greeted with the same hostility a king would show some young pretender to his throne. Who steps outside the framework of the master narrative commits treason to its rule.

It's on account of this resistance that change comes only in fits and starts, usually belatedly, often by revolution or by power-brokered compromise, and disagreement is endemic to the process. No meaningful single story can be told of how either of these processes, the cognitive and the practical, has come to its present state or whither each might be trending. Politics is an inherently "agonistic" enterprise and so is education.

The masters always want to extend their suzerainty as far as possible. Pyramids are what pharaohs strive to realize. But once we realize that there's nothing sacrosanct about pyramids, we can simply refuse to build them anymore. We can opt instead for "little narratives," for houses of knowledge and of politics that are scaled down to human size, which would mean acknowledging that we are always telling stories of our own making. We would need to confess that we invent things for our own purposes. Some of our stories build structures that house acceptable assertions about the world; some tell us how we should relate to one another. But all these narratives are partial, temporary, human artifacts. By including only some ideas or only some individuals, they leave others out; "whose truth?" and "whose liberty?" are important questions we always need to ask.

Everything would be fine if we respected one another's narratives about truth and liberty, delighting in our differences and from time to time joining in another's storytelling, making it our own, because we found it a helpful or a fun way to orient ourselves. The problem comes when we decide to wear a pharaoh's mask and insist that others help in building us our pyramid while we tear theirs down.

You complain that we're not consistent. You say that we say, on the one hand, that modernity destroys wholeness, separates us from nature, from ourselves and from one another, sends each of us out into lonely exile. Then you say that we say, on the other hand, that totalities of every sort are hegemonic impositions which need to be deconstructed, that each person has his or her own unique perspective and this uniqueness is what is primary, sacred, inviolable. Yes, you're quite right: we say the one hand and we say the other hand. But the two hands are perfectly consistent. We each have our unique worlds, but they are all interrelated. Postmodern holism is about creating a world in which differences are woven together into a single fabric, a totality made possible by, and valued because of, the richly varied character of its fibers. Let me show you what I mean by talking about schooling in America.

What I mean by "ethnic tribalists" are folks who think and feel and act as though their ethnic group were the only one that counted. Tribalists are clannish, conformist, uncritical of themselves, prejudicially critical of others, paranoid, and fiercely loyal to whatever beliefs and practices they think essential to their group's survival and well-being. So take a look at the textbooks used by K–12 teachers, and surely you'll agree that a horde of European ethnic tribalists are in the saddle. American history begins with the coming of the Europeans and the subsequent story is about their interactions with non-Europeans whom they assimilate, exploit, thrust aside, or simply eradicate. In our schools, the American literature courses begin by reading Washington Irving and continue right on through to John Updike. And so it goes, lily-white all the way.

In a lot of schools, the saddle is filled by evangelical Christian ethnic tribalists who have forgotten their grandparents' European origins and think of themselves as without ethnicity. They insist that the United States is a Christian nation, so that it's wrong for school textbooks to be secular. Students aren't educated unless the schools teach them that it's in God we trust; it says so, right there on our dollar bills. These evangelical ethnics want textbooks that look from the City on a Hill across the American prairie toward our Manifest Destiny, but things should be centered around matters of personal morality and public piety rather than just the bare course of history.

If your ancestors were African or your religion Jewish, if you fancy yourself a modern secularist or your English is too heavily accented, then it's hard not to feel like an outsider when people argue like that. Feel, hell: you *are* an outsider. The proof is that you're not likely to see any American in the textbooks who looks like you or whose name is spelled like yours.

A tribalist response to these WASP-ish tribalisms would be to demand the same arrangements for anyone's own ethnic group. Separate schools, separate textbooks. You go your way, we'll go ours. And certainly there is enough of this separatism going on, and it's quite understandable because it's how the colonized always respond to the colonizers: by imitating them. "Separate but equal" has never worked, however. So be suspicious of it, no matter what its form, remembering that tribes don't always need to be ethnic, that there are lots of kinds of ghettos.

"Creative ethnicists" are folks who use their ethnic background as a point of departure, a foundation upon which to build. Learning to live beyond your roots doesn't mean giving them up; a tree trunk, don't forget, is living beyond its roots. What it means is entering into genuine communication and interchange with people who believe and act differently than you do. This approach means appreciating other ethnic traditions and respecting people because of, not despite, their different cultural backgrounds. But it also means learning to function within other ethnic frameworks. It's one thing to stop sneering at the Latinos across the tracks; it's something else to learn Spanish and visit in their homes. Learning about the coming of the Europeans through their intrusions into the lands of the Zuñi and Hopi will free you from thinking the story is primarily about English settlements at Jamestown and Plymouth. But better yet is learning the history of your own region and contributing some of your time and talent to a more pluralistic account of the peoples who have lived there.

Yet this growth in understanding and in firsthand involvement is still not sufficient if our goal is to get beyond single-ethnic domination and multiethnic separation. Our multiculturalism needs to be "emancipatory": what we learn about other ethnic groups and how we relate to people different from us has to have an impact on the current social conditions. We have constructed a framework for American self-understanding that excludes, subordinates, or seeks to eliminate whole groups of people. Our growing knowledge and our widening friendships need to be translated into finding the most effective ways to reconstruct our framework so that these old prejudicial ways no longer work.

The uninstitutionalized experiences of marginalized people need to be brought into the school curriculum. I mean having long-silenced voices speak in our assemblies. I mean finding counterhegemonic poets, painters, and philosophers and giving them equal standing in our courses with the usual stable of "great minds." I mean exposing the biases, the unthinking ones and the deliberate ones, in the writings and the actions of the dominant European ethnics, investigating the alternatives that are a part of our collective cultural treasure, and then discovering how to construct fresh frameworks that mold these differences together into a vibrantly pluralistic union.

❖   ❖   ❖   ❖   ❖

Suppose a college were a democracy. Suppose it were democratic because its mission was to educate democratic citizens, and it was thought that providing them with role models at all levels of what democracy is all about was crucial to that education.

Right now, a student residence hall functions as a democracy: elected officers enforcing collectively agreed upon rules. The same goes for some student extracurricular organizations and obviously for student government. Faculty meetings and college senates are parliamentary systems. But the real power centers in the college are not fountains of democracy. Academic departments are more hierarchial than they like to admit: chairs are typically administrative appointments, and when it comes to evaluation and tenure issues the junior faculty have no say. The faculty is a feudal guild system, and the administration is a corporate hierarchy.

And then there's the board of trustees. Trustees are a self-perpetuating group that is in no way beholden to the college's faculty, administrative staff, or students and alumni. It has full fiduciary responsibility and so the power to make whatever decisions are necessary to preserve and enhance the college's fiscal position. More often than not this fiduciary responsibility means that the board of trustees has final authority in all fundamental matters of college policy as well.

Suppose a college were a democracy and actually implemented these four organizational principles:

1. The College is a community. A decision affecting some members affects, to varying degrees, all members.
2. Those affected by decisions should have a say in formulating and implementing them. It is important that diverse perspectives be adequately represented in the various decision-making bodies. But adequacy does not necessarily imply parity.
3. Those with competence in particular areas should have a say in formulating and implementing decisions related to those areas. The members of the college community have differing needs, differing talents, differing responsibilities. These differences should be respected and used for the common good. The members of the community are interdependent, but their roles are not interchangeable.
4. Government in the college community should be representative. For the process of decision-making to be effective, some must act on behalf of all. But those who make decisions should be responsive to the interests of the rest through procedures of accountability and distributed responsibility.

Take any of the following currently acceptable models of democratic procedure and expand it to encompass the whole college: governing boards elected by the vote of community citizens, college presidents elected by majority vote of governing boards, faculty committee members elected by vote of the whole faculty, student representatives elected by residence halls. Suppose, in keeping with the spirit of these models, classes were organized and taught as a teacher-student democracy. Suppose academic deans and college presidents were elected by vote of faculty and alumni. Suppose trustees were appointed and evaluated with the consent of the governed.

Suppose a college were a democracy. Maybe we'd learn that way how to make the United States a democracy.

❖   ❖   ❖   ❖   ❖

I'm out duck hunting, and at the sound of the birds overhead I raise my shotgun and without looking fire both barrels. My hope is that some of the buckshot on its way up or on its way back down might happen to kill a passing duck. You would think me crazy, or at least silly, to do something so aimless and still call it duck hunting. To have any reasonable chance of bagging some game, my shotgun would need to be carefully aimed and fired so that its packet of shot is sent in a trajectory designed to intercept the anticipated trajectory of the duck. I may misjudge either trajectory or both, but at least my means will have been chosen because of its relevance to the end I had in mind. It would be seen as a reasonable way to operationalize my desire for roast duck on next week's table.

What goes on in your classroom, professor, is pretty much a matter of your randomly spraying ideas and facts into the air, with the pious hope that some of what you're tossing about will bring down the winged ignorance encircling the assembled students. Sometimes this outcome occurs but usually not. Surprisingly, you are amazed that you have managed to bag so few of your quarry. It's a good thing you don't hunt like you teach, or you'd soon starve to death. Which is what happens to your students' minds. Intellectual starvation is not a pretty sight, especially when it happens to someone who has paid a lot of money in anticipation of a feast.

You show up on the first day of class with a syllabus carefully prepared in advance, indicating the assignments for each day, from a preliminary overview of the topic on through to a final concluding lecture. The knowledge packeted in your course is more orderly than the pile of unrelated units of buckshot in the shotgun shell. Indeed, your topics are carefully linked together, sometimes so tightly that to miss a single class session, or even when present to fail to understand what was being said, is to be thenceforth confused. But you propel that knowledge into the space of the semester without any particular regard for the student ignorance it is supposed to destroy. You presume that if the gun is well oiled and the shell properly charged, simply firing it off will do the job.

The ducks are never all in a line, however, and even if they were the line would need aiming at. If you are ignorant of where the students' ignorance lies, how can your course be aimed to do what it is supposed to do? This question of what you're aiming at applies not just to your course as a whole or simply to each class session; it applies directly and emphatically to what goes on each time you open your mouth and speak. Those words of yours convey some idea or fact, which you are attempting to relate to earlier ideas and facts and which are set forth at this point because they prepare the way for what you wish to introduce next. Those relationships are crucial to the knowledge; they give it its integrity. But if this knowledge of yours is to be taught, another relationship is equally important. You need to relate these ideas and facts to those known or not known by your students, which means anticipating the trajectories of the students' learning curves and then aiming your words to intercept those trajectories. Obviously, however, if you neither know nor care to know what your students know and care to know, it will be hard to aim your words.

I need to know where the ducks are in order to anticipate the direction, angle, and velocity of their flight pattern so that I can tailor the aim of my shotgun accordingly. Thus I learn from the ducks how to kill them, just as you must learn from your students how to slay their ignorance.

So your *prix fixe* meal this evening includes a required entrée: a single no-choice item or maybe a group of items from which you must select at least one. And the professor on the first day hands out the instructions for how this fare is to be consumed. Start with this, work your way along in the following manner, and by the end of the semester your tummy will be full and your plate will be empty.

Too bad if you weren't hungry just now, or if that sort of food disagrees with you, or if you'd have benefited by an appetizer, or if you are having trouble manipulating the necessary utensils. Too bad if the other food items on the plate don't happen to complement the entrée or if you stupidly ended up with two kinds of starches and no fruit. Just be quiet and eat your peas, and don't think you're going to be allowed up from the table until you've cleaned your plate.

When the cafeteria is a college and the entrées are the courses composing its curriculum, the resulting nutritional value of the baccalaureate degree may not be anywhere as good as advertised. You've been sold a bill of goods if you're actually paying someone to starve you to death. You might well ask, "Where's the beef?"

Yes, but look at it this way. The coin of the realm in colleges is academic credits. Three-hour chits, four-hour chits; add them up and eventually you have accumulated enough capital to buy yourself a bachelor's degree. It's the degree that's your meal ticket: it gets you into the banquet, but it isn't itself the banquet. Forget the courses; they're just how you pay for the degree. I suppose it would be fair enough if you could just plunk down the full asking price and get your diploma right off. Why bother with the middleman? Why spend four years twiddling your thumbs? Or is the enforced servitude part of the price you have to pay? Bang! goes the judge's gavel: I find you guilty of illegal possession of ignorance, for which the mandatory penalty is tuition plus four. Well, at least that's better than a life sentence.

Let me take a peek at this coin of the realm, okay? Interesting. On its obverse it's got a body of knowledge that someone is insisting you need to learn whether you want to or not. On the reverse, this body of knowledge is taught in a way someone knows in advance to be the right way to learn such things. It would seem the cash value of the coin is that the educational mission of a college is something that can and should be carried out without regard for the students whose increased knowledge is its objective. Hey, let me see that coin again. Uh-oh, it looks like confederate currency to me.

I'm not happy about having to say this, but my shoe pinches.
I'm the only one who knows if my shoe pinches.
I'm also the only one who knows if my shoe fits comfortably.
I'm quite interested in avoiding pinches and finding comfortable fits.
I'm justified in seeking experiences I find enjoyable and avoiding painful
    ones.

I'm willing to hurt a little bit in the wallet if it will increase my pleasure.

I'm willing to forgo some pleasure now if it's likely I may have even more later.

I'm told your course is about shoes and how to make them work to your advantage.

I'm looking forward to your course because it's said to be a fun experience.

I'm looking forward to learning how to avoid the usual shoe mistakes.

I'm finding the homework difficult, but "no pain no gain."

I'm encouraged by the good grade you gave me on the last exam.

I'm more motivated than ever to do well in this course.

I'm convinced that this information will serve me well for years to come.

I'm happy I had you as a professor.

I'm even thinking about the benefit of taking another course with you.

I'm not sure I could handle the course you're planning to teach, however.

I'm afraid it's too much work for what I'll get out of it.

I'm not going to take your course after all, but I didn't really need it anyway.

I'm feeling pretty comfortable about what I've learned in college.

I'm ready to start job hunting.

I'm confident my transcript and recommendations will look impressive.

I'm pleased that I got such a good job: good wages, nice boss, friendly coworkers.

I'm happy to say that my shoe doesn't pinch anymore.

Date: 15 November 1996 00.05:14 -0500 (EST)
From: George Allan <allang@dickinson.edu>
To: Philosophers <somelist@someplace.edu>
Subject: The Electronic Text

Richard Jones said on 14 November:
> I've tended to be more a "lurker" than a contributor to this
> discussion group, but I decided I'd better speak up before I burst
> my gut. In response to Ivan's overwrought metaphor: it's sure a
> lot quicker sending ideas back and forth on our "list" than using
> snail mail; cheaper too. But I'm not ready to believe that e-mail
> has metaphysical implications, as though we needed a new
> ontology or something. Give me a break! And if you're going to
> get into the rhetorical flourish stuff, at least don't use old-world

> nautical metaphors. How about some new-world cybernetic
> metaphors instead!!
> —rj

> Ivan Illich said on 12 November:
>
> >>   Like the signals from a phantom schooner, its digital strings
> >>   form arbitrary font-shapes on the screen, ghosts which appear
> >>   and then vanish.

I don't agree with those of you, Richard in particular, who have been attacking Ivan's nautical metaphor concerning e-mail messages. Ivan just wants to get across how different posting and receiving messages on this "list" is from writing and reading books. On the "list," we transact whatever exchanges of information we want, then move on to other things. My message, and whatever avatars it causes on my own and other people's computer screens, remains throughout nothing but electronic signals in cyberspace. It's all very ethereal.

Back when an essay by Augustine was a vellum parchment on which inky letters were inscribed by monks, the text was inseparable from the physical object, the book, which held it. A book was the solid "ground" in which words were "rooted" that told us of our salvation. The textual meaning and its book were an organic whole: we held the sacred plant with trembling hands and ate its fruit by reading it.

When writing materials became cheaper, the text no longer needed to be tied so closely to any particular object. Augustine's text was easily multiplied and parts of it routinely extracted in order to be quoted and commented upon in other texts. Texts were intangible meanings no longer rooted in a single book. Nonetheless the physical page still functioned as the vessel by which those meanings were transported through space. Books were the tangible "harbors" where the intangible text, like a "sailing ship," could put down its anchor, and where people like you and I could come to receive the truth that it was carrying from place to place.

So that was quite a revolutionary transformation. From meanings that grew up like flowers out of a solid bookish soil to meanings as a motile treasure temporarily located in this or that bookish harbor. From the book as the home of the text to the book as a motel stop.

It sure makes sense to me when Ivan then argues that there's now another revolution going on, a third kind of text emerging: texts produced and transmitted electronically. Electronic texts can be sent

from place to place without needing a book to carry them. There's no
need to smuggle a copy of Augustine through customs, no need for the
dissident author to hide his manuscript in a loose brick behind the
chimney. Just put it out on the Web and it is everywhere someone has
a modem connected to a phone line or can download from a
communications satellite.

Well, I'll grant that the electronic signals are physical and that so
are the files on floppy disks and the phosphors on the computer
screen. Those are Ivan's flickering ghosts, the phantom occasions for
the text. An Augustine manuscript, the closer to the original autograph
the better, is worth a fortune; some manuscripts are even national
treasures valuable beyond all possible price. Bibliophiles collect first
editions of books, some of which if in good condition and bearing the
author's signature can command a pretty price at a book auction. But
it doesn't even make sense to talk about the original computer
message; we may want to be sure our version is accurate, but neither
authors nor recipients know or care which electrons provided the
initial configuration. The text neither rests nor roots in any physical
place or object.

So I think Ivan's right, and I like his metaphor . . .
—ga

Uncle Stan worked for the Iowa State University Extension Service until
he retired recently. When he started with them, back in the 1930s, he was
part of a cadre of young agricultural experts stirred by a vision of saving
farmers from bankruptcy by teaching them up-to-date methods of agriculture. You weren't going to do that standing behind a lecture podium
back on campus. The farmers had their hands full trying to make ends
meet. They had no time to waste on the arcane ideas of professors who
were probably unable to tell a pig from a poke. Nor could they spare their
sons from the fields to pursue college studies, even if they might be able
to afford the cost. Farming was a no-nonsense practical matter, far
removed from the world of academe.

So the Extension Service went to the farmers. Stan gassed up his Ford,
drove out to John Smith's farm, and spent the day helping him with the
plowing or the weeding, with slopping the hogs or with whatever was the
task at hand. Slowly over the months, Stan would gain Smith's confidence

and at the same time learn the details of his farming style, his implicit management system, how he went about making the myriad decisions by which a farmer seeks to turn spring's possibilities into an autumnal harvest.

In this context of mutual trust and understanding, Stan would begin to slip in a few suggestions. Have you noticed how the corn along that depression grows shorter than the rest? The ears are mostly puny and the yield on an acre is hardly worth the seed. Now what do you suppose is causing that? Could be the soil's too moist out there. Or maybe the soil erosion has been carrying off the nutrients needed for the crop to thrive. Or it could be your seed: have you ever tried a hybrid? Respectfully but persistently, Stan would help Smith see his farm in terms of questions relating possible alternatives to expected results and current practices. After enough questioning, enough supposings-that, Smith might agree to have a soil sample sent back to Iowa State for analysis, to read a pamphlet on contour plowing, or to attend a special evening class on erosion prevention being offered by the Extension Service without fee at a nearby high school. Eventually he might agree to laying drainage tile in the depression or trying out an early-maturing hybrid on a twenty-acre section.

Nothing succeeds like success, of course, and when the corn yields in the drained area jump dramatically and the hybrid saves the season after a wet spring has delayed planting by nearly a month, the other farmers have questions for Stan when he next drops by. These days the farmers are no less skeptical about innovations than they were before, but they trust Stan's successor to work the issues through with them prudently and fairly. And the slow increments of sixty years have made a difference in the sophistication of the accepted practices against which the current innovations pull. The issues now have to do with no-till planting, infrared satellite photography of the fields, variable rate seeding and fertilizing using global positioning systems, and whether the co-op should pay its members' fees for an on-line link to the futures quotations at the Chicago Commodities Exchange.

The Extension Service took education out of the university classroom and brought it onto the farm. Agricultural science became a new farm implement to go with the green John Deere tractor and the red International Harvester harrow. It was a tool for the farmer to bring out as needed. You need a tractor to pull the plow, but you need more intangible tools to help you decide whether the furrows should be straight or contoured, whether last year's stubble should be turned under or just planted through, and whether the harvest should be sold now or held off the market for a while. The farmers had a living to make, and in the course of doing so they found that laboratory scientists could be of help.

Knowledge rooted in firsthand experience, tailored to address real-world problems, and available in usable form as needed: that's a kind of education worth the tax dollars it costs. That's education functioning as an investment that had shown it can return its value a hundredfold. Every discipline should have its Extension Service, with a research staff back on the home campus and a cadre of Uncle Stans out among the people helping them discover the educational tools best suited to their various needs.

Education should be on a need-to-know basis. Bernard Samson works for British Intelligence, but he never sees the whole picture because Uncle Silas and the other powers-that-be work from the premise that an agent should only know what he needs to know in order to carry out his orders. Bernard's wife Fiona defects to the Soviets without anyone ever telling Bernard that she is actually a double agent still loyal to the British. Even Fiona doesn't confide in him. It is decided that Bernard doesn't need to know and so, no matter what the personal and familial anguish that will result, he isn't told.

This subterfuge is always happening in spy novels, and I presume that's the way things happen in the real world of international espionage as well. It's what happens in any world where a goal can be reached only if a complex procedure is broken down into simpler procedures, each of which can then be completed independently. That's how a Boeing assembly line works. That's how the Manhattan Project was organized. That's how Microsoft designs a computer program like Windows 95. The people responsible for one of the component procedures need to be expert in running that procedure: whether it is a matter of tightening a bolt to a prescribed torque, or developing a metal that can withstand specified temperature and pressure extremes, or writing a subroutine. But the expert isn't expected to know what's going on elsewhere, except to know that there are certain things that can be counted on to arrive from other component procedures when needed, and that there is a certain result, within defined specifications, which the expert is to deliver at an appointed time.

Bernard's knowledge is limited because MI5 doesn't want its secrets leaked to the enemy; the Manhattan Project worked the same way. The assembly-line worker's efforts are limited to the bolt-tightening task because it is thought more efficient to put a jumbo jet together by a large number of people each doing a few small tasks than by a few people doing a large number of tasks. The Microsoft approach is simply an acknowledgment that the whole program is too complex for one or two people to conceive and develop by themselves.

Differentiated processing can be motivated by the need for secrecy, efficiency, or adequate understanding. But even though the motives are very different, the contexts are the same. Very complex systems require very complex procedures for their creation and maintenance, and the complexity is beyond the capacity of anyone to know completely. Like Uncle Silas or Bill Gates, those who manage the whole system can't be expected to know, much less know how to use, all the details. Those who have complete know-how about a detail lack the skills and knowledge requisite for overall system design and critique. And so we all develop different competencies. Some of us have a competence marked by considerable depth but not much breadth; we have a focused skill and know how to use it. Some of us are competent in handling breadth but lack depth; like any manager, we know a little about a lot of things, but we are masters of none. There isn't a one of us who can fully see the whole picture in all its details. The forest obscures the trees and the trees the forest. Although we sometimes try to be, none of us is Superman or Wonder Woman.

Society is a very complex system composed of very complex systems. To function within it, we all need to have some socially useful competence. If the job of America's colleges and universities is to prepare young people to become productive citizens, and to make it possible for adults and even old people to continue being productive citizens, then the primary task of teachers should be to teach students how to be competent in at least one of the ever-changing skills a dynamic nation needs.

When I arranged with a local contractor, Mr. Meyers, to build an addition to our house, we began our negotiations with a consideration of my goals. I wanted a bigger kitchen and more bedroom space. We agreed that extending the back of the house on both the first and second stories would meet that need. Mr. Meyers then went over my options with respect to building materials, the location of outlets and fixtures, how I wanted the walls finished, carpeting, shelving, interior decorating. Since the borough has a building code, there were certain options over which I had little choice, although in many cases there were a range of increasingly expensive alternatives, all of which met code. Also, because we were located in a "historical district," I had to comply with the rule that my addition remain in keeping with the traditional look of the house, that its footprint, height, windows, trim, and brick façade would undergo no radical alterations. Once Mr. Meyers and I had agreed on these matters, he drew up a contract, we went over it item by item, determined a starting time and a completion date, and haggled over the escape clauses in his estimated price. When this was all worked out, we both signed the contract, and at 7:00 A.M. one Tuesday morning a few weeks later the first workmen showed up.

This contractual procedure is exactly how education should be marketed. I want to learn something. The college provides the service, and it charges me a fee based on the character of the resources I will use and the amount of time it takes me to master the material. The only difference between a college and Mr. Meyers is that the college is modifying me whereas Mr. Meyers modified my house.

In some cases, the criteria for success in the educational venture may be completely up to me. Perhaps I've been asked to become more involved with the local symphony orchestra, and I'm a bit embarrassed that I really don't know much about music. So I decide that it would be helpful to sit in on a music history course, but no tests and papers, please. The college agrees to assign me a seat in its Music 101 lecture course, the relevant books are for sale in the bookstore, and I'm given checkout privileges at the library and listening privileges in its audiovisual center. I can take the course seriously, come to class, read the assignments and listen to CDs in the library, talk with the professor when I'm confused, and maybe even decide to take an exam after all or write a paper in order to get informal feedback. Or I can treat the whole thing as a lark, cut class on occasion, get behind in my reading, and never ask anything of the professor except to be entertaining during the class sessions. I suppose I could pay my money and then never get around to doing anything at all. The college only agreed to provide me with access to an experience, not to measure the quality of what I may have learned during that experience.

My goals could be quite different, however. I might want to obtain certification as a nurse. Nursing standards are established by a professional organization and include such things as a prescribed list of subjects that must be mastered and a sequence of increasingly more extensive apprenticeship and internship experiences that must be successfully completed. The college offers a formal four-year nursing degree, and if I enroll in it I am promised access to courses that cover the prescribed topics in general science, health care, psychology, and management. I'm also promised access to appropriate fieldwork opportunities at nearby hospitals and care facilities. Throughout, I will be taught, supervised, and advised by professionals whose expertise has been properly certified, and these experts will evaluate my work and validate its quality through a mix of letter grades and written assessments. If I successfully complete the course of study, I will be awarded a nursing degree from the college, a degree accepted anywhere in the United States as prima facie proof of my competence to be employed as a nurse. The college might provide some sort of placement service; some schools even guarantee a first job to their graduates.

There's no reason why a traditional B.A. or B.S. degree couldn't be contractually negotiated. For each course I take, I might contract with the professor regarding assignments and mode of evaluation, in many cases even regarding topic. The discipline in which I major could have requirements that the department and I would agree upon contractually, or a major could be completed merely by taking a specified number of courses of my own choosing from the list of offerings provided each semester. Such arrangements would lie somewhere between a program like nursing, which dances to the tune of an external credentialing body, and a self-defined program without external standards such as people want who are only satisfying their own personal aspirations.

But neither is there any reason why offering a baccalaureate degree should be the primary mission of a college nor even part of its mission. The two-year community colleges don't have a baccalaureate mission, for instance, and they're doing quite well. The same goes for institutions devoted entirely to continuing education and concentrating on educational packages designed for adults who need or want to upgrade their skills in order to be eligible for promotion or to shift to a different field of work. And elderhostel, after all, is a sort of college without walls that caters to people no longer interested in credentialing but very interested in intellectually stimulating experiences in the company of other like-minded folk.

Contract education serves all this myriad of reasons for going to school. So let's break out of the unnecessary straitjackets of predetermined set-piece courses and programs of study. Let's be as protean in our ways of delivering education as our students are in defining what they want. That would give a meaning to "universal education" which makes good sense. It's what we should mean when we claim as a nation or as a college that we are preparing people for living in the twenty-first century.

❖   ❖   ❖   ❖   ❖

Date: 02 December 1996 11:26:33 -0500 (EST)
From: George Allan <allang@dickinson.edu>
To: Text Course <texts@someplace.edu>
Subject: Our Course on the Text

I'm excited by your response to my invitation to participate in an on-line course dealing with the issues Ivan raised about how ancient, modern, and postmodern kinds of textuality differ from one another. I'm working on finding a college that will agree to give academic credit to anyone who needs it, so let me know right away if you would like a course credit for this (it'll cost you something, though).

I've set up a new list on the server called "texts" and this is the first test to see if it's working. Please post a message to the list indicating that you're hooked in and ready to go. We can continue some of our discussions on the list, but I think all of us by now have access to the Web, so we should also think about having our own page. Anyone want to volunteer to create one?

I know we'll have time zone problems with you folks in Australia, and actually the time difference between Bremen and Portland isn't going to be easy to handle. But I think we can still manage to schedule a few real-time conferences. If we all use the right communications software, maybe we can do a split-screen shtick with each of us in our own little window on everyone's screens. But if we're not quite up to that yet, we can at least set up a teleconference. Most of us have access to the necessary high-tech room either at the university or through Kinko's. Two or three of you might need to be linked in by audio only. More on that soon.

Ivan suggests that we begin with the monastic scriptorium. He's going to work up a list of topics about how medieval manuscripts were prepared, used, and preserved. Maybe we can focus in on some specific monastery or even a specific manuscript and do a case study, as it were, so that our ideas stay tethered down to something concrete.

Maybe the Bodleian Library at Oxford has some material on-line; certainly some of the museums will have images from illuminated manuscripts that we can download. Once we settle on our first nest of topics, we can each pick one to explore—and then we're up and running! We'll use our Web page as a dump site for anything each of us finds that we want to share with the rest of the class right off, but we'll use our discussions to shape what information we want to keep long-term at the site.

Ivan has a few colleagues who are into textuality. He's going to contact them about joining our course or at least agreeing to interact with us on occasion. Do any of you know, or at least know of, people who would have some expertise on these matters?

Well, enough for the moment.

—ga

The traditional college and university arrangement is for the institution to employ a sizable work force of faculty, guarantee most of them a life-long salary, and then hope that they will earn their keep by attracting sufficient numbers of tuition-paying students. Where tax dollars or endowments pay some of the salary costs, the issue is more complicated, but the results are the same. Faculty are a fixed expense, student-generated or student-justified income a variable.

The traditional system works in a stable environment. It also works wonderfully in a growth situation, because overenrollments mean full classes and additional hiring need only be done at the margin: the students generate more income than is required to service their needs. The system doesn't work when enrollments fall short of expectations, however, because the result is too many underemployed faculty: tuition income drops but salary expenses remain unchanged.

Crafty academic administrators have tried to address this problem by increasing proportionately the number of part-time and temporary faculty they employ. Some union arrangements permit a last-hired layoff policy. But these efforts to increase flexibility in the faculty salary budget don't get at the heart of the matter. There's no better proof of this deficiency than the Sturm und Drang surrounding campus decisions (in ascending order of tempestuousness) to insist that a replacement be hired at the entry level, to freeze new hirings in a department, to deny renewal of an untenured faculty contract for "institutional reasons," or to abolish a department that has only minimal enrollments.

The basic premise is all wrong. Instead of being responsible for a roster of employees whose costs are largely independent of what they do, educational institutions should be hiring faculty on a consultancy basis. That's the best way to use experts, after all: bring them in when they're needed. Faculty in a number of academic disciplines and those in the professional schools already make quite a lot of money serving as consultants to businesses and government. Why shouldn't their relation to colleges and universities be on the same fee-for-service basis?

I'm not talking about hiring part-time faculty. Administrations use this ploy because the current surplus of teachers permits them to call the shots. A full-time faculty member, teaching six courses a year, earns a salary that goes up each year as the person works along the seniority scale, plus there's the increasingly expensive fringe benefits package. It's cheaper to hire six part-timers whose total cost will be less than half the full-time cost, plus no fringe benefits expenses. That's a cynical, exploitative strategy because either it underpays good faculty who deserve to be paid at full-time rates or it replaces them with second-rate faculty who will teach inferior courses.

Consultants, in contrast, are very well paid. Their fees take into account the likelihood that they will not always be employed and that they have to make their own arrangements for medical insurance, retirement annuities, and the like. Indeed, very successful consultants can make far more money than they would ever be able to command for a traditional full-time job.

The financial savings for the institution should not come from underpaying the education experts. It should come from not having to bear unnecessary fixed costs. If the American education system is going to be first rate it won't come about by cutting corners. If faculty are poorly paid, good people will cease making college teaching their career. Second-rate education is the hidden cost in the seemingly smart discount-store strategy of selling courses taught by second-rate faculty hired at second-rate prices. Penny wise, pound foolish. So pay the faculty at consultant-fee rates: pay for the best and get the best. Then simply don't hire consultants where and when you don't need them.

The result, of course, will be to reduce the number of people earning their living as faculty. But the ones forced to seek alternative fields of endeavor will be those who, relative to their peers, are not as good at the teaching profession rather than those who, as now, received their Ph.D. in a lean season and have found the job slots already filled by others fortunate enough to have been hired (and then tenured) in fatter times.

The consultancy model dovetails nicely with a curriculum that emphasizes student choice. Obviously, the more students are herded into required courses in predefined numbers, the more a college can count on sufficient enrollments to keep its predefined faculty busy. But if students have the flexibility to design their own programs of study, to determine what they need to study in order to meet their personal educational objectives, then colleges need the capacity to respond flexibly. The ideal would be individually contracted tutorial courses: for each course, the student contracts through the college with an appropriate expert who on a consultancy fee then provides the educational experience agreed upon. And with the Internet, the consulting experts wouldn't even have to be on campus all the time—indeed, they wouldn't have to be there at all!

Date: 31 December 1996 23:59:30 -0500 (EST)
From: George Allan <allang@dickinson.edu>
To: Text Course <texts@someplace.edu>
Subject: Thought for the Day!!

You might like this comment I just found while out browsing on the Net. . . .

> "Once we all have computers, modems, and phone lines, the
> colleges can sell their campuses to entrepreneurs wanting to turn
> the facilities into low-security prisons, entertainment complexes,
> and retirement villages. Which is what, more or less, they already
> are." :-)
—ga

BIBLIOGRAPHICAL ESSAY

The invidious distinction between the liberal and servile arts is a recurrent theme in the writings of John Dewey. I recommend in particular his *Philosophy of Edu-*

cation; its original title, under which it is also available, is *Problems of Men.* You'll discover that Dewey's ideas on the proper role of education in a democracy have influenced many of the arguments in this chapter. For instance, he's the source of the duck hunting example.

Aristotle's argument that men are superior to women is at *Politics* I.5 ("the male is by nature superior, and the female inferior; and the one rules, and the other is ruled"). Dickinson College's quota on women was originally set at 15 percent, eventually raised to a third of the student body, and set in 1963 at a third of the entering class (which meant a much higher percentage of the graduates, since men were more likely not to complete their course of study). The quota was dropped in 1968 and thereafter admission was gender-blind. In 1990, when the proportion of women students approached 60 percent, Dickinson considered imposing a quota on women once more, but fortunately the idea was never taken seriously.

I haven't been able to find a textual source for the Black Muslim anthropogenic myth. The story of Ham's curse is recorded in Genesis 9:20–27, just after (ironically) the rainbow covenant. Henri Bergson's distinction between an "open society" and a "closed society" is found in his *The Two Sources of Morality and Religion.*

The selections from the poetry of Alfred Lord Tennyson are from *In Memoriam A.H.H.,* except for the dying swan lines that are the opening to *Tithonus* and the "Am I mad" couplet that is from *Locksley Hall.* For more on the critique of modern science because of its bifurcation of nature, read Alfred North Whitehead, *Science and the Modern World;* for the link to Tennyson, see chapter 5, "The Romantic Reaction."

The world of Flatland, including its epistemology and its social pecking order, is the invention of Edwin A. Abbott in *Flatland: A Romance of Many Dimensions.* Lineland is also discussed. The narrator is thrown into prison as a madman for claiming that he had been visited by a Sphere, a stranger from the Third Dimension. The William James quote is from *Pragmatism,* his Lowell Lectures given at Boston in 1906.

The critique of "master narratives" is based on the arguments in Jean-François Lyotard's *The Postmodern Condition: A Report on Knowledge.* Lyotard argues that the cognitive and practical versions of the modern Western "master narrative"—or "metanarrative" or "grand narrative"—are being undermined. The "postmodern" worldview that is arising as modernism collapses is a view marked by an "incredulity toward metanarrative" and a celebration of "little narratives." Lyotard interchanges his "narrative" metaphor with a "language game" metaphor drawn from Ludwig Wittgenstein. You might also be interested in a related book, a series of interviews with Lyotard conducted by Jean-Loup Thébaud, *Just Gaming.* My underlying argument in this chapter is as much influenced by Lyotard as by Dewey.

The distinction between "ethnic tribalists" and "creative ethnicists" comes from an article by Richard Gambino, "The Ethnic Revolution and Public Policy," in Sidney Hook, Paul Kurtz, and Miro Todorovich, eds., *The Idea of a Modern University* (I suspect this hardback book is long out of print, so check at your nearest university library). The notion of "critical emancipatory multiculturalism" is from Cameron McCarthy, "After the Canon: Knowledge and Ideological Representation in the Multicultural Discourse on Curriculum Reform," in a 1993 hardback edited by Cameron McCarthy and Warren Crichhow entitled *Race, Identity, and Representation in Education.*

The four organizational principles for campus governance cited in the section about colleges as democracies compose the statement on "Guiding Principles" for Dickinson College's committee system, *Academic Handbook,* chapter 3, section I,1.

Ivan Illich's very interesting *In the Vineyard of the Text: A Commentary to Hugh's Didascalicon* explores the difference between the presuppositions of the "monkish book" and the "scholastic text." Toward the end of his book, Illich has a few hurried things to say about electronic texts; the quote is from page 118.

Uncle Stan is my wife's uncle, Stanley A. Collins, but he worked in northern Iowa for the government Soil Conservation Service rather than for Iowa State's Extension Service. The two agencies did related work, each in their own way helping to further the general goal of ensuring an adequate and safe food supply for the nation and the world. I have used considerable poetic license in depicting what Uncle Stan actually did, and I've interpolated into my profile some of the interpersonal techniques used by Pete Bechtel, a close friend who for long years was an agricultural consultant in Swaziland. For anyone preferring historical accuracy, I recommend a hardcover book from Iowa State University Press: Wayne D. Rasmussen's *Taking the University to the People: Seventy-Five Years of Cooperative Extension.*

Len Deighton is currently publishing his third trilogy of spy novels featuring Bernard Samson: *Mexico Game, London Set, Berlin Match; Spy Hook, Spy Line, Spy Sinker; Faith, Hope, Charity.*

Unless indicated otherwise, the books I've mentioned are available in paperback. None are on-line, but it's only a matter of time before that'll change.

4

The Essence of a College

When you understand an educational institution as part of a Faithful Community, you presume that its purposes are defined by the community it serves. The ends of education reflect the ends of the wider society; the means a college uses to further its ends are those the community applauds or at least accepts. One People, one God, one Faith, one State—and so, inexorably, one educational Mission.

Such a mission need not be as monolithic as it sounds, however. As a college administrator or member of a board of overseers, you could tolerate considerable variation in the beliefs and practices of faculty and students as long as the variety were in the details and not the basics. For instance, your community could mandate one of the college's purposes to be that of a gadfly. You and your colleagues decide that the community would benefit from a certain amount of pestering and so you institutionalize the pest. You envision colleges as an important instrument of critique by means of which society expects continually to purge itself of inefficiencies and provide a safety valve for dissent. The independence of the medieval universities from routine civil controls and the semiautonomy of American faculty under the current academic freedom and tenure system are examples of how Western societies have tolerated a modicum of social and intellectual deviance for the sake of the common good it presumably furthers. Controlled dissent, like controlled fusion, is a subtle art. If it does not get out of hand, the benefits for the community are substantial.

But you cannot allow it to get out of hand. You and your faithful compatriots are unable to cope with significant genuine pluralism because you cannot tolerate disagreements about the core of your shared worldview. Foundational answers to the fundamental "whys" of a faithful community cannot be at issue. There can be no dispute about why the world is this way rather than some other way, why as a people you came into existence and for what ultimate end you have been permitted to endure, why as individuals you are born and live and die as you do. The answers to these questions compose a framework of meaning essential to your community's distinctive character. They are its reason for existing, and to undermine the reason justifying a community's existence is, of course, to undermine that existence itself.

Hence, as the guild masters' critique in Chapter 2 so devastatingly pointed out, under conditions of incipient pluralism a Faithful Community has only two options. You can systematically exclude deviants from the community or you can make the conditions of membership more inclusive. The exclusion option narrows the community, however, forcing you to parochialize values you had once thought universal. Your catholic faith becomes sectarian, the chosen people an ethnic enclave. The inclusion option pays the opposite price, forcing you to define your community's transcendent values in terms of superficial rather than fundamental unities. Your hope for the creation of an ecumenical church and for world federation are degraded from urgent visions of a better tomorrow to pious platitudes about some far-off utopia.

The educational version of this cruel dilemma, as the Guild's critique tauntingly put it, was a choice between the college as a denominational or as a nonsectarian school. Either you must abandon the traditional role of educating your nation's next generation of leaders, allowing the Faithful Community to shrink from a people or a civilization to a faction or a special interest group. Or you can retain the traditional role, but only if you agree to abandon the pretense of having anything important to say, any unifying meaning or orienting purpose to teach the nation's and the civilization's new leaders.

If you forsake the Faithful Community and join with the Guild of Inquirers, you will be susceptible to this same critique, however. Once again you will be forced into a cruel dilemma from which there is no viable escape. The Guild promises you an institutional realization of the great Enlightenment dream that people can be freed from both the parochial and the superficial. Properly educated men and women should give their primary allegiance to an unfettered search for the universal truths that lie hidden deep beneath surface plausibilities. Here you will belong to a community in its truest sense: the community of truth-seekers, the community of science. This community transcends historical contingencies, arbitrary geographic distinctions, and political and religious ideologies, binding its citizens together in a cosmopolis governed by a moral law to which all positive laws must be subordinate.

The fatal flaw in this ideal, however, is that you and your enlightened colleagues require experts rigorously trained in scientific method in order for you to be able to expand the suzerainty of objective truth over a world easily deceived by the lure of emotional and self-serving pretenders to the truth. Expertise is of necessity a narrowing enterprise, one that excludes in order to organize effectively and then to explore thoroughly a particular region of experience. So what makes your scientific community a community is only the method of inquiry everyone uses. Scientists in different scientific disciplines define their knowledge goals differently; they are united only by the methodological regimen under which they all labor. Expertise fragments your goals, although not your means.

A common method is an insufficient constraint on the centrifugal pull of the multiplicity of ends, however. As an expert, you end up wearing the blinders of parochial belief, expelling from serious consideration everything outside the scope of your expertise, either by anathema if it be unscientific or by indifference if it be an unrelated science. You leave it up to amateurs to carry out the task of integrating all these truths, not merely with each other but most importantly with the questions of meaning and destiny that your science does not, nor can, address.

So those of you in the Guild colleges end up lying to yourselves and to others, claiming an ideal of scientific community while practicing an anarchy of disciplinary special-interest narrowness. You can call the Tower of Babel that houses your academic departments a Cathedral of Learning, but no one takes you seriously when you do. Or you can trivialize the Enlightenment ideal by calling indifference toleration and arguing that a mastery of technique is the same as intellectual excellence. With exquisite irony, you and your colleagues in the Guild, while continuing to be the scourge of those unwilling or unable to distinguish appearance from reality, end up justifying yourselves by boasting that your educational system is really what it merely appears to be.

The vice of the Faithful Community, its narrowed and trivializing vision of the world, reappears as the vice of the Guild of Inquirers as well. The focusing language of mission and the freeing language of experimental method, the emphasis on ends and the emphasis on means, both prove inadequate and, oddly enough, for the same reason. They each by different pathways lead faculty and students into narrow back alleys of scholarship and teaching.

So you reject both Community and Guild, undertaking a postmodern critique of them. Your criticisms vividly point to the weak foundations underlying their claims to universal significance. You are able to expose the vicious implications of their hypocritical insistence on the truth of what they themselves know to be false. But your postmodern alternative, the college as Resource Center, is no better. You and your friends blather on about deconstructing hegemonic claims to universalism, exposing them as unseemly assertions of special privilege. But you end up making universal claims of your own, which are as insipid or vile as those of the models you have repudiated.

Because Resource Centers emphasize the practical value of an education tailored to the needs of each individual student, you may attempt to validate these services by pointing to outcomes. For instance, you might boast of your college's success rates in job placement. In doing so, you will probably correlate placement information, subsequent employment history, and income level with a student's undergraduate major. The implication, which you are quick to assert, is that the education the college provided is the reason why the job was secured and why the student's salary has been rising so steadily. As an alternative to this egregious post hoc ergo propter hoc reasoning, should you find its illogic too embarrassing, you might prefer to deploy an argument on behalf of the general skills and background of information provided by the college experience. But this line of reasoning threatens to become little more than the truism that anything one learns is relevant in some way or another to one's life and lifework. A stint in the military or two years in the Peace Corps might have been equally relevant. So once again you have embraced an educational model that requires you either to lie or to trivialize in an attempt to avoid facing up to the narrowing dynamic it imposes.

When you and your associates transform your college into a resource center, you make it an instrument for reinforcing a narrowed vision of life and its possibilities. The adolescents in your student body are prone to closure. Their very ignorance of their ignorance impels them down clearly defined but clearly confining career paths. They think that they must *be* something in order to have an identity. It is no better with the adults among your students, who came back to college wanting to upgrade their skills and acquire new credentials in order to get a salary increase or a promotion or to find themselves a better job. They think that they already are who they are, and that education is an instrument for reaffirming that identity or making sure that its worth is properly recognized.

Your students are convinced that living creatively and openly, always in the process of becoming something they know not what, would mean for them to *be* nothing at all, a nobody, a mere cipher. How embarrassing to your adolescent students—and maybe even more so to their parents—should they have no ready answer to the omnipresent question asked at family reunions and neighborhood cookouts: "And so what are you going to *be* when you grow up?" How embarrassing to your adult students should they have no answer to the usual cocktail party question: "So what's the payoff for spending your evenings reading those turgid tomes?" Unless you resist your students' rush toward closure, their college years will be fully given over to learning the skills and securing the credentials they need in order to be no more than what they came to college already convinced they were or were meant to be.

In the absence of a required curriculum pulling your students out of their parochial worlds into the wider worldview of their culture and its traditions, they will remain as though they were still children intent on fulfilling nothing more than their narrowly defined desires. They will never truly grow up, never become genuine adults fit by virtue of their knowledge and commitment to assume the burdens of leadership required by the wider community. In the absence of a demanding method that must be mastered as a prerequisite for pursuing these goals, your students will continue to expect that the world will supply their wants automatically. They will never become aware that a hard-won expertise is their best pathway to personal satisfaction and that it is crucial as well to the continued viability of the sophisticated social order they take for granted. This Resource Center of yours, having denied that there are any nonnegotiable ends or nonnegotiable means to success, has lost the authority it needs to educate its students. It cannot lead them from what is to what could be; it cannot "e-ducate" them out of childishness into mature citizenship. For the Resource Center, the limited horizons of youth are translated into the limited horizons of adulthood.

Three models of institutional purpose thus present themselves, each claiming to offer higher education in America the paradigm it needs to survive the crisis of this century's waning years. Whether as Faithful Community, as Guild of Inquirers, or as Resource Center, however, these colleges have been forced to make a debilitating choice between deceit and triviality in the way they articulate their purposes, and they have been led with seeming inexorability into an ever-narrowing sense of what those purposes are or even ought to be. If the story of the first decade of the new century is to be an account of the struggle among these three models for the hearts and minds of citizens, educators, and students, then it will be a sorry tale indeed that must be told. For it would seem that whichever model is victorious, the result will be the same. By the beginning of the next century our colleges will have lost the ennobling breadth and depth of meaning that were the sources of their importance to the nation. Narrow-visioned shadows of their former selves, America's fin de siècle colleges have become either the advocates or the servants of narrow interests.

But where there is no longer vision, the people perish.

II

The way out from this dead end is certainly not for me to propose a fourth model as the proper paradigm of educational purpose. I cannot imagine at the moment what such a model might be, nor would it help if I could. The problem is not the inadequacy of any of the models for academic purpose we have been examining. The problem is thinking that the essence of a college lies in the purposes it serves. Having a purpose is necessary to any college being a college, but it is not sufficient. A college, perhaps any social institution of significance, must find its meaning not only in what it serves but in what it is. There must be more to a college than even its most fundamental purposes. It must have purposes, but it must not allow itself to be defined by them.

Missions, methods, and outcomes are all extrinsic matters. They orient a group toward what lies outside itself, toward the future and the possibilities that await realization there. The process is for the sake of the product, the servant for what it serves. The character of any means-ends structure has a beginning and a middle which find their relevance in the Promised Land they make possible but which like Moses they cannot possess. For the Faithful Community, both ends and means are specified by the mandate of the founders: the purpose of a college is to prepare a society's new generation of leaders by teaching them a specific heritage of beliefs and practices. The Guild of Inquirers specifies the means but permits each individual to determine the ends desired: the purpose of a college is to provide the analytic and synthetic skills of problem-solving necessary to acquire the knowledge requisite for whatever theoretical or practical ends a person might pursue. The Resource Center allows individuals to specify both means and ends: its purpose is to provide whatever skills, beliefs, and practical experiences a person may want for whatever reason. In all three cases, the result of the process is distinguished carefully from the process itself, and it is the result that legitimates the process. The end justifies the means. The final judgment of success or failure is always a matter of the bottom line: has the mission been accomplished, has the method become an effective habit, have the conditions of the contract been fulfilled?

A means-ends structure is teleological. A possibility is identified as worthy of being made actual, and a process is initiated which strives to turn that possibility into an actuality. The whole point of having purposes is to realize them. The aim of the process is always at closure, the transmutation of what could be into what actually is. The purposes to which a college is committed, therefore, should be judged worthy or unworthy by assessing the likelihood, character, and consequences of their realization. Did the students grow up to become leaders in their community, did they become recognized experts in their field, did they make lots of money? Similarly the means employed by a college in attaining its purposes should be judged in terms of their effectiveness in bringing about that realization. Does requiring your students to read Shakespeare and Plato really help them cope with today's world? Is a chemistry major adequately prepared for graduate school without having had a chance to do work on an NMR? Will graduates be better prepared for the job market if they have had at least one internship experience? A purposive institution should be evaluated by reference not to what it is in itself but by reference to how worthy its purposes are and how effectively it serves them.[1]

The purpose essential to a Faithful Community is to do whatever is necessary to attain an end of absolute worth. So valuable is this end that the reasonable likelihood of its possession is alone what gives life meaning. Educationally, a commitment to this purpose implies teaching young people and adults to believe in the importance of the institutionally specified end, then making sure they are familiar with the means that can legitimately be utilized for achieving it. The end is invaluable, an intrinsic good. The means most conducive to obtaining this good then becomes good as well but instrumentally so: it is good because it provides you with a pathway to what is good. In the special case where there is only one good and only one way to obtain it, the means becomes priceless because the end is: for you to lose that means would be to lose the end only it can guarantee.

A college should therefore be judged by the success of its graduates: by their achievements as leaders in the community, as exemplars of the intrinsic values the community celebrates. Where the graduates fail to realize such ends, the college can be chastised for not carrying out its mission properly. The problem, however, may not be a matter of whether students were taught what they need to know in order to be exemplars. The problem could be a matter of will. Students may have been taught in school that their aim in life should be to attain eternal life or to love their neighbor as themselves, to be persons of strong character or to bring about a just social order. But they may not care to do so; they may willfully turn their back on such goals. The judgment of others that their deeds fall short of acceptable standards, or their own inner doubt about the righteousness of their motives, is supposed to be devastating. Graduates of your college who do not measure up should know that they are in danger of not gaining possession of the value without which other values have no worth. If the end for which they were born has become an impossible dream, then their lives will have been for naught. To the members of a Faithful Community, despair is the price paid by those who fall short of what is expected of them. The wages of sin is death.

As soon as a community tolerates, and a college teaches about, ends other than the ones it holds sacrosanct, there is no way to prevent its students and graduates from redefining the requirements for living a meaningful life. It should be that if they are unable or unwilling to seek salvation, they know they will end up eternally damned. If they are not willing to do their duty, to serve God and country to the best of their ability, they should be aware that their actions will be thought treasonous and that the penalty for their misbehavior is death or at least permanent banishment from the community. But if the end that is the source of life's meaning can be chosen at will, then reasonable people will tailor that end to suit themselves. They will not despair if they do not love their neighbor as themselves but instead will find it quite satisfying to be successful in the pursuit of their own interests—and the devil take the hindmost. And anyway, why should a college not honor its mavericks as well as those who follow the established paths to fame and fortune?

If there is no single end shared by the members of a community, necessary to their sense of what a meaningful life entails, then anything goes.

As Karamazov says, if there be no God, then all is permissible. In the absence of a common normative end, the only alternative to moral anarchy is to find your standard of value, your necessary condition for meaningfulness, in the means utilized rather than the end sought. The Guild of Inquirers is permissive about ends because it has come to the conclusion that there is only one best means for obtaining any and all worthwhile ends. Faculty should teach, and students should learn, that the scientific method is invaluable, the sole intrinsic good, because it is the only route to ends the value of which are assured by the value of the means by which they are realized. The ends they seek are derivatively good, therefore, not intrinsically good. Even were they to discover an end that was invaluable, its value would still be a function of the method for possessing it because only the method can validate it as invaluable: its significance is not self-validating.

So the Guild judges every action by the same normative standard: adherence to the proper method. What is important in life is the pursuit of truth, whether or not it can ever be obtained. The college's graduates can be said to have lived a meaningful life if they were committed to improving the social good, even if their efforts ended in failure. Salvation is not a matter of good works but of faith, of intentions not achievements. But the whole point of the scientific method is that it has been designed to secure the end sought: a system of verified knowledge. This method is claimed by some to be the best way for doing so, by others the only way. Consequently the Guild's method is imbued with intrinsic rather than merely instrumental value. Its end, paradoxically, is a means.

This is only an apparent paradox, however. The means-ends structure is what is important, not which element of that structure happens to be emphasized. The only difference between the Faithful Community and the Guild of Inquirers is that the one has emphasized the ends dimension of the means-ends structure whereas the other has emphasized the means dimension. This comparison is paralleled in ethical theory by the similarity between utilitarianism and deontology. Bentham[2] argues that pleasure is the intrinsic good and any action conducive to its realization is instrumentally good, whereas Kant[3] argues that any action conforming to the categorical imperative is intrinsically good and any pleasure that might result is derivatively good. But for both, the good has to do with a combination of ends and means. A meaningful life is one lived in pursuit of worthwhile ends by worthwhile means. A top-flight college inculcates the highest aspirations in its students and provides them with the best possible tools available for realizing those aspirations.

But the problem of an absolute method is the same as the problem of an absolute end: how to enforce its authority. Once religious pluralism has been accepted, there is no one faith for you to believe as a prerequisite for salvation. Once an appeal to reason, self-evidence, common sense, or intuition has been discredited as a way to validate the claim that you are doing the right thing if your actions were motivated by good intentions, there is no way you can expect to be respected for what you only hope someday to accomplish. Once the history of science has exposed the myth of the scientific method as an objective instrument for determining truths independent of individual or cultural bias, you are free to insist that other ways of knowing should be given equal status. So who is to say anymore that there is one right method or attitude or procedure that needs to be taught and learned, without which people's actions are likely to be misdirected, their work a waste of time, their dreams mere fantasies? Who is to say there are any prerequisites to the good life or to an effectively functioning society? The Guild, become permissive, has no answer.

A Resource Center affirms no intrinsic goods. Means are valued by the ends they help realize, but the ends turn out merely to be means to further ends. Nothing is valued in itself because its value is always a function of a particular purpose, which is a function of a given situational context. No possibility is such that it would be good were it to be realized at any time in any situation; no method is such that were it to be effectively applied at any time in any situation the result would be worthwhile. The Biblical admonition[4] that everything has its season and every activity its time is transmuted into the claim that there is no such thing as the right time or the appropriate place, the proper method or the worthwhile end. Every good is instrumental, none intrinsic. Pleasure is good if that is your thing; treating others as ends rather than merely as means is good if that is how you want it.

Within the context of a Resource Center, the means-ends structure has been completely relativized. But the structure remains, and it is as powerfully present as in the other two kinds of college. Indeed, it is more evident because not obscured by the idolization of particular ends or means. Where there is no content to the commitment, where neither the Great Community nor the Universal Calculus guides your hopes and focuses your energies, the means-ends structure is all that remains. To be committed to serving educational needs defined by others in ways defined by others can be taken as a dignified profession, however, only if you think of service as the pearl beyond price. What is invaluable is for you to make it your life-purpose to help others realize their purposes. "Whatever end by whatever means" is a celebration of the means-ends structure as such as the sole intrinsic good.

Because of this inherent instability in the absolute affirmation of ends or means, any institution defined solely in terms of its purposes will gravitate naturally toward the Resource Center model. The resulting servitude of an institution to its means-ends structure rather than to any particular means or ends is most clearly revealed in a time of institutional crisis. Your college finds itself in a situation where in order to survive it must abandon its traditional beliefs and practices, must break free from the constraints of its original mandate. At first you might think it unseemly for your college to place mere survival as its highest priority. Is it not more noble to commit institutional seppuku if need be than to forsake one's founding purpose or one's historical commitment to an agreed upon standard of academic excellence? Yet in the crisis moments of a college's struggle for survival, you and your friends at the college learn that its existence and its purposes are quite separable. Its purposes are extrinsic to it.

Therefore one way for your college to survive, and to do so with dignity and verve, is by the simple expedient of altering the purposes it serves. A college defined essentially by missions, methods, or outcomes is essentially an instrument. But an instrument, although always first created with some purpose in mind that it was designed to help accomplish, is in fact independent of that purpose. This college of yours, whatever its past purposes, can be used in the future to realize a quite different purpose, and in the process it can be altered in marginal or in fundamental ways to better suit its new usage.

And so your college as Faithful Community, confronted by the collapse of the unified commonwealth whose leaders it was designed to nurture, proposes adjusting its mandate to suit the new realities. Wanting it to survive, you encourage your college to change its mandate. And so it alters its fundamental commitments, remakes itself with a new image, and goes on surviving for a time. And eventually a new crisis arises, and your college again adjusts its mandate. And adjusts it, and adjusts it, always tacking into the winds of change, doing whatever is necessary to assure sufficient resources to remain afloat as an educational institution.

And so your college as Guild of Inquirers, confounded by a declining willingness on the part of students to pay the price in self-discipline necessary for mastering the scientific method, buffeted by people more interested in enjoying what they have than in searching for an intangible truth they lack, adjusts its expectations. You applaud your college when it narrows the scope of those it educates to a chosen few or when it waters down its requirements for mastery in order to provide greater relevance. So that it might survive, it changes its standards enough to be assured of fully enrolled classes that justify the salaries of its faculty, and it compromises its commitment to the unfettered pursuit of truth by contracting out its services to businesses and industries able to provide it with a continued flow of research grants. You are happy that these outside companies are paying your college's pipers so handsomely, ignoring their quiet insistence that this commitment means they can stipulate which tune is henceforth to be played. And thus your college changes its standards, and it changes them, until it is no longer master of its method.

And so the college as Faithful Community gives up its absolute ends and the college as Guild of Inquirers gives up its absolute means, and what remains are versions of the college as Resource Center. Tell us our mission, coos your Resource Center seductively, prescribe for us our method. Then turn us loose so that we can do as you want. We are absolutely sure you will be pleased with the results.

This sword cuts both ways, of course. A mandate to educate the nation's youth in the skills of social leadership might better be served by the executive training programs of business corporations than by the curricula of the traditional colleges. Public and commercial television might be more effective media than the lecture hall for transmitting scientific information. Weekend encounter groups run by for-profit institutes might provide a more attractive environment than the residential campus for exploring and inculcating values. When you turn your college into a Resource Center, you are freed from the shackles of any predetermining sense of what sort of outcomes you and your associates should advocate or even to what sort of methods you and they should conform. But at the same time other institutions, designed originally for purposes having nothing to do with education, are freed likewise from any predetermining constraints that make it inappropriate for them to adapt their own specialized instrumentalities to serve an educational purpose. Where the raison d'être of an institution is extrinsic to it, the primary virtue will be an eye for the opportune advantage combined with the boldness, skill, and resources needed to translate that opportunity into practical reality.

Educational institutions in this country are singularly unsuited to playing this role, however. They are unsuited not because they are outdated, inept, cowardly, or underfunded but because they are not essentially purposeful. The essence of a college does not lie in the purposes it serves. Its essence is not extrinsic but intrinsic.

III

Colleges that serve no essential purpose are their own masters. Since they are defined in terms of intrinsic qualities, in terms of what they are and not what ends they serve, their worth lies within their control. Like a lover, they are cherished for what they were and are and will be, and this value is not conditional upon their general or specific usefulness. The deep meaning of "alma mater" is that for those who attend a college its utility is not what makes it important to them. We do not love our mothers because they raised us to adulthood.

The virtue of a college is that it is not reducible to the ways by which it assists individual students to achieve their life goals and the ways it contributes to society's need for a continuing supply of educated citizens. Nor is it reducible to the contributions of its faculty to the national welfare or to the ever-growing body of scientific and humanistic knowledge. By having intrinsic worth as well as any of these various extrinsic relevancies, a college is able to resist two dangers. First of all, it is able to fend off the zealots who in the heyday of their success either seek to equate the college with the triumphant purposes they celebrate or to condemn it as the enemy of those purposes. Second, the appeal to intrinsic worth preserves a college from the prostitution of its purposes that times of crisis or decline make tempting. To avoid the rigidity of the former and the flaccidity of the latter, a college must have more than a purpose.

The virtue of a college should be that it is virtuous. Being virtuous may sound oddly dated, however, besides being something applicable to individuals but not to institutions. It used to be said that a woman's virtue is her chastity, and that for a man *virtu* is the quality that makes him manly. In each case, the reference is to a characteristic that is thought to be crucial to the person being who she or he is and so something of inestimable worth to that person. The excellence of a man lies in his virility, his willingness to act incisively and to persist in pursuit of his goals despite dangers and difficulties. He who so acts is a virtuous man. An unmarried woman's excellence lies in her purity, expressed physically in her virginity and morally in her refusal to succumb to the worldly temptations that would rob her of that virginity or of the spiritual and mental qualities associated with it. She who so acts is a virtuous woman.

The characteristics that nowadays we think essential to manliness and femininity are no longer valor and chastity. Indeed, you may well doubt if there are any characteristics essential to being a man or a woman, or even to being human. But you probably still speak of someone behaving or thinking in a characteristic fashion, by which you mean that this person responds to a variety of different situations in consistent, even predictable, ways. The person's actions or beliefs are not random or arbitrary; they are neither unthinking nor ungrounded. He acted that way for principled reasons, because it was what squared with who he thinks he is and what he stands for. She stuck by her beliefs despite the hostile reaction, because they reflect the sort of person she knows herself to be. It is because these people tend to act in characteristic ways that we say they have character. They have a sense of themselves to which they are loyal, an ideal by which they judge as appropriate or inappropriate the alternative courses of action available to them. How out of character, you say, when one of them does something not in keeping with that self-image or not in keeping with your sense of it: she just is not herself today; it is just not like him to act that way.

So you are likely to speak of character rather than virtue when pointing out the qualities essential to a person's identity. Also, you are probably more willing to think of a person's character as self-ascribed and as unique to that person than to think of it as a genetic inheritance or a natural necessity. You agree that people should be true to themselves and not allow others to define them, but you hesitate to agree that people are true to themselves only if they act in an essentially human way. And even if you did think there was some quality essential to your humanity, it is not likely that you would find general agreement about what it might be. Perhaps what is characteristic of humans is that they seek to maximize their own pleasure, or that they act rationally, or that they love their neighbors as themselves. Amid our disagreements, however, on this we agree: there is something normative about being a mature adult—being a "person" in the honorific sense of that word. There is something that centers the actions and beliefs of a person, something that integrates them so that the person is "a" person and not merely a congeries of unconnected, unfocused responses to environmental stimuli. Let us call this something a person's essence or character, leaving unresolved for the moment whether it is natural or invented, unique to each individual or unique to the species.

Can we extend this notion of character from individuals to institutions? Can the college be a person writ large? Can it have a character, have not just interesting or idiosyncratic features but have a feature that is essential to what it is? And if so, does each college fashion its own character or is there a single generic character that all colleges must possess if they are to be a college?

I think these are legitimate questions, for which there are no a priori answers. Let me hypothesize that there is no sharp demarcation between persons and groups with respect to whether or not they have an essence. Any group, whether informal or institutionalized, if it has a collective sense of itself, a sense to which its members are loyal and which they use to assess the appropriateness of what the group did or does or might possibly do, can be said to have character. In a world where anything might happen and probably will, the actions of a college, its policies and practices, would be seen as merely reactive, merely hit-or-miss, were the only criterion for evaluating them whether or not they helped the college attain some stated purpose, including that of mere survival. For a college where anything goes as long as it works, its nature is necessarily defined by the external forces against which it reacts. The college is the anything by which it goes. In contrast, the policies and practices of a college with character can be judged fitting or not, appropriate or inappropriate for it as a college to be doing, because it has a normative and not only a descriptive dimension.

It was once thought by those who worked for IBM that the company's character included a commitment to treat its employees as more than costs of operation. IBM said that it was sensitive to various intangible values having to do with respect and loyalty, values that it expected its employees to reciprocate. This agreement was only tacit, to be sure, as much a mix of myth and rumor as of any explicit promises. But it was a palpable feature of the IBM ethos and was expressed in such things as the confidence employees had that the company thought its people so important they need not fear periods of economic downturn. After all, even during the Great Depression IBM's employees had not been laid off.

When IBM in the mid-1990s began a significant retrenchment in its work force, the shock to its employees and to the general public was not what it was doing but that these actions seemed to violate one of the company's guiding principles. Other companies might dismiss workers without regard for past loyalty, but IBM was a different sort of place: it had a certain character that could be counted on to prevent such practices. In abruptly terminating employees who had thought their years of loyalty provided job protection or at least justified an explanation and even some compassion, IBM was not simply doing something unpleasant yet necessary, something neither it nor its workers liked. Far worse, it was doing what it had said it ought not to do: the Big Blue had lost its virtue.

Neither a person's nor a college's character need be rigid, however. What it would be in character to do in a given situation is necessarily fuzzy around the edges and so involves interpretation. A characteristic way of behaving, a policy governing the actions of a college's members, is abstract and needs further determinations in order to be concretely realized. Simply applying a policy in the way it was previously applied, without regard to the contextual peculiarities and with insufficient imagination to see the full range of acceptable alternative determinations, is to misunderstand what it means to be under the guidance of norms. Treating normative principles as though they were specific instructions, treating policies as though they were courses of action, is what gives bureaucracies a bad name. So a college governed by a normative sense of itself might do bold and daring things in an attempt to remain true to its character in the particular situation where it finds itself, or it might do very traditional, even rigidly repetitive, things. But there is a difference between, on the one hand, a college's decision-makers doing something out of the ordinary because they think that it is fitting for the college to proceed in such a fashion, and, on the other hand, a college doing something without its decision-makers thinking about what might be fitting, without them thinking normatively at all. This distinction is what IBM executives, it would seem, failed to appreciate when the pink slips came without any attempt to justify the firings as somehow still in keeping with the company's long-standing commitment to its workers.

A college, if it has no essential purpose, is able to develop a character of its own. I am not arguing that colleges should not have purposes; there could be no such thing as an institution without purposes. My claim is that what is essential to a college should not be its purposes. It may be proper for a business enterprise to be defined by a goal of maximizing its profits or optimizing the total return on its stocks, so that such matters as the quality of its products, or even what its products are, can be altered as its defining goal is altered. But it was not proper for IBM, which had a character in addition to its purposes, to have allowed itself to become a function of its goals. Nor would it be proper for a college, which has no choice except to adhere to the character without which it is not a college, to allow itself to be defined by its purposes. Its purpose might be to produce tomorrow's leaders, to increase knowledge, or to train workers, but an institution could do all of these and yet not be a college. And a college might shift from one to another of these purposes, or invent a radically new kind of purpose, and still remain fully and genuinely a college.

When current purposes falter or fail and the members of a college community agree that its directions must be reassessed and possibly reoriented, it should not be the identity of the college that is at issue but only its current goals. Colleges with character should be able to undertake this difficult task with an equanimity derived from the knowledge that they are centered elsewhere than in the purposes being called into question. Colleges that understand themselves as having an intrinsic meaning should be willing to affirm that identity and its value even in the midst of danger and even, if necessary, past the brink of their destruction. Where purposes are the only value for a college, survival becomes ultimately the only purpose. Yet surely there is a higher meaning to education than the indefinite perpetuation of its institutional structures.

I want to argue on behalf of the educational character of colleges and to do so in the strong sense: that there is a generic feature that any college must possess and to which it must be loyal in order for that college truly to be a college. The character of a college is something intrinsic to it as a particular institution with a particular history and a particular palette of purposes arising from that history, but that character is also something intrinsic to it as a college rather than some other kind of institution. The fact that colleges have a generic feature they share and because of which they are colleges does not mean that all colleges need express this feature identically nor that they could even if they wished to. Colleges vary not only in their nonessential features—for instance, with respect to their purposes. They also incarnate their essence as a college in specifically divergent ways. There are more ways than one to be a virtuous college even though all the ways are expressions of the same essential feature without which none of them would be, in the genuine sense, a college.[5]

I would also want to insist that this generic essence is a historical artifact, although one not easily scrapped or recast because so long tempered
in the fires of cultural meaning.[6] But this line of argument would carry me
too far afield and so I will not pursue it further. I want instead to pin
down more precisely what this essential quality of a college is. I then will
argue that the reason a college must possess such a character is because
what makes it a college is that students in the presence of this virtue can
come to acquire it themselves.

IV

It is important for what I am trying to say that you understand the difference between an action and a practice.[7] An action is something done by an
agent in a situation in order to realize a purpose. An action is a particular
deed concretely performed by a specific individual within an identifiable
context for a specifiable reason. The deed you do is always specific: a student asks his professor to repeat her question; a poet alters the second word
in a line of his own verse as he recites it at a reading; a dean signs a letter
in the presence of the department chair authorizing a new faculty appoint-
ment. And your doing is always done for the sake of a specific end: whether
it be to secure information the professor possesses or to curry her favor, to
improve the lilt of the poem or to exhibit your creative restlessness, to sig-
nal the end of a rancorous dispute over appointments or to reward the
department for its support in a prior curricular battle.

When what happens is instinctual or involuntary, the transaction
between the person and environment is not an action but merely a behavior, a physical process. An action requires an agent, a human being, who
is conscious: aware of the given concrete situation, finding it in some sense
inadequate, even if only because the situation is in danger of perishing and
needs to be sustained or recovered, aware of specific possibilities that if
realized would likely remove that inadequacy. The agent, thusly aware,
intervenes in the situation, interacting with what is given in order to actu-
alize at least one of those available possibilities and so create a different,
more satisfactory situation.[8] An action is a here-and-now occurrence occa-
sioned by an agent.

For every verb of action, there has to be an adverb modifying it. How
you do these things, how you entertain those possibilities and make those

choices, is also specific, a specific characteristic qualifying a specific action. For every doing there must be the way in which it was done. You cannot just take action: you must always do so in some manner. The student politely asks his questions of the professor; the poet impatiently crosses out the offending words; the dean hypocritically masks her Machiavellian purposes with a pleasant smile.

There are no verbs without adverbs, but the forms of their connection are various. At one extreme are actions that can only be done in a certain way and ways of acting that are only compatible with one sort of end or means. The professor will not answer questions unless they are addressed to her politely; poets who view their first drafts uncritically will never write anything publishable; no dean can get anywhere with that department chair by speaking candidly. At the other extreme are actions that can be done in almost any way and ways in which any action could be done. The same question can be asked impolitely instead of politely; the poem can be altered not in a genuinely spontaneous manner but with a studied spontaneity intended mainly for effect; the document could be signed reluctantly and with refreshingly candid protests rather than incisively with a deceptive smile. There are lots of ways to skin a cat, but the only way to feed a 400-pound canary is carefully.

More relevant to our inquiry are connections between verbs and adverbs lying far from such extremes. These include connections where an action tolerates a wide variety of manners of action but excludes others, and connections where a way of doing things constrains but does not predetermine what can be done. If you want to do whatever it takes to become a prosperous Wall Street broker or a Nobel laureate or a college president, there are a variety of routes you could take in order to reach your goal. But you will not succeed unless along your route you learn the attitudes and habits of mind appropriate to those social roles. Brokers who tend to make too many investment judgments carelessly, who do not ask their questions pointedly and in timely fashion, end up selling pencils. Poets who are too easily enamored by their own words, and so do not think their verses deeply, are not likely to be invited to Stockholm. Deans who have a penchant for speaking deviously and acting deceptively tend not to be trusted and so to their puzzlement never make it onto anyone's short list of presidential candidates. Deans whose purposes are explained honestly and implemented forthrightly may not become presidents either, but their aspiration for higher office is at least compatible with their manner of pursuing it. Honest folks can be poets or brokers as well, but not government spies or rip-off artists.

Let us look more closely at one particular kind of relationship between verbs and their associated adverbs: where you are committed to a certain manner of acting, one that does not specifically determine your actions although it constrains them. For in these situations the adverbs of action have become practices.

A practice is a generalized adverb, available to an agent who is choosing a possible end to realize and a means for doing so. A practice is a general procedure you can follow when performing an action: a set of considerations—customs, maxims, rules, standards—that guide you in determining how an action should be done, that shepherd the manner in which you perform your deed. If how you do something tends to be similar to how you did that sort of thing previously, the adverbs of your actions are probably tutored by a practice. If the student is usually polite, if the poet hardly ever sets down a verse without reworking it a dozen times, if the dean seems always to have a hidden agenda, then they can be said to have each developed a practice of acting in a certain way.

The manner of an action could be simply uncontrolled, spontaneous, errant, something to which you have given no thought. But the absence of a conscious choice of how you will act is more likely to trigger a controlling habit. A practice is something to which an agent subscribes, something chosen because of its general helpfulness in making specific choices about ends and means. Habits are the residues of practices, ways of acting chosen so frequently that they have become the familiar default manner of doing things. A habit is a practice selected without giving much thought to its relevance, without weighing it against alternatives, without deliberately choosing to be guided by it. It never occurred to the student not to be polite; the poet does not realize he is such a fussbudget about his texts; the dean probably smiles like that even when she is informing a faculty member that he has just been denied tenure.

The practice in your classes is that students are to raise their hand when they wish to be called upon, and then when you have acknowledged their hand they are to stand by their desks and ask a question or reply to one in a clear but quiet voice. This practice has nothing to do with what question you or they might ask or answer. Indeed, the whole point of your insistence on this way of proceeding is that it sets the conditions under which any exchange whatsoever is to go on within the confines of your classroom. Students may curse you loudly once they have left the sphere of your authority, and you may think mean-spirited thoughts about their diligence or their intelligence even while they are answering your question, but the ground rules for classroom discourse are clearly understood by everyone, and they are to be followed not only when discussing literature but also when studying geometry and even when seeking permission to go to the rest room.

You may think this practice is a simple matter of good manners, of being courteous, although you probably recognize that an orderly classroom atmosphere is also an efficient way for you to stick to your lesson plan. I might think that my classroom practices also require that students be polite, although my rules are not clearly stipulated and are far more flexible than yours in deciding what counts as a proper way in which to ask or answer questions. The actions of students in my classes may even appear to you as uncontrolled, guided by no proper practice at all and so giving free rein to student unruliness. We might find ourselves arguing in the faculty lounge about your suggestion that each teacher post explicit rules and then expect the students to be able to recite them by heart as well as to obey them. Our argument would be over whether practices should be explicit and whether knowing how to follow them entails also knowing how to say what they are. Where we would agree is that there must be a practice that shapes how our classroom activities are conducted, that without being polite and respecting one another, without some constraints on what students and teachers may do in a classroom, there can be no effective learning.

A practice can be the direct outcome of an action, as when, for the sake of creating a good learning environment, you write down the explicit politeness rules for your class to follow. Another classroom down the hall might also produce a practice as the outcome of specific actions, but whereas you created and imposed your list of rules unilaterally, they arrived at theirs by group consensus. Most procedures, however, are not the consequence of a purposeful action. They arise as by-products of actions that had other kinds of outcomes in mind. Having conducted her literature sessions by asking students to pull their chairs into a circle, and by working hard to make sure that everyone in the circle contributed at least twice to any day's discussion, the teacher down the hall turned what may at first have been a spontaneous suggestion into an expected format for such discussions. She found herself, without ever having explicitly intended it, following the practice of teaching literature in a discussion format, then found it natural to use that same practice for other subject matters, and eventually even for teaching geometry. This pedagogical practice was then readily available to her as a practice to be used when deciding what the other, nonpedagogical, practices of the class should be: she elevated a practice to a practice for determining practices.

You will agree, I am sure, that your quite distinctive classroom practice is hardly your own invention. What you did was adapt to your situation practices that had long since become traditional in the schools, practices deriving most likely from how adults in your community usually act toward one another. The good manners you learned at home, around town, and in your own schooling, and which you now seek to apply in your classroom, are an accretion over the generations of a typical way of interacting. No one set about purposefully formulating these social conventions, although many people may on occasion have tried to influence one or another limited feature of the wider practices, and some may have succeeded sufficiently to be remembered for the changes they effected. Others are remembered, for good or ill, because of changes that came as unintended consequences of actions they took with no thought for their relevance to your community's accepted practices. The practices that you adapted to your classroom, precisely because they were so pervasive, so seemingly obvious as to be taken for granted, are not likely to be written down anywhere except in highly specified cases such as legislative acts or the newspaper columns of Miss Manners and her ilk. That is what makes it so difficult to be accepted in a strange community: its practices are very hard to learn because they are for the most part unspoken, nuanced in ways that often defy verbal articulation. Yet nonetheless they are expected to be the conditions for your every action.

So particular individuals perform specific actions in specific ways, and by a process more of accretion than conscious fabrication these ways of acting are generalized into practices of which these individuals avail themselves when they are determining the specific ways in which they go about doing what they do. Games are played by the rules, informal interactions are shaped by habit and custom, government policies must be in accord with the Constitution. For any action, there are practices associated with it of which you are expected to make use. The association may be conventional or natural, or so deeply rooted a convention as to seem natural, but what is important about a practice is that it is invoked as a mentor whenever its associated kind of action has become an imminent possibility.

It will now be helpful to distinguish two kinds of practices; I will refer to one kind as "prudential" and the other as "moral." So far our discussion of practices has been primarily about those of a prudential sort. I want first to elaborate on what has been said about such practices in order then to draw the contrast with moral practices. These latter are what the essence of a college is all about.

Prudential practices provide guidance in how best to achieve certain purposes. Carpenters who are cabinetmakers, for instance, pursue their craft under the tutelage of techniques, sensibilities, conventions, and tricks of the trade that centuries of experience have validated as those most conducive to guiding them in their effort to create wooden cabinets suited to the needs of their customers. These practices range from rules of thumb for how to sense the flaws and virtues in a piece of lumber to knowing the best ways for selecting, utilizing, and maintaining their various tools. The rules of conduct in your classroom had an explicit educational purpose in mind. The dean's hypocrisy was a style she had found helpful in pursuing her announced goal of improving the quality of the academic program at her college; it also was helping her advance her career, which was an equally important purpose for her if not a higher one. The poet's dream was to write great poetry, and he knew that only by constantly reworking his material would he ever be likely to realize that dream.

For each expertise there are the certain practices that must be learned as prerequisites for mastering it: basic techniques that it is necessary to make use of when doing the things expected of the expert, but also critiques and adjustments and varied subtleties crucial in applying those basic techniques in a manner sensitive to the particular features of each actual situation. An expert pianist is skilled in striking the proper keys accurately and at the appropriate time. But truly excellent piano playing calls for more than technique; it requires art, the higher practices of enunciation, interpretation, and expression. These practices, both technical and artful, are relevant, whether the pianist's purpose is to play a Bach fugue, a Chopin prelude, or an improvisation in the style of Scott Joplin. Good pianists are good not because of what compositions they can play, but because they are effective at using well the appropriate musical practices no matter what they are playing.

The scientific method is a prudential practice, a complex of protocols and techniques and ways of seeing, designed first to secure accurate empirical information about objects and events and then to formulate and test general hypotheses about their interrelationships. The goal for which the method of experimental inquiry is a prudential practice is being able to predict the behavior of those objects and to anticipate those events in order to control them—or, at least, to gain sufficient opportunity to adapt to what cannot be controlled. The biochemist in the laboratory or the entomologist in the field should be as well versed in the art of inquiry as in its techniques, for scientific expertise involves more than skill in following a procedure. It also calls for subtle adaptations of general laboratory or field practices in a manner sensitive to the particular features of each actual situation.

The notion of a scientific method, of course, is a highly abstracted and idealized description of the more specific practices of particular disciplines, which are in turn abstract summaries of the concrete practices of specific laboratories and individual scientists. But this abstractness should not obscure the fact that the scientific method is prudential: its authority derives from its track record in helping to guide the actual inquiries of actual scientists in such a way that their factual claims and their predictions meet appropriate tests of criticism and evidence.

I have been generating in these comments a little hierarchy of abstractions with regard to the adverbs of an action. Most concretely, there are the features of an action that constitute how it was performed: quietly, fussily, secretively. They could be salient or barely noticed, flat-footed or exquisitely adjusted to the action's situational context. Then there are the prudential practices that generalize those manners of acting and return them back to agents as recommendations for how subsequent actions might be done: politely, relentlessly, hypocritically. Such practices can be thoughtlessly selected, more taken for granted than chosen, or they can be deliberately chosen, and the deliberation might be foolish or wise.

Practices can themselves be generalized, as when we speak of the student's manners, the poet's compositional style, the dean's approach to management. We could then generalize across all the kinds of ways of a person's various kinds of doings, and we would be describing that person's character: the inquisitive student, the perfectionist poet, the unprincipled dean. And we could continue to abstract until our generalization was about a community or an era or a civilization: the pragmatic Americans, the rational Enlightenment, the Faustian West. Were we then to generalize to include human beings of every community, era, and civilization, we would be well on our way toward an understanding of human conduct, perhaps ready to develop a metaphysical theory of action.

My concern, however, is with only one level and kind of abstraction, that of the practices which are ready at hand for concrete human agents when determining how they should act in a given situation. I have tried to suggest how important prudential practices are for action, that they are crucial resources for us as we decide how to make a good choice among the possible goals relevant to our purposes, how we should select the best means for realizing those purposes, and how we might most effectively apply those means. These prudential frameworks constrain how we act, insofar as we heed their suggestions, but in doing so they improve the likelihood that we will realize our purposes. Good-mannered citizens make for a good society; great poems are never written by people who are easily satisfied with their work; nice deans finish last. With regard to prudential practices, the proof is in the pudding. If the practices help get you there, use them; if not, then you would be smart to get yourself some better ones.

The second important kind of practices, our moral practices, set conditions for action without regard to the ends or means the agent of the action might have in view. There are certain practices people should follow no matter what they are doing, practices that should govern their actions not because of the purposes those actions seek to realize but simply because they are actions. Not only when functioning as scientists in the laboratory but also when performing any other social function and even when in solitary meditation, a person simply because of being a person should act in certain ways and not in others. Those practices that guide our every action can be called moral because, as Kant puts it, they are categorical rather than hypothetical. They do not condition our actions "if" we have this or that purpose in mind; they condition our actions no matter what our purpose might be. They are the adverbial advisers that simply by their presence as possibilities for conditioning action transform an agent's actions into morally acceptable actions. Moral practices point us toward adverbs of actions that express what is most fully human about a human being, adverbs that when characterizing our actions make them actions worthy of our humanity.

A mentor relevant to any and every action, a guideline that guides toward no particular goal nor oversees the use of any particular method, cannot be about how those goals and methods are enacted. What moral practices are about is how such goals and methods are selected. It is not the ends to which you are committed that make your actions moral nor how you pursue those ends, but how you go about determining in the first place that they are appropriate, and how you determine whether to remain constant in their pursuit or to alter or repudiate them. It is not the means you use to achieve your ends nor how you implement those means that make your actions moral, but how you determine them in the first place as appropriate means, and how you decide to stay with them or to modify or abandon them as the pursuit of your ends matures toward realization or failure. Moral practices are not up a level of abstraction from prudential practices; they simply have a different clientele. They advise us on how we should choose a possibility to realize rather than advising us on what that choice should be or on how the possibility we choose should be realized.

In arguing that the essence of a college should lie in something other than its purposes, I want to propose that its essence should be a matter of its and its society's moral practices. Students in attending a college should find themselves interacting with others in a milieu marked by human actions that are, or should be, conditioned by moral practices, by the resources that help people decide to do whatever they do in an appropriate manner. A college is where students go in order to learn things. Among those things, indeed most important among them, is learning how to act properly. Students certainly need to learn the proper things to do and the proper ways to get those things done—that is where prudential practices come in handy. But more important, students need to learn how properly to go about doing all of those proper things in proper ways.

What you should do, in the sense of what ends you should pursue and what the best means are for doing so: these are teachable subjects. However, the moral practices guiding such actions, the question of how properly to go about determining those ends and those means, and how properly to determine how to realize those ends by those means, cannot be taught. But, if moral practices are unteachable, then it cannot be the purpose of a college to teach students how to act morally nor can it be a student's aim to learn how. And yet unless the moral education of its students is more fundamental for a college than any educational goals it and its students pursue, the college will have betrayed what it is essentially. It will no longer be a college but merely a purveyor of certain interesting and important prudential practices.

You cannot be taught how to act morally because moral practices are not a subject matter. Subject matters are made up of nouns and verbs. The purpose of a college should be to teach you the content of certain subject matters: the ancient Athenian educational system and how it worked, the structure and dynamics of the hydrogen atom, meter and meaning in Tennyson's nature poetry. In addition to having you study the forms and contents of things, and the transactional and developmental processes into which they enter, a college could go further and expect you to know something about the moral practices of the human beings involved. Having learned what Isocrates and Plato taught their students and having learned what their pedagogical techniques were, you might next be expected to learn by what limits or imperatives they felt constrained when selecting some particular concept or fact to teach and when using a certain instructional technique. That is part of a first-class education: to get beyond names and dates and to include, where appropriate, the study of a person's or a people's moral practices.

Yet in doing so, you would still be studying only nouns and verbs, for you would be studying about "what" Isocrates probably intended when he conducted a class and "what" practices Plato might have had in mind when determining a pedagogical course of action and attempting to realize it. This knowledge would be difficult to acquire since it has to do with intentions, with personal attitudes, sensibilities, and habits of mind, rather than with publicly verifiable facts. But it would still be part of the content of a subject matter. You would be learning about the moral practices of Athenians, just as you might study contemporary America and learn about your own moral practices. But that is different from learning those moral practices, from acting such that your actions are conditioned by them.

Our concern here is not with the accuracy or precision of your knowledge about others' moral practices or your own, but only with the character of moral practices as a subject matter for inquiry. Whether the questions are about the social status of the Athenian students, the truth of the ideas they studied, or the pedagogical practices of Isocrates and Plato, the appropriate answers will be in terms of what happened to whom and when, where, and by what means. If you ask your professor these questions politely, you will get the answers she thinks correct and you can carefully write them down in your notebook and, who knows, perhaps you might make good use of this information in an essay on the final examination. But you did not learn how to ask her politely by writing down that this behavior is what you should do and then memorizing what you had written.

Hydrogen atoms have no purposes nor any practices governing their behavior, so it is easy to teach you what you need to know about them. The subject matter of your inquiry, however, might not be the hydrogen atoms running blindly but rather the moral practices of scientists who have studied hydrogen, or the moral practices of students attempting to understand the significance of hydrogen's location at the top of the Periodic Table. But the difference between studying about the atom and studying about a scientist studying the atom is only a difference in the source, precision, and verifiability of the relevant evidence, a difference in degree but not in kind. It is still a matter of nouns and verbs, including in this case those descriptive of the practices guiding the scientist's inquiry. If you want to do science properly, however, you will need to learn to determine and to enact your scientific purposes under the constraint of certain adverbial conditions. But that is quite different from learning how scientists act.

Where the subject matter is the meaning of a text rather than the description of an object, event, or mental state, the method of inquiry will need to change accordingly. In regard to moral practices, you may interpret Tennyson's *In Memoriam* as being about the moral quality of beloved Arthur's actions when he was still alive. Or the poem might turn out on your analysis to be about the moral practices that shaped or should have shaped Tennyson's own actions as he mourned his friend's death. Or the poem may be read as alluding to a moral practice that Tennyson advocates; it might even be read as showing such a practice without alluding to it. The poem may express Tennyson's moral practice when he was composing it or the poem could enigmatically hide those practices from all but the most discerning readers. All of these different kinds of moral practice—these qualifiers on Tennyson's acts of writing poetry and on the actions his poems describe, disclose, and propose—are relevant to your understanding of his poetry. What Tennyson sought to teach you about how to reconcile yourself to the blind flight of the atoms, and how he sought to teach you this moral truth, can only be learned by reading, analyzing, and discussing his poems. You cannot ascertain Tennyson's moral vision by applying an abstract standard to his poetry or to his actions in writing each poem, but only by attempting to discern in the particular what the practices might have been by which he felt himself constrained when writing or by which he hoped his readers would be constrained once they had finished reading or hearing what he wrote. But even this subtle hermeneutical task remains within the circle of nouns and verbs. It is the way for you to learn about moral practices relevant to Tennyson's poetry, but that is quite different from learning those practices.

It is possible for you to insist that we become more abstract, that we inquire not about Tennyson's moral practices nor those of a student studying under Isocrates, but that we learn about moral practices as such and that we do so not only to describe but also to recommend. In keeping with your admonition, I might offer a course in ethics that attempts to define its subject matter as having a normative dimension. I could design my assignments so that they move from the moral quality of particular actions to the moral practices derived from them, then to general kinds of actions and the moral practices appropriate to that level of generalization, and finally to moral practice as such.

So I might begin my course with an anthropological survey of particular cultures, trying to discern the actual moral practices of peoples both from their own descriptive and normative statements and from the anthropologists' descriptions of how these people behave and what they say about why they behave that way. My course could conceivably then rise slowly up a ladder of abstraction until it arrived at a metaphysical account of the dimension of moral practice in human conduct. Or the anthropological information could be deemed irrelevant to this metaphysical account on the grounds that the only proper way to study about moral practices is through purely rational self-reflection. But the ethics course in either of these forms would be about nominal things. Among the descriptive information we study would be accounts of what particular people in particular cultures recommend as appropriate moral practices to guide not merely their own actions but ours as well. And as the professor in this course, if I thought it proper I could make my own moral recommendations based on what you and your fellow students could be expected to know about the ethical positions studied throughout the semester. I might argue that faculty should respond to student questions by asking them even tougher questions, that poets should be the conscience of societies, and that deans should be honest. Some students would write my moral recommendations down, impressed by their sagacity or shrewdly thinking that by feeding them back to me on the final they might improve their grade.

Yet none of these activities would teach you how to act properly. The ethics course would be from beginning to end a nouns and verbs course, for the obvious reason that it would be a course in which things are taught—and the only things that can be taught are nominal and verbal.

But learning how to act properly is learning an adverb, and adverbs cannot be taught. Besides, an ethics course on how you should go about deciding how to do anything whatsoever sounds incredibly vapid. If there are no real problems to analyze, no possible solutions to imagine, no results to assess concretely, then how can there be any relevant moral practices for you as a student to learn, much less for me as an instructor to talk about?

Just as a technique or any other prudential practice can be learned only by doing it, so also a moral practice. But if moral practices are the conditions we should bring to bear on our every action, then anything you do as a conscious agent has a moral practice or its habitual residue guiding you in how you decide what you should do and how you should be doing it. You have a moral practice already at hand and are using it, although you may wish to critique the practice or to critique your use of it. These are important differences to be clear about: recognizing yourself as being guided by a moral practice, in fact being guided by it, being guided well by it, thinking it is well that you are so guided. So there is much to learn, even if it cannot be taught.

If a college is supposed to be—essentially—where you learn how better to be guided by the best available moral practices, what can it do to make sure this learning occurs? But that is precisely the wrong question! The question is not what can the college do, since to ask "what" is to ask about an end or a means for accomplishing an end. The answer to a "what" is minimally to propose a purpose and a method and preferably to launch forth toward the one on the wings of the other. The question is not what a college can do but how it should go about determining to do whatever it does. How can a college go about pursuing whatever purposes it pursues, and utilizing whatever means it utilizes in their pursuit, such that its students will learn within the collegiate milieu thereby created how to act virtuously, how to act in ways worthy of their humanity? How can a college make it possible for a student to develop character?

But if answers are composed of nouns and verbs, it is not likely that the proper response to a question about moral practices is to answer it.

V

Aristotle may be of some help here.[9] He distinguishes scientific activities *(theōria)* from productive activities *(poiēsis):* the one a matter of understanding based on deductions from first principles established by rational reflection, the other a matter of skills for transforming natural things into artifacts. Scientific theory is concerned with universals; it satisfies our need to know how things really are by providing certain knowledge of the unchanging realities that govern the uncertain world of ever-changing particulars. The practice that guides this kind of activity is wisdom *(sophia)*: a person who reflects wisely will achieve excellence in thinking and is most likely to reach the goal of theoretical reflection, which is the contemplation of first principles. Productive activity, in contrast, is concerned with the ever-changing particulars science seeks to transcend. Whether in the fine arts or the practical arts, it is interested in the possibilities particulars have for yielding, through the artifice of human imagination and dexterity, resources for fulfilling our needs and assuaging our desires. The practice guiding these activities is competence *(technē)*: a person who works skillfully has achieved excellence as an artist or a craftsman and is most likely to produce things of great utility and exquisite beauty.

This distinction between thinking and making is familiar. Unfortunately but typically, it leads to a judgment that one of these two kinds of activity is better than the other: *Homo sapiens* versus *Homo faber;* science versus technology; the search for truth versus the search for fulfillment; the purity of abstract reasoning versus the practicality of preprofessional and vocational training; the Guild of Inquirers versus the Resource Center. Aristotle fell into this trap at times himself, arguing on occasion that wisdom is a higher excellence than competence.

Aristotle identifies a third kind of activity, that of doing *(praxis)*. Doing is civic activity, the actions by which citizens in a community conduct their mutual affairs, the ways they determine together the character of their intermingled lives. The practice guiding civic activity is *phronēsis,* which is usually translated as practical wisdom but can more accurately be called good sense.[10] Good sense is the practice of making thoughtful decisions conducive to the proper functioning of a community, a community in which individuals, alone and in groups, can attain those proximate ends that best serve the highest of human ends: individual happiness and the common good. A person whose civic choices show good sense thereby demonstrates excellence in matters of governance and public service. That person would be a good candidate for being placed in a leadership position and charged with important collective responsibility. So a person who engages in civic activity well is *Homo oratiens,* the good person whose virtue is neither as a thinker nor a maker but as a citizen.

The salient feature of civic activities is that they are intrinsically valuable. What is important is the activity itself and not what results from it. In contrast, the point of engaging in critical reflection is to arrive at knowledge: the addition of a new element to the Periodic Table, a theory of gravitation more adequate to the experimental data than Newton's, a proof that no consistent logical system can also be complete. The reason for making something lies not in the making but in what is made: the eulogistic poem, the rightly hung cabinet, the bumper crop of corn. But civility is how people interact within communities; it is the style of their social relationships. If the result is happiness for the participants, this happiness comes as a by-product of their activities rather than as its goal, a retrospective judgment concerning the excellence of their civil intercourse in combination with the excellence of their theoretical and productive efforts and accomplishments. The purpose of *praxis,* of doing, is the doing itself. Wisdom and competence are prudential practices since they provide advisories on how best to gain certain knowledge or to create valuable objects, whereas good sense is a practice advising persons on how best to interact with others in determining and effecting their purposes. Aristotelian good sense is what I mean by moral practice.

As a person engaged in purposeful activities, whether for private or communal ends, you are normally engaged simultaneously in civic activities, interacting with others to secure their assistance or acquiescence in your endeavors. You deal with corporate executives, day laborers, politicians, clerks, students, crooks, bureaucrats, artisans, philanthropists, engineers, factory workers, unpaid volunteers, police officers, so that you might be able to buy a new pair of shoes, make better laws, mollify your neighbor, increase productivity, earn an honest wage, develop a winning team, make your community a better place in which to live. Whatever your aims, in your pursuit of them you are constantly crossing paths with other persons pursuing aims of their own that are compatible with your aims, opposed to them, or irrelevant. The aspect of these activities that is civic has to do not with where you or they are headed but with your interactions with them while headed there.

Good sense is a repertoire of ways to interact. You may know where you want to go and that you will have to deal with this and that person in order to get there, so prudential choices must be made regarding the best technique by which to convince these people to cooperate with you. But your manipulative purposes will be intertwined with how you deal with them as persons, the style of your interactions apart from your purposes. The relevance of your civic practices, your good sense in dealing with others, is particularly obvious in situations where your goals and your means for realizing them are obscure to you, where there are no clear or final answers to what the prudent things to do might be, but where nonetheless you are required to interact with others as you grope your way along. On such occasions, your way of interacting comes more into focus precisely because the means-ends structure of your actions has been momentarily occluded.

The problematics of purposive activity, in forcing you to shift your focus from what is done to how it is done, also force you to recognize the fragility of what you purpose. The wins and losses in life, after all, usually cannot be guaranteed nor often even foreseen as possible eventualities. If they could, a science of that sort of situation could be fashioned, outcomes predicted, and the sequence of events controlled to assure the desired results. The pathology of leadership is that entrepreneurs, soldiers, and politicians, students, poets, and deans, too often think too highly of their ability to control events; they forget that pride goeth before a fall. To be sure, the quest for truth can be organized into a science and its results certified as certain knowledge. Productive activities, at least where the products have a use, are also amenable to scientific organization and management. There are limits to the extent of this control, however, although it may be long in revealing itself.

In contrast, control is never more than proximate in matters of civic interaction. There are always people opposed to your course of action, no matter how right-headed you may think it to be, and they are likely to do something unexpected to counter your aims. The enemy may still have a trick or two up its sleeve; the craziest things can happen. Call it Murphy's Law, call it *fortuna,* call it the radical indeterminacy of temporal transition: in the realm of human affairs

> The best laid schemes o' mice an' men
> Gang aft a-gley.[11]

All too often the context of actions is too contingent to permit even probability calculations and optimization strategies. In those situations, when best guesses are the best that can be managed, you want a person with good sense making the choices. The moral practices of our common life are the advisories by which such a person is guided under such circumstances. More important than what decisions are made is that they are rightly made.

People appreciated for their good sense are those whose choices have often proved useful to themselves and others, yet what impresses you about them is not their record of success but the sensitive, perceptive, clever, thoughtful, insightful manner in which, within the given social milieu, they go about making their decisions. You appreciate not whether they won or lost but how they played the game. You like their style, their character, the cut of their jib. They are the sort of people you would want as friends, colleagues, or compatriots: it is them you appreciate, not what they have done. It is people of that sort, people with character, whom you want in positions of civic responsibility.

You want sensible people in the sciences and arts as well, but because the truths that can be known and the artifacts that can be made loom so large on the horizon of these kinds of action, you tend to pay less attention than you should to their moral quality. Truth is truth, after all; there is nothing scientifically relevant in the biographies of the scientists who discovered or fashioned scientific truths. The pyramid of knowledge was built by human hands, but whose hands and how is beside the point. Yet it is not completely beside the point: the scientists' procedures need to be known so that the experiments validating their hypotheses can be confirmed by being replicated, and the prudential practices guiding scientists in their choice of problems and in the design of their experiments may suggest topics, strategies, and styles useful for determining the direction of further research. You should not neglect, however, to ask if the scientists went about their activities of selecting, designing, testing, reporting in a way guided by moral practices. You should not forget to inquire if they thought themselves constrained by a requirement that they do these things honestly, candidly, graciously, and with their love of glory subordinated to their love for truth. Such adverbs, you might think, have no bearing on whether the claims are true that the scientists make about the results of their experiments. And yet, unless most scientists most of the time take their bearings from such moral practices, the scientific enterprise itself will eventually be undermined.

So also those who make things. Rilke was a horrid human being, but his *Duino Elegies* is great poetry. You do not have to be a form critic to be enthralled by the power and beauty of his poems and in this experience to find the man Rilke irrelevant. You might think that no one need care whether the architects of the cathedral at Chartres were good men or even if they believed in God. The exquisite way in which the incredible complexities of its formal details and their iconographic meanings are integrated by the cathedral's structural harmonies and orientation inspires an aesthetic response that only those afraid of belief would fail to call religious awe. But the beauty of Chartres, you might think, could just as easily have been made by atheists. And yet, without the moral practices of the Christian faith informing the actions of most people in the communities of medieval Europe, no cathedrals would have been built. Unless through their actions people are able to experience their world profoundly, in ways imbued with the deepest human meanings, there can be neither great poetry nor monumental architecture.

When it comes to politicians, lawyers, tax collectors, academic deans, military heroes, and all their kind, you are painfully aware of the relevance of how they go about their actions. You know that they have far less control than they are willing to acknowledge over what problems they face, what they are trying to accomplish, and by what means. You think that we would all be better off if they at least do these things they do properly. Should they fail in their efforts, let it at least be the case that they did so honestly, fairly, nobly.

The most important things we do, those having to do with the interactions among human beings that express their sense of meaning and further the ends inscribed by that meaning, occur in a context of indeterminacy. However valuable the sciences and the productive arts, they are ultimately secondary to the primary art of deciding, individually and collectively, who we are, what our place is in the scheme of things, and what we should do on account of who and where and when we are. Because these decisions are so important and because they are never once and for all but are constantly in need of reiteration and reformulation, because they are the organizing, essential, meaning-expressing dimension of all our activities, making good communal choices is the most important thing we do. Yet there is one thing more important than learning how to make the best choices for a community, and that is learning how to make them rightly. It is more important that our actions be meaningful than that they fill our bellies or our minds.

Our primary task as educators is to nurture neither learned scientists nor talented artists and artisans but good citizens. Our common life cannot be guided by a science of society nor can it be turned over to craftsmen and technocrats. Both alternatives have been suggested; the advocates of one or the other dominate our politics and have contributed tragically to the world's turmoil throughout this century. But social good is neither a truth to be perceived nor a product to be engineered. It is an activity to be done, and its excellence lies in the adverbial character of the actions performed, in the capacity of persons to choose sensibly among complex and always changing possibilities.

Educating tomorrow's good citizens does not just mean teaching talented young people and adults how to become successful statesmen and CEOs. It does not just mean teaching the others to be dutiful followers. It also means providing everyone with a moral education. For no matter what their station in life and no matter what their attainments, we will need to rely upon their good sense in the civil deliberations by which our collective ends are shaped for good or ill. The question is: How can students learn the requisite moral practices so crucial for their good and for our collective good? How can they learn what is essential to them if they are to succeed in finding their theoretical and practical activities meaningful? How can they learn what alone will assure the rest of us that in their scientific and productive endeavors they will be serving the common weal?

The answer to these questions returns us to the paradox that the most important thing for students to learn at college is something they cannot be taught. The adverbial features of actions are quite different from the intellectual and productive means-ends features taught in the sciences and the arts. The adverbs will attach themselves willy-nilly to the verbs of action if you act unaware of how you are acting. You are properly educated, therefore, if you are aware of the adverbial dimension of what you do, if you decide the manner in which you pursue your purposes at the same time as you are determining your goals and methods, and if you have a repertoire of appropriate moral practices as well as prudential ones to draw from in doing so.

These moral and prudential practices are learned, and hence the particular qualities that adhere to your actions as a result of availing yourself of those practices define you as a person. And if what you have learned is well-learned and well-utilized, then your actions can be characterized as marked by moral excellence, just as they will be judged wise and competent actions if you fully understand your situation and its possibilities and if you are guided by appropriate prudential practices in choosing your ends and choosing means well-suited to effect those ends. You cannot be taught to be prudent or moral, and yet unless you have learned how to act prudently and morally you will not have been properly educated. Power in the hands of wise fools, no matter how competent they might be, is the bane of a civilization. A college that willfully graduates its "sophomores" betrays the culture for which it was meant to be a bulwark.

A college education should provide understanding; it should provide technical competence; it should provide training in the skills required for making difficult choices among conflicting goods; and it should also provide instruction concerning ends worthy of pursuit. But a college should refrain from attempting to teach good sense so that it might flourish. You must resist the temptation to attempt giving your students the one thing no one can provide another, a capacity for acting properly. As someone who teaches, in order for you to act sensibly with respect to how best to help your students learn how to act sensibly, you will need to learn how to refrain from attempting to teach them how thusly to act.

The essence of a college lies not in what it teaches but in fostering an environment in which making the best choices is thought less important than learning the moral conditions for doing so.

NOTES

1. This standard is precisely the basis upon which any school, college, or university in the United States is assessed by the agencies currently responsible for determining its accreditation. For instance, the first four criteria listed by the Middle States Association of Colleges and Schools as needing to be met are that the institution "is guided by well-defined and appropriate goals; that it has established conditions and procedures under which its goals can be realized; that it is accomplishing its goals substantially; [and] that it is so organized, staffed, and supported that it can be expected to continue to accomplish its goals" (*Characteristics of Excellence in Higher Education: Standards for Accreditation* [Philadelphia: Commission on Higher Education, Middle States Association of Colleges and Schools, 1994], p. 1).

2. Jeremy Bentham, *An Introduction to the Principles of Morals and Legislation* (Garden City, N.Y.: Doubleday, 1961 [1789]).

3. Immanuel Kant, *Grounding for the Metaphysics of Morals* (Indianapolis: Hackett, 1981 [1785]).

4. Eccles. 3:1.

5. See my book, *The Realizations of the Future: An Inquiry into the Authority of Praxis* (Albany: State University of New York Press, 1990), chap. 6, "The Creating of Self," especially the discussion of what Søren Kierkegaard's Judge William has to say about incarnating the universal in the particular (pp. 126–32).

6. This discussion is the burden of my argument in *The Importances of the Past: A Meditation on the Authority of Tradition* (Albany: SUNY Press, 1986).

7. Throughout this section I am drawing from Michael Oakeshott's arguments in *On Human Conduct* (Oxford: Oxford University Press, 1975). However, except for the terms 'moral practice' and 'prudential practice', I have not hewed to Oakeshott's precise if somewhat idiosyncratic vocabulary, and I focus less on the epistemology and more on the ontology of human conduct than he does.

8. The notions of an 'action' and of a 'situation' derive as much from John Dewey as from Oakeshott, although on this point the two philosophers are very similar. Almost any of Dewey's books includes an analysis of situated actions, especially as they should be understood when the action is performed intelligently, i.e., as an instance of experimental inquiry. See, for example, *Experience and Nature* (New York: Dover Publications, 1958). For more on Dewey's theory and its relation to other philosophers including Oakeshott, Whitehead, and Sartre, see my *The Realizations of the Future,* chap. 1, "The Nature of Praxis."

9. Primarily, *Nichomachean Ethics,* book 6. I am trying to clarify my own argument by recasting it somewhat within an Aristotelian vocabulary; in no sense am I attempting to provide a careful analysis of the text of *NE*. The distinction among *'praxis'* (conduct of one's life), *'poiēsis'* (productive activity), and *'theōria'* (theoretical activity) is well established. The notion that each of these activities has an associated way by which they are properly performed—*'phronēsis'* for *'praxis',* *'technē'* for *'poiēsis', 'sophia'* for *'theōria'*—is supported by Joseph Dunne, *Back to the Rough Ground: 'Phronesis' and 'Techne' in Modern Philosophy and Aristotle* (Notre Dame: University of Notre Dame Press, 1993), part 2, pp. 237–356.

10. Martin Ostwald translates *'gnome'* as "good sense," Ross translates it as "judgment," and J. A. K. Thomson as "fellow feeling." Aristotle compares *'gnome'* with *'phronēsis',* concluding that they mean just about the same thing. The emphasis in *'gnome'* seems more on the sympathetic character of the judgments whereas *'phronēsis'* is pointing up their insightfulness. But Aristotle never actually makes this distinction. I prefer "good sense" because "practical wisdom" resonates with "prudential practices" whereas I am after a "moral practices" resonance.

11. Robert Burns, "To a Mouse."

5
The Playfulness of a College

It is difficult
to get the news from poems
yet men die miserably every day
for lack
of what is found there.[1]

Moral practices can obviously be learned in the same way prudential practices are learned: while engaged in the serious pursuit of practical ends. Indeed, that is typically how they are learned. The faucet on the kitchen sink is dripping: I find the sound annoying, I do not like its implications for my water bill, and, besides, I just think that things ought to work right in my house. So I get a screwdriver and wrench, turn off the valve on the water line under the sink, remove the faucet handle and stem, replace the washer, reassemble the faucet, turn the water back on, and give myself a smug pat on the back for having solved the problem so expeditiously. There was a time when I would have let something like this go; it seemed easier to adjust my actions to the dripping than to do anything about it (a strategically placed sponge nicely muffles the annoying sound). But I have learned over the years that these little compromises do not really work. Once I have actually fixed the problem, it is usually a surprise to discover how much convenience I had sacrificed in order to avoid dealing with it. Laziness exacts a subtle price.

Other problems are not as easily solved as leaking faucets are. Some persist interminably, and others keep coming back to haunt me long after I had thought them safely and permanently interred. Nor are the simple mechanical problems simply solved whereas the complex, interpersonal, intercivilizational ones seem insolvable. A leaky faucet can sometimes be as impossible a puzzle as a Middle Eastern peace initiative, the chances of success seemingly on a par with winning the war on poverty.

147

Nonetheless, the pattern to my actions is the same in every situation: needs and desires, possibilities for satisfying them, methods for realizing those possibilities, one possibility made into a new actuality. The repetitions of this pattern accrete prudential practices that help me make the choices of means and ends most likely over the long run to bring me the satisfaction I seek. They also, and at the same time, accrete moral practices shaping how I should best make those choices.

All these elements of action are interfused and taken for granted. My orientation is toward accomplishing what I have set out to do. My aims are several and intertwining: a dripless faucet, a full stomach, a sense of well-being, my personal survival, my sacred honor. These are results and conditions I very much desire, one or another of the insistent and often overweeningly important things I want to get or keep. They are at issue and command my full attention. Rarely do I have occasion to reflect on what I am doing and to wonder if I might do it better. Such moments of self-understanding and critique are most likely to occur when things are going badly. If my normal way of doing things is proving to be inadequate, so that I am failing to satisfy my desires or finding that what used to satisfy me no longer does, then I may find it necessary to step back and to reassess things.

Dewey[2] argues that consciousness emerges only when the smooth workings of habit are derailed. I have learned what to do in familiar sorts of situations: my repertoire of appropriate responses is ready at hand. The situation is concretely unique, however, whereas my repertoire of responses is generic. So I also have a repertoire of practices that help me make the best possible use of my possible responses, tailoring them to the peculiarities of the particular situation. I am used to dealing with leaky faucets and I am handy with tools, so it is fairly obvious to me why the faucet is dripping. The remedy is equally straightforward, although I may have to think for a moment where I have put the spare washers, and a stubborn nut might call for some minor adjustments in how I handle my wrench. I sense what is going on, I know what to do under these conditions, I do it, and so things flow on into the next situation without my having given any thought to what happened.

If the situation is not familiar, however, then I no longer have a way ready at hand for dealing with it. The instructions say to turn right at the next corner, but the cross street does not run that direction; it is suddenly clear to me that she did not take my sarcastic comment like I thought she would; I stomp on the brakes but nothing happens. Aft a-gley, indeed. When I do not know what to do or do not know how best to do it, the course of my action grinds to a halt. I could try the same thing over again: I could let up on the pedal and then stomp down on it once more, only harder. Failing this simple solution, I will need to extricate myself from the rush of things for a moment, take stock of the situation, and figure out some new response. Maybe the instructions said to turn left; maybe I should apologize to her for what I said.

Thinking, says Dewey, is figuring out where the problem is, taking stock of it, sizing up the situation, imagining different possibilities, weighing alternatives, and whatever else is involved in getting my derailed purposes back on track. This interlude of thinking may only take a split second, because if my brakes really are not working, then either I immediately twist the steering wheel sharply to the left or I will plow into the slow-moving truck just ahead of me. In other situations, I may have more time to consider the options and even to invent new ones. But the whole point of thinking, whatever form it might take and whatever its duration, is to provide resources necessary to restore the smooth flow of actions guided by habit. And the quicker the better: thinking is hard work, and the unfamiliar world that has called it forth is an uncomfortable place. I want to get back to the tried and true as soon as I can.

The one other occasion for reflection is the opposite of a crisis. With my needs reasonably well satisfied, I have breathing room to set aside for a brief moment the constant press for results. I can take a respite from the incessant pursuit of my immediate purposes in order for a different sort of purpose to emerge. The accident avoided and my brakes repaired, I now have time to explore what should be done to reduce the likelihood in the future that they will fail me again. The faucet fixed, I can begin to wonder if a ball faucet might not be a good idea, and soon I am flipping through catalogues to get a sense of how they work and what they cost.

Times of leisure lure forth my powers of critical thinking. Concepts are sharpened, presuppositions explicated, contexts widened and deepened, actual achievements contrasted with those that were intended, and all of this mental activity is articulated in order the better to be remembered, shared with others, and put to use in confirming, reforming, or revolutionizing what I had been doing and how I had been doing it. These moments of reflective critique may be brief or extended, they may be superficial or insightful, the results may be useful or irrelevant, the problem may pass or despite my best efforts nonetheless eventually prove itself overwhelming. I may have lost her respect because of what I said so thoughtlessly, and my resolve to clean up my act may not last beyond our next conversation; or it could be that this blunder marks a turning point in my life, that since then I have worked hard to overcome my sexist habits and have even begun to earn her respect. The reflective turn may not actually lead to any improvements, but without disengagement and critique I will simply continue to do things in the same old unimproved ways. Nothing ventured, nothing gained.

Only in these out-of-gear moments of critical reflection can my moral practices appear as objects for my consideration. Just as tools are not noticed when they do what they were designed to do, so practices go unnoticed when the conditions they set to my choices expedite what I am doing. Only when these conditions are not the case do they come to my attention, and only then can the double question be asked: am I using these moral practices properly, and are these moral practices the proper ones for me to use? I can wait until I am forced to stop working because I have accidentally inflicted myself with a wicked puncture wound, or I can ask right off for help in how to use the new nail gun. I can wait until these strangers ostracize me for acting wickedly, or I can ask a friend right off for pointers on how to read their faces for the proper social cues. A reflective turn is the best way for me to get better at what I do.

The advantage that leisure has over crisis is that a crisis needs to be resolved as quickly as possible. The emergency has forced me into reflection, but the situation gives me precious little time to think. I must come up with a solution quickly; it is imperative that things get working again. My emphasis is on the immediate utility of the reflection as a problem-solving instrument. The mode of inquiry is pragmatic. In contrast, a leisured consideration of how I am acting has no such urgency. I need not reflect on these matters, but nonetheless I choose to do so. My curiosity is pricked, my imagination stirred; longer-term desires make their appearance, those not immediately crucial to living but which ask instead about living better or living well. My belly full, I have the luxury to wonder if the usual dinner fare might be enhanced. In such moments of reflective leisure, I am able, if I wish, to distinguish my desires from my needs, to invent and test new methods for attaining them, and to scrutinize practices that I have long assumed without question or that I had not before even noticed I was utilizing. Leisure provides the opportunity for a different order of critique than is permitted under crisis conditions. Although less vivid because less urgent, leisure is ultimately a far more important mode of reflectivity than crisis.

When adult students matriculate into a college they set aside for a time their practical pursuits in order to enjoy the leisure required for reflective critique. Or, if they are late adolescents, they postpone their transition to adulthood in order to acquire ideas, skills, and practices crucial to their capacity to function fully as adults. In either case, nothing is immediately at stake. The serious practical activities of life and their guiding practices have been temporarily mothballed; neither life nor death hangs in the balance. In this bucolic, impractical interlude, students have a brief opportunity to learn how to live well. The school of hard knocks with its stern schoolmaster, practical experience, can teach them all they need to know, but a college makes it possible to acquire that knowledge less painfully, more quickly, and more adequately.

I speak ideally, of course. This example is the normative model, not a description of what actually goes on in a college. Obviously the problem with leisure is that it has the very same smooth features that characterize successful practical activities. Why should I go to the effort to reflect critically if my needs and desires are being fully met? So as a student I could very well come to college and simply enjoy my leisure for its own sake rather than for the learning opportunities it makes possible. Or pressed by circumstances that seem to preclude setting aside the practical for a sufficient time, I could continue to devote substantial portions of my energies to practical matters. I may have to earn the money I need in order to buy access to what the college offers, or I may want to satisfy desires I think more immediately important than the extra study time made possible by not working. So to some extent students have only themselves to blame when they fall short of the ideal for how best to use their college-time leisure. But the colleges are the real culprits. They do not understand leisured reflection as their educational ideal and therefore do not articulate for students a sense of what it is and why it is so important.

In order for me to be able to critique the moral practices I have learned from birth, I must step back from what I am doing. In order for me to recognize the way my culture has wrapped me in a world that sets the fundamental contours of my desires and my needs, my aspirations and my efforts to realize them, I must extricate myself from it sufficiently to see it as an artifactual rather than a natural force. In order for me to appreciate why it is important that my desires be conditioned by moral practices rather than merely express themselves naturally, why my purposes should be properly determined rather than chosen in any way imaginable, it is crucial that I be able to suspend belief in my moral practices even while practicing them. To achieve this result, I must find myself in an environment where the desires that drive me and the possibilities that lure me no longer predominate. I must find myself in an environment not concerned primarily with purposes: neither its own nor those of its students nor those of the wider world.

This requirement is why a college must recognize that it is essentially without purpose. Its heart and soul, its primary focus, its center, needs to be an environment in which the conditions for purposive action take precedence over the purposive actions themselves. In the silence of suspended practicality, I will be able to hear the still small voice of moral practice. In the absence of the usual noisy marketplace of practical considerations, I can find a quiet space conducive to critical reflection and so begin to realize that my actions have a moral frame which I have acquired, the use of which I could perfect, and the contents of which are subject to reformulation by exercising the same critical powers by which I have discovered them.

In times of crisis I am least disposed to put in question the practices that root and reflect my deepest convictions about the meaning of life. The most traumatic kind of crisis I could experience, therefore, would be a crisis in my faith in my moral practices: a situation so problematic that my moral practices no longer seem trustworthy, no longer seem to orient me relevantly. I had been getting along just fine, thank you, pursuing my various goals with verve, suffering some failures, to be sure, but on the whole quite optimistic about things and quite pleased with myself. Then suddenly everything seems to have collapsed. The times are out of joint and so am I. I do not know what it is proper for me to do in this situation: as a dutiful son, as a parent, as a faculty member with my professional responsibilities, as American citizen, as a human being. And yet it is as though the brake pedal is all the way to the floor: unless I do something right away, I am lost. This moment is hardly the time to begin wondering if I should have installed an automatic braking system after all or to muse about the adequacy of Newton's first law of motion. My moral practices have let me down. Either I can flee from that truth by believing that there is nothing really wrong, or I can leap in desperation into another practice even though I have no sense for it, or I can slide into despair, bereft of an old faith with no new faith to save me. Some choice!

Far better then that college campuses provide noncrisis occasions where as a student I might learn to use, and learn to question, my moral practices. In the classrooms, in the libraries and the laboratories, in the residence halls and the athletic fields, I should be invited by the college to engage in activities of little practical consequence. I am at play, which is to say I am functioning as an agent in a context where I can experiment with new desires, new skills, new goals, new techniques, without having to abide by the results. And so I can modulate the accustomed prudential practices that have for so long advised me on how to make the best choices and the trusted moral practices that have over the years advised me on how best to make those choices. If the new practices with which I have been fooling around do not do their job, no lasting harm need result. Social degradation, physical debilitation, imprisonment, or death are not the wages of these sins.

College is a time for me to play because playing mimics life without its penalties and so serves as a place for me to practice my practices, to try them on, to test them out, to assess their virtues and explore previously unimagined alternatives. College is a time for casual conversation, for bull sessions and discussion groups, because words permit me and my fellow students to fashion images of action collaboratively, which we can then explore together, assess, adjust, or discard without leaving an irreversible scar on the face of things.[3]

The only justification for playfulness is in the playing. Many ends may well be served by leisure activity: refreshment from labor, rehearsal for subsequent serious involvements, rhythmic centering that rests the body and coordinated striving that heightens its functional capacities. But insofar as the activity is truly play and not merely unrecompensed work, it is undertaken for itself and not merely for these beneficial and often very much desired outcomes. Play is its own reward.

An athletic contest, of course, is not play; it is driven by explicit purpose. In professional sports, the purpose of the owners and players is to make money by providing an entertainment for which people will pay a fee and to fashion an idol toward which they will develop loyalties that translate into various indirect expenditures to the metropole, sponsors, auxiliary enterprises, and the like. Big-time intercollegiate sports have the same goal, except that the players do not receive a share of the profits. In such contexts, winning is all. "It's not whether you win or lose" is thought by most people to be a shibboleth because sports are no longer playful, no longer focused on the process instead of the product.

Where the value of a game lies in the activity rather than in what it accomplishes, the question of how well I did takes on a different meaning. It refers not to whether I won nor even to how effectively I played, but rather to the character of my play. In an important sense, the moral practices of a game are its rules. The rules of the game serve as guides to how a player acts; they do not predetermine those actions but rather set conditions on them. I can bring the ball to the goal by an infinity of routes, so I fake the goalie by looking toward a possible route on the left while kicking the ball with my off-foot along a route to the right. But whatever my plan of attack and however well I execute it, to play the game I must condition my actions on the requirement that I not touch the ball with my hands nor receive a pass forward of the last defender other than the goalie. My prudential practices are utilized in the skill with which I move the ball, fake the goalie, place the kick, constantly adjusting general ball-handling techniques to the special demands of a fast-breaking particular situation. My moral practices, of which my character as a soccer player is composed, are disclosed in how I relate myself to the rules: whether I am willing to break a rule if it is advantageous to do so and no one notices, whether I live by the spirit or the letter, whether I find satisfaction in doing my best to turn the limitations on action imposed by the rules into an ordered world of intense although momentary value for everyone involved.

The athletic metaphor is finally inadequate, however. The rules of a game are crystal clear and inviolate, no matter how much room for interpretation there might be in their application to a particular situation. Wittgenstein[4] says that cultural worldviews, forms of life, are "language games." Groups of people share the same view of things by means of a common language, a discourse that defines in its grammar and vocabulary the shape and content of what counts for them as meaningful. But here the rules of the game are no longer explicit. Precisely the opposite. The conditions for my worldview are taken for granted, unnoticed because so ubiquitous.[5] I have been playing this game since I was born and have nothing with which to contrast it, so although I know how to use the rules I have never had to think about them. I have trouble explaining to others, much less to myself, what I am doing. Moreover, any attempt to articulate precisely what the rules are will of necessity have abstracted from the richness of their multiform and often incompatible expressions; the saying will never quite be adequate to the lived reality.

Lyotard[6] enthuses about a world without a dominant worldview, a world of a thousand different language games, any of which I may join by choosing for a time to play by its rules, then bowing out of the game when my interests turn elsewhere. This food court approach to language games is an attractive way to relate to groups defined by a variety of specific purposes. As long as I am interested in a particular goal, I should join a relevant special interest group, then pitch in and help in the struggle to bring about its goals. As long as I am happy to work within its frame of reference, I should stay around and do the sorts of things the group finds acceptable. But as with any voluntary society, when my interests change so should my memberships.

The problem with this benign anarchy in worldviews, however, is that the dominant cultural worldview cannot be so easily wished away. The language game of the culture into which I was born defines my character apart from my purposes. I can change my physical, economic, and social location, my purposes and my loyalties, but the old ways of my culture persist because they have to do with my sense of myself. If I am to change the cultural language games I play, I will have to change my self, redefine who essentially I am. This alteration can be done, but it is not like channel surfing on the television. It is not a change external to my sense of who I am but rather one constitutive of that sense. They can take me out of the country, but they will never quite take this country out of me because without it I am no longer me.

Does this mean that I am a slave to the cultural language game in which I was born, forced to play by its rules without even quite knowing what they are and how they work? The answer is no: moral freedom is possible. But liberation from my moral practices, whether in order to forsake them or to reaffirm them, is the most difficult of all human endeavors. College is one of the few institutions in our culture designed to provide people with an opportunity for developing into morally free persons. It would be too much to expect college seniors to be genuinely free, but we can expect them to have learned how to go about becoming free. And we can hope, for their good and for our common good, that by graduation their ambitions will be undergirded by an aspiration to the excellence which freedom represents: the ability to act within a critically assessed framework of appropriate moral practices.

The obvious immediate consequence of putting aside my practical concerns by enrolling in a college, by suspending for the moment any question of relevance in what I do, is that this decision leaves me free to explore things that are irrelevant and impractical. What makes something relevant is its place within the means-ends structure of my actions. If that structure is no longer at work, if it has been put out to pasture, then other means-ends structures can slip in and replace it. Were they to present themselves as candidates for a permanent replacement, the occasion would be extremely serious, a struggle between orienting frameworks for defining myself and my purposes. But if my familiar structure of meaning is at rest because the game I am about to play is not the game of life but only some temporary exploration game, then it is okay to mess around a bit, to try on some other structures to see what they might be like. I can take a course in Buddhism without it meaning that I intend to convert to a new religion. I can study Enlightenment despotism without having to think of it as a viable alternative to liberal democracy. I can learn how to interpret a Picasso without thinking of my lessons as a preparatory course for launching myself on a new career as an art historian. I am free to take these courses just because they seem interesting, for purely aesthetic reasons—but only if, for the moment, there are no important practical implications to my doing so.

In fooling around with such irrelevancies, I find myself learning about alternative heritages, values, ways of understanding. I soon discover that the ways in which I habitually think and behave are only some among the many ways in which human beings have comported themselves. My purposes, methods, and practices, it seems, are very like those of people I never knew existed. I discover that there are faraway peoples and ancient customs that resonate with my own world, different and yet the same, like meeting a distant cousin for the first time. And I also come to realize that my ways are radically different from those of many other people, including sometimes those I thought most like myself. I learn there is nothing so strange that some philosopher has not advocated it and some culture practiced it.

This immersion in the variegated pluralism of humankind's accomplishments and failures, this introduction to the eye-popping insights and blind stupidities that mark every known cultural perspective, mine included, is exhilarating. It would be unsettling, if not outright terrifying, to be thrust unceremoniously into some of these worlds and told to make my way as best I could from here on out. But I am comforted to know that college is not the "real world." It is safe to muck about in these other worlds knowing that my own will not be damaged by my doing so, that it waits patiently for me to be done with my fun and, tired of playing around, to return home at last, ready to take up again with its assistance the serious pursuit of serious purposes.

How magnificent is my awakening as a student: when I suddenly understand why Plato thought the Forms more real than the empirical world; or when I see the familiar Mount St. Victoire afresh through the eyes of Cézanne; or appreciate the plausibility of the theory of an interstellar ether; or grasp with a sense of immediacy the life-world of a totem worshiper; or tremble with Conrad at the horror of it all. How shocking for me when I am confronted by the evidence that there are human beings like myself who deny "obvious" truths and values, who deplore democracy, tonality, absolute time, or the exterior world, and who instead willingly consent to such madness as Marxism, chromatic tone rows, Minkowski world-lines, or solipsism. Yet from the shock of these experiences comes at last the sobering discovery that even obvious truths stand in need of justification, that some truths which are self-evident cannot withstand the test of sustained dispassionate scrutiny. And that some madness is profoundest truth.

Mere awareness of these alternatives, merely acquiring information about them, is not enough. They can only be truly appreciated if they are adequately understood and they can only be understood interactively. It is fairly easy to learn in a college course that Plato believed there were eternal realities called Forms, which could be known only by rational reflection, and that he thought they were more real than the things we can see and touch. But it is hard to believe that Plato or anyone else could actually believe such nonsense. This proud stallion, stomping its foot and blowing its nostrils in the cold morning air, can carry me around the lake and out across the long sweep of grassland, up into those distant hills. He could kill me with the sharp hoof on that stomping foot were I to torment him, or his hoof might protect me from being mauled by an angered mountain lion. Does Plato actually believe that this wonderful beast and his life-and-death world are far less real than some fleshless, bloodless, generic Horseness in the sky? Sheer madness! The ancients, it would seem, had weird beliefs, but fortunately we now know better. Nonetheless, if it is a matter for a test of being able to answer true or false whether Plato thought the Forms more real than particulars, then I will know enough to mark the statement with a "T."

Information-transfer courses of this sort fail to educate the students who enroll in them. Such courses turn Plato's philosophy into a pile of facts that have no practical value beyond their relevance to doing well on examinations. By means of knowing my Plato, I may earn a good grade in the course and so improve my chances of getting into law school, which is a key step in my long-range plan of becoming a successful big-time lawyer and living the good life. The problem with this approach, however, is that the professor teaches without ever asking me to put aside my practical pursuits. My classroom experience remains within the accustomed framework of purposes I brought with me to college. The professor reinforces that framework and helps entrap me in its structure of ends and means by presuming that the point of studying Plato, that the point of studying anything, is to improve my ability to operate within it more effectively.

If pressed to justify the presence of a course on Plato in its curriculum, the college will have to mumble something about how sometimes the strangest things can prove relevant. I am left with the impression that for reasons which do not bear close scrutiny, my society makes knowing a bit of philosophy one of the hurdles that must be jumped on the fast track to success, which explains why Cliff's Notes will often do quite well as a resource for learning Plato. Or maybe it would be smarter to borrow a good, clear textbook on the history of philosophy, something that will provide me with a simplified systematic summary of his views. If the fraternity files have old copies of the course exams, even better, because then what I should learn from Plato will have been already filtered for me in terms of its relevance to the professor's purposes for the course and hence to mine for passing it.

If throughout this course my frame of reference has been unquestioned, Plato's beliefs will continue to seem weird because so out of kilter with what I have presumed, and my professor and the college have encouraged me to presume, makes sense. I have studied hard in this course, and I am confident I understand what Plato said. But the more I know what he said, the more I am convinced of the foolishness of his ideas. And yet—surely Plato was no dummy. Surely the simplest criterion for knowing whether or not I have understood him is that I find his theory believable. It cannot be that I understand him for whom all Western thought is but a series of footnotes[7] if, even though I can recite "the Platonic doctrine of Forms,"

I think it is all a bunch of bull. If I am ever to understand Plato, I am going to need to step away from my framework of beliefs and learn to operate within his. Since from where I now stand what Plato says is utter nonsense, it will only be by standing somewhere else that I can ever think he might speak utter truth instead. My first concern should be to ask how my way of seeing things must change in order for Plato's talk of Forms to make good sense—and for what I know to be obviously the case to seem ridiculous instead.

It is true this morning that my stallion is a wonderful horse; it was true yesterday, and it will be true tomorrow. But from the perspective of a thousand years, this stallion's reality is a short truth compared to the truth that throughout the millennium the genus *Equus caballus* has remained extant. In spring, the swans return to the lake and the trees are bedecked in green, but after a summer the leaves fade and fall. And in the next spring, with the return of the swans, new leaves paint the trees once again with green, and the colors last until the fall. And although after too few years my stallion will die and after many a summer dies the swan, the trees will go on blooming green. And with the passing of the trees, the lake, and even the hills, there are still the meadow grasses sprouting green. For a thousand years, one long recurrent green truth and a billion brief organic truths. Is this leaf or that horse or these swan really more real than the timelessly recurrent qualities for which they are but momentary receptacles?

It takes more than empathy to see the world as Plato invites me to see it. It requires analytic skills as well: to be clear about the precise meaning of his terms; to know how the grammar of his Greek transforms those meanings into claims, portraits, assessments, arguments; to be alert to the place of dramatic setting and dialogical interchange in how these sentences and paragraphs are to be interpreted; to embed, as far as possible, these paragraphs in the fuller context of the dialogue and of Plato's other writings, the cultural climate of his times, and the history of interpretation leading from him to me. To do all of this analysis is not to be engaged in any easy task. My desk is cluttered with conflicting data, and even the right question hides itself amid the confusion. After the critics and the commentaries have had their say, after my classmates and I have talked the thing to death, the meaning and significance remain obscure to me, even though dimly felt. Yet nonetheless, in the library some rainy afternoon an impossibly vague and yet illuminating idea begins to be articulated in the illegible medium of my yellow tablet sheets. Occasionally, perhaps only glimpsed as a receding dream not appreciated when it was at my side, I see the world with Plato's eyes and am for the moment confident I know what he would have told me about the meaning of an event that because it is occurring at this endpoint of the twentieth century would actually be far beyond his ken.

Plato at last makes sense to me because I have gotten inside the means-ends structure of his thinking. Plato is trying to understand the world as he experiences it, trying to come to terms with his own tradition of what the truth, goodness, and beauty of it are, and trying to convince his readers that he has got it right. If I am intimate enough with how Plato goes about his philosophizing, I can discern these goals with considerable clarity and appreciate their relation to the means he has deployed in pursuit of them. And thusly located, I will become aware of Plato's practices. Where I can begin to anticipate what Plato's understanding of an issue might be before having read what he actually said about it, and where there is a smile of recognition as I see him unfolding the dialogical moves that will bring along both the interlocutors in the dialogue and myself as reader, I know that I must have a handle on prudential practices that reflect, even if only in a glass darkly, the ones with which he worked. And where I become concerned with why Plato should have chosen such ends and means, where I start probing his texts for indications of how he may have gone about making such choices, I am trying to sense, to appreciate, to grasp the moral practices that guided his thinking and his writing. And only then can I ask if it might have been Plato's intent in his dialogues to persuade me of the value of those moral practices, not by what he ever explicitly says but by his showing me, in my encounter with his text, truths that he knows are unsayable because foundational to the language game that makes whatever he actually says sayable.[8]

It is unusually difficult for any of us to work our way through to an understanding of Plato's good sense, but the manner by which we learn about the practices of less complex, less indirect thinkers is no different. Nor is it significantly different when our concern is with a person's productive and civic activities. The moral practices of Napoleon killing Englishmen at Waterloo, of the clerk at the checkout desk counting out my change, or of my daughter at home playing with her children, are features of what they do, features that I can know only by being able to inhabit imaginatively and with appropriate precision the inside of the means-ends structure of their actions, gaining through that knowledge an awareness of the practices that might have guided those actions. The generalizations of such individual activities, which is what anthropologists or economists do, merely move the challenge of learning the moral practices to a more abstract level. The focus is now on statistical patterns, on social trends, rather than on individual actions. But there are still things to know in addition to the trends if the moral underpinning of what is happening is to be grasped. For instance, gaining a sense for how a cohort of people behave—a generation, gender, class, or ethnicity—involves becoming aware of how they understand themselves as this understanding is reflected in their moral practices.

The hallmark of barbarism is an attitude that treats cultural variety as unfortunate or quaint and reacts to it dogmatically and parochially. The reason why I need to know appreciatively other worlds, other culturally fundamental means-ends structures, why I need to be aware of them as living forms of life, as worlds really at work for real people, is because only in this way are the worldviews of cultures alternative to my own able to combat my proclivity to dismiss them dogmatically. But the only way to experience a cultural worldview at work, to see it up close and for what it is, is for my own worldview not to be at work. Only if my way of doing things is not at issue can I tolerate the presence of other ways. I can embrace an alien world, take it seriously into my open arms, only if my actions are set within a framework of playfulness. I am willing to entertain such strangeness imaginatively, empathetically, experimentally, precisely because I know that at any time I can call a halt to the game, pick up my bat and ball, and go home.

There is no better way for me to learn another culture than to spend some time living there, and there is no better way of doing so than through a college junior-year-abroad program where my immersion is complete but in the mode of playfulness. I am immersed, yet I know that eventually the year will end and it will be time to climb out of those cultural waters. Tourists dart like water striders across the surface of a form of life, moving too fast, too lightly, for the up-close knowing required by an immersion. Refugees have had the protecting framework of playfulness torn away from them; they are thrust from a familiar into an unfamiliar world without a chance ever to come back home again. The junior year experience permits me to explore the unknown with enough seriousness to become aware of the moral practices at work but with enough playfulness to lure me into running the risk of finding those practices a challenge to my own.

Some worlds are long since dead and gone, others difficult to approach, and some live only in the imagination of their authors. So junior year immersion programs are not in a literal sense the answer to how best to educate students, but they are the answer figuratively. Every college course should be like an immersion program, leading students into worlds where, unthreatened, they can discover that the various features of their own world have real, viable, and even attractive alternatives.

So far my argument has emphasized the reflective turn in which moral practices reveal themselves. I have said that I am not critical of my practices while I am using them, that I need to disengage from the pursuit of my various ends in order to turn my practices from adverbs into nouns, to make them into objects for investigation. When something has gone wrong, one of the ways to see how I might fix things is to scrutinize my practices to see if they are functioning adequately as guides to how I should be going about whatever I am doing. But it is always difficult to put the tire chains on in the middle of a snowstorm, so I advocated the value of examining practices in the more leisurely context of a time when things were going along just fine. Colleges, I said, are institutions in our culture designed to play precisely that educative role.

Self-examination, in the strong sense of taking a good look at the conditions of my selfhood, is a freeing experience. Because I am born into a culture, I learn its practices in learning how to gain the attention of those who can cater to my wants, in learning how to walk and talk, to recognize the otherness of others and to interact with them. Bringing these taken-for-granteds out into the open, putting them on the examining table to be dissected and assessed, frees me from being dependent upon them without knowing they are there, or rather without realizing that they are not as natural as my sucking and breathing. I argued that a mode of playfulness was crucial to the process of getting moral practices onto the table: first, because play is one of the few activities in which purposes are sufficiently hushed to permit me to hear the whisper of the practices that determine their conditions; and second, because I can tolerate alternatives to what is most important for me if the alternatives are not seen as threats but as playthings.

The conservative response to these reflections on my moral practices, these playings with worlds and their meanings, is for me to reaffirm the value of the old ways. When done in a manner that has made those practices clear to me and has situated them comparatively, such a reaffirmation will have been well-earned, and in making that choice I will have moved from childhood to adulthood, from subservience to independence. Or, as Kant would put it, from heteronomy to autonomy. The reformative response, in contrast, would be for me to find fault with the old ways, to find attractive resources in the alternatives, and, in the play of imagination and reason with both the old and its alternatives, to remake my practices. Only by making my own world can I make it my own; the path to adulthood, independence, autonomy is always away from the familiar and into the unknown.

Critical reflection, however, is rarely just conservative or so radically reformative that the old is completely swept away. More than likely, the changes in my character, in my way of taking my world, will be very small. We usually change who we are by taking baby steps, not by leaps and bounds. But we usually change.

The only way I can alter my moral practices, or even take up the old familiar ones with new understanding, is to put them into practice. Knowing the conditions for judging an action fitting is no more to be able to make judgments fittingly than knowing what arm motions are required to swim the crawl is actually to be able to swim it. The information is helpful, but the skill is only learned in the doing. By an up-close look at texts, stories, and interpretive descriptions that show moral practices at work, I am brought to an understanding of my own practices and to some resolve concerning them. But to turn that resolve into reality, I must act with the adverbial character of my actions tutored by what I now take to be suitable moral practices. At first, this change will be awkward. When I am learning a new skill, too much of my attention is directed initially to how I am doing. In trying to improve my golf game, I become so concerned about stance, grip, and arc that my score actually deteriorates; after putting on my first pair of bifocal glasses, I am so engrossed in coordinating the different focal points that the pace of my walking slows to a crawl. My moral practices, like a tool, should be transparent to me, assisting me in determining the how of my actions without my having to pay them any attention. As soon as I am sensitive to their presence, the transparency becomes streaked with opacity. The smooth competence of my engine begins running roughly. Eventually, I will get used to doing things this new way, however, and then my moral practices will blend into the background of features determining the parameters of my pursuits. My engine runs smoothly again; my glasses are forgotten; my golf score improves.

People usually do not change practices in quite such a linear fashion, however. It is not that I select an altered style for my actions and from then on the only issue is getting those practices down pat. My critical mode is not likely to be shut off as soon as I have resolved to effect a change; the altered style as it begins to be implemented needs to be the constant occasion for assessing and reassessing how it works. I am not only learning to make the best possible use of these altered conditions for the proper ways in which to make my choices of ends and means, but I am also learning whether these conditions are actually as sensible as I thought they would be. What looks good on the rack may look terrible when worn; the change may sound better in prospect than it is in reality. So how I am doing needs to be critiqued by others and by myself. No one can teach me how, but they can certainly do a full-dress Monday morning quarterbacking routine on where I was inept in exercising the practice, confused about its meaning and function, obtuse about its possibilities or implications. I learn by doing, but by then reflecting, with the help of others, on how I did, I can refine how good I am at doing what I do. And so without their teaching me, my friends—and, indeed, my enemies—help me learn how to act properly.

Playfulness is as valuable for acquiring new practices as it is for discovering, critiquing, and reformulating the old ones. Since beginners in a learning process are always going to make lots of mistakes, it is better that the mistakes occur where they will do no harm or relatively little harm. The college classroom is a specially designed arena for making harmless mistakes. The penalties for ineptitude are embarrassment or a poor grade, but nothing that cannot be lived down or overcome. And even if I fail the course, the next semester I get to start all over again, the slate wiped almost clean. Any course will do, and every course should do, just so long as it is structured and taught in a way that calls for making choices and then fosters occasions where what is critiqued is not only the choices but how they were made.

The intellectual skills I learn in college for assessing information are both analytic and interpretive. The former clarify and sharpen my grasp of a situation by isolating its elements, making fruitful distinctions, reorganizing them in terms of a principle of order; the latter thicken my grasp of that same situation by drawing out its inner connections, embedding them contextually, altering the vantage point, letting be what is. Values of relevance, importance, significance, and suitability shape and in turn are shaped by my activities of clarification and thickening. The ability to exercise prudential judgments, guided by prudential practices, is then required of me if I am to transform the fluidity of this complexity into a determinate outcome realizing some envisioned human good. Good sense is my ability to make those judgments in a properly human manner.

The challenge for faculty is to design courses in which students are put into situations requiring moral and prudential judgments as well as analytic and interpretive ones. To give me practice in making prudential judgments, these should be situations that require me and my classmates to make choices that sift the worth and the relevancy of materials, improving their clarity or profundity as needed, that reconcile divergences, and that attain outcomes which realize worthwhile ends. These choices should be critiqued by reference to their effectiveness in using prudential practices that guide my actions wisely and efficiently toward the desired results. To give me practice in making moral judgments, these should be situations that require me and my classmates to be alert to how I arrived at those prudentially guided choices, and to ask if I did so in a way consonant with my character and alert to the fundamental presumptions of my culture concerning what counts as meaningful and what is required to secure, perpetuate, or alter those meanings.

Faculty can set out schematic diagrams reminding me of the moral and prudential practices likely put into play on such occasions, and they can even arrange matters to put more emphasis than normal upon skills and sensibilities that I have been neglecting or that the years of my schooling have distorted. Faculty can be sensitive to the stages in my personal development and educational maturation in order to create contexts that call for sophistications in choice and in the use of practices that will expand but not overwhelm my confidence and adeptness. Simulations are convenient, cross-cultural perspectives crucial, self-consciousness concerning the languages of articulation a prerequisite. But faculty can do no more than provide this groundwork. Growth in the good sense guiding how these choices are made, how the relevant ends are proposed and the appropriate skills utilized, will be my doing if it occurs, not the faculty's.

Somewhat ironically, therefore, the most important thing I can learn in these leisured, playful classroom settings is not gradable and often not even commented on. I can receive a grade of A in a course for giving the correct answers regarding the facts, concepts, processes, and relationships which it is the aim of the course that the professor teach and that I learn.

Where correct answers are not the aim but rather explanatory acumen, I can earn a high grade by giving a plausible answer, by constructing a well-argued interpretation based on warranted judgments. But that the choices of my answers and of my reasons were conditioned by proper attention to the relevant moral practices is an ungradable achievement. This ungradability of the moral practices I have learned applies even in classes where it might have been for the purpose of creating such a moral learning opportunity that the professor assigned the questions for which gradable answers were required.

The reason why classes need to be small, composed of about a dozen or so students and their instructor, is because of this indirection essential to learning practices. Not that it is not important for professors to transfer information to their students; if students are going to appreciate, understand, and explore cultural or professional worldviews, they need to know as much as possible about the means-ends structures of those worlds. Not that it is not important for professors to be role models, inviting students to learn from their mentors by imitating them. But no matter how refined or crass my purposes, in trying to acquire that information and trying to emulate those behaviors I will have missed their keystone if I am baffled by the relevant moral practices or, worse, do not have a clue what they are or that there are such features to things. When I take courses in the social sciences, this requirement applies to the moral practices that conditioned the actions I am studying; when I take courses in the natural sciences and technology, it applies to the moral practices conditioning the actions that made apparent what I am studying; when taking courses in the humanities, it applies to the moral practices conditioning the moral practices advocated by argument or expression in what I study. It applies as well to my own moral practices in going about my studies.

My access to the keystone of a cultural worldview or other more focused point of view, to its moral practices in any of the senses just mentioned, comes only by inhabiting the perspectives they condition in a critical and reflective way, discovering them at work by trying with mixed success to function actually or imaginatively within those worldviews and points of view, and learning thereby how they work and how to work them. It is this direct participation, this involvement, the critical appreciation and empathetic generalizations rooted in these firsthand experiences, that permits the requisite learning to occur. Only slowly, in a painfully interactive manner, does a student break through the information and the methods to their conditions and so learns how the arches of a culture, working together, manage to support the heavy traffic in purposes that busily move back and forth across them from one solid shore of outcomes to the other.

So why do we insist in the name of efficiency to make it harder and harder for students to see the keystone to these arches, to appreciate their nature and function, to learn how to make them? For when new arches are poorly constructed and old ones allowed to fall into disrepair, because keystones are thought unimportant or their presence not even seen, the societal bridge will eventually collapse and all the busy people's purposes will be left stranded. The efficiency of large classes, easily verified standards of knowledge, and a faculty paid for their productivity is a strange kind of efficiency. It is an efficiency that thinks it is okay to pull the bridges down because that is cheaper than making them work properly.

Moral practices provide the conditions for how the members of a society interact while pursuing their various purposes. It is important that people hold certain moral practices in common so that they can further their divergent aims by interacting with one another. Societies, unlike special interest groups of every sort, cannot expect to limit their members to those who share a common purpose. But unless they can share a common way for interacting despite their different purposes, the realization of their aims will be far too problematic, their lives more than likely nasty, short, and brutish. In even the most basic kind of barter, the conditions for exchanging goods, the moral practices of the marketplace, must be agreed upon so that the antithetical purposes of the parties to the barter can be made over into complementary purposes and hence the likelihood increased that their aims might both be realized.

But a society does not even need to insist that its citizens hold all their moral practices in common. Or at least such is the American dream. Therefore the moral practices it is most important for me to learn as a citizen in a pluralistic society like America are those having to do with the clash of moral practices.

When other people and I share the same worldview, we are still going to find ourselves at odds over ends and means. I want to raise the minimum wage and you want to abolish it; they are opposed to the federal government using tax dollars to support private colleges and we are strong advocates of federally supported financial aid. But at least we agree on how people should act in such adversarial situations: no hitting below the belt, back to your corner between rounds, and be as gracious in defeat as you are humble in victory. When those I disagree with do not share my basic beliefs about what is proper, however, the problem becomes much more difficult. And where the dispute over moral practices cannot be avoided, where both sides cannot finesse their profound differences on fundamental matters in order to get some routine practical problem solved, the integrity of the social order is brought into question.[9]

The rules of a game are its boundary conditions. Although they have nothing to say about the specific game plans of groups or individuals nor about the strategies they might devise for realizing their plans, the rules nonetheless, by stipulating how these activities are to be conducted, set limits to what sorts of plans and strategies, ends and means, are acceptable. My soccer game plan should not include seeking to injure the key players on my opponent's team, although the rules in excluding this style of play as a proper practice also disclose it as a possibility. Trying to knock an opponent out of the game is, after all, the acceptable practice of playing hard, pushed beyond the horizon of acceptability by introducing an intent to harm. I collide with my opponent not in order to regain possession of the ball but to do injury. My bodily contact is not a by-product of an attempt to undermine his control of the space of his ball handling. Instead, the contact is the object of my action, its harmful consequences my intent. This intention being so, my moral practices are inappropriate to the game. My teammates, insofar as they encourage or merely tolerate my actions, have ceased to play the old game and have joined me in playing a new and different game. We are playing by different rules even though we pretend to be playing by the same rules as our opponents are.

Critical reflection on my moral practices is thus, as I have already suggested, both conservative and reformist. The rules of the game always permit me to envision other rules that if implemented would change the game. The change might result in no more than a local variation, but it could produce a significant alternative form of the game, or the change might be substantial enough to create a new, quite different kind of game. The rules, the moral practices, are conservative because by setting conditions on what is acceptable, they police the exuberance of desire and reason, restrain the restless inventions of novel ends and experimental means. Moral practices say of certain actions that they are not meaningful even if possible, that because they step beyond the pale of how I may properly go about doing whatever I am doing, to practice them is no longer to be a player in the game, no longer to be a member of the community. But since the rules make possible envisioning their violation, they have a reformist and even a radical function as well, for they point me in the direction of a way to change the game for the better, to initiate new games, begin new traditions, found brave new worlds.

Moral practices are thus engines of conflict. They exclude whatever does not measure up to the standards that give their game or their community its distinctive character, that mark its defining characteristics, that constitute its essence. But in doing so they provide whatever is excluded with the alternative practices that constitute them as an alternative game or community. Therefore, repression or separation would seem to be the only ways to deal with moral deviance: you do things my way or we go our separate ways. But there is no reason why moral practices cannot be self-referential, not only providing the conditions for reconciling differences in means and ends but also providing the conditions for reconciling divergent moral practices. Moral practices need not always result in agonistic situations, this worldview pitted relentlessly against another, struggling to determine whose meanings will be foundational for a group, a nation, a culture. Why should not moral practices instead be able to provide the participants in these clashes with a practice for the reconciliation of conflicting practices? Given certain purposes and the means-ends structure that frames them, and aware of opposing purposes framed by an alternative means-ends structure, how might we go about finding a middle way between them, one that takes both sets of purposes into account, building a single new structure in place of the two incompatible ones?

Creating such a reconciling practice is what the Hegelian dialectic is all about, but I prefer here Josiah Royce's notion of the "between" and the "community of reconciliation" it makes possible.[10] My development as a self, the process by which I become a person with character, requires for Royce not only my capacity to acquire the moral practices of the community into which I was born but a capacity to go beyond those practices. I begin to become a self primarily by imitation: finding a role model, I learn by mimicking it. But if I am to do this, I need to be able to discriminate between the model and myself, to contrast its implicit description of how I ought to be acting with a description of how in fact I have actually been acting. I recognize that I have not accurately imitated the person whose ways of acting I have taken as normative, and I try to do better. Or I could cease trying to imitate that person and instead pick someone else as my role model.

But if I am to develop into more than merely a reflection of my cultural environment, I will need to go beyond simply striving to emulate those around me. Instead, I could refocus my discriminating skills, contrast my model with the alternative practices it implicitly harbors, and then imagine myself guided by those different practices. This change would only be to take the antimodel as my model, however; it would only be another kind of imitation. I would not yet have become my own self, a dynamic ever-growing self. My growth as a self, says Royce, comes only in the creative act of reconciliation. Growth involves seeing what lies between the old model and its alternative, thereby discerning the contours of their difference as suggesting a direction, a pathway, along which I might reshape the old in the light of the new, creating a self that is the old self stretched by the pull of its alternative, the self transformed into something new without abandoning what it was.

This process of finding new intermediaries is, for Royce, the essence of a self: for selves are dynamic activities, not static substances. But the dynamism is not linear in the sense of a well-ordered sequence of intermediate purposes marching toward the realization of some ultimate life-purpose. The dynamism of growth is indirect, a series of exploratory actions involving a recurring search for some conciliatory middle way between what has been given and what is taken to be a better possibility. Were I to come to college with my life already mapped out, seeking only to acquire the tools necessary to follow the route prescribed, my college years would be composed of a well-ordered sequence of purposes, indifferent to alternatives, undisturbed by unsettling doubts about the hows and whys and wherefores of what I did. There would be no time for playfulness, for wasted hours exploring interesting alternatives that lead nowhere in particular, for being tempted to try a reach that might exceed my grasp. There would be no time, that is, for growth.

What is true of selves is true of communities. Our common life is not based in any simple way on a shared tradition or shared hopes. Communities of memory and communities of hope, as Royce calls them, require those unities of past and future. But such unities are achievements rather than necessities, and having been achieved they are constantly needing to be remade. Times change, things happen, remembered agreements become irrelevant, old wounds fester, and promises of cooperation collapse under the weight of too much distrust and fear. The importances of my past are not the same as yours; the future you would have us realize is not what I would want. Our moral practices are at odds, because what you think proper I find obscene or frivolous. In order that it might be possible for us to share the same community, we will need to find a "between," a way to reconcile your memories and dreams with mine. If we succeed in this reconciliation, we will find the new world we share to be one that offers both the proper fulfillment of what we had each wanted and a place for new horizons that properly challenge each of us. Ours must be first and constantly a community of reconciliation so that it might be a community of memory and of hope.

Consider the ways in which the face of American society these days is lacerated by sharply divergent moral practices. For example, those who think of the country's natural resources as resources for use, as raw materials to be exploited, see their activities as morally justified. They think they have a right to make use in whatever way they see fit of what they have acquired legally. Furthermore, the products created from those resources, and the processes by which they are created, improve the national economy and increase the ways by which the quality of everyone's life is enhanced. Contrary to those who hold this point of view are those who think of the country's natural resources as resources to be preserved, as finite aspects of an environment to be respected for its own sake as well as enjoyed for ours. These people think we have a responsibility to future generations that requires pacing the use of resources so that the present will not benefit unfairly at the expense of the future. Furthermore, the earth is not ours to own. We are not its masters but only one among its many tenants. And so we need to learn to dwell beside and amid creatures and things whose existence is every bit as precious as our own.

Obviously we have here a clash of two worldviews, a conflict between the moral practices that deploy the meanings crucial to each. Within one frame of reference it is incomprehensible how an endangered species such as the spotted owl could be thought more valuable than the livelihood of workers threatened by a ban on further logging activity; from the standpoint of the alternative frame of reference, it makes no sense that people would be unwilling to forego marginal short-term gains for the sake of longer-range goods. Each side rightly demonizes the other, since from each perspective the others are not playing by the rules but are violating what is obviously right for reasons that can only be suspect. Indeed, reasons are of no avail against those whose actions repudiate so clearly the good sense that gives credence and persuasiveness to reasons. So each side turns to other modes of power than reasoned argument, using the ballot box and the checkbook to pressure politicians into passing laws and regulations that will favor their ends at the expense of those sought by their opponents. And if the power of votes and dollars should also fail, a more directly coercive kind of power still remains available.

Such dyads threaten the social fabric, and if left to unravel of their own momentum, too often lead to rents and tears that are increasingly difficult to mend. And people die of these dyads every day, these tear-stained holes in the social fabric. They die for lack of political poets willing to teach them that new verses might be added to their ancient sagas, for lack of weavers to remind them that they have had the skill all along to make new garments out of old. When two moral practices are at loggerheads, the power of one needs to be met with the countervailing power of the other. Otherwise, the more powerful of the two will simply carry the day, no matter how right or wrong its cause. But people whose purposes are at cross-purposes, who pursue their ends in direct sequential actions with unrelenting passion, have inoculated themselves against any possibilities for growth. No matter how noble their causes, the dyads clash like ignorant armies in the night. Like atoms, blindly running, they lack the eyes exploratory actions provide, eyes with which to see a creative between.

We are not always well served by our ideals. The antienvironmentalists work from purposes, methods, and practices suited for a world long gone; the environmentalists work from antipodean purposes, methods, and practices that take their meaning more from what they oppose than from what they are. A question needs to be asked regarding what uncriticized fundamental beliefs and unquestioned moral practices might be shared by both environmentalists and antienvironmentalists. Is there a vantage unimaginable to either of these earnest parties that might radically transform their polarized situation? Is there a world in which the problem of either/or dissolves, a world in which the environmental wars can be won rather than just another battle waged, a war won in the only way wars are ever truly won: by creating the conditions for peace? Can these enemies be reconciled within a wider, deeper, more valuable practice of community?

Critical reflection of this sort is no ivory tower occupation, but neither is it the activism of the barricades. Exploratory action requires reflection that arises in the context of real human problems and that is tested constantly in the fires of concrete conflict and resolution. The difference is that the practical aims of the activists, pro and con, work out of moral practices taken as givens in order to effect ideal ends taken as givens for the sake of effecting a greater conformity of the actual world to their ideals. In sharp contrast, the ambitions of a reconciling moral practice utilize the assumed characteristics of the given world and the reigning ideals as malleable resources for molding a new way of life, for remaking the world closer to our heart's desire. They call up from the vasty deep a transformative interpretation more adequate to the given and its possibilities. Those whose purposes are guided by the moral practices appropriate to a community of reconciliation are poets of our worldview so that they might be conjurers of its successor.

If our society is to be an organic community, a living creature and neither a fossil nor a machine dedicated to fixed ends, it needs moral practices for reconciling the conflicting moral practices that its dynamism will always be churning up. And those reconciling practices will need to be learned by each rising generation, and learned critically. Our society not only needs constantly to be turning its proliferation of pluralisms into unities but also needs constantly to be altering the moral practices by which it is guided in doing so. For each new reconciliation with its new practices puts in question the viability of the accepted practices for reconciling future practices.

Colleges are places for leisurely reflection, for playing around with alternatives that are interesting or worthless and often both. The leisure and the play are important antidotes to the poison destroying communities devoid of any moral practices for reconciling the moral practices of groups united only by their memories or their hopes. Those ethnic memories and special-interest hopes need to be celebrated on a college campus but not taken too seriously. For they need also to be criticized, poked and pawed, joked about, played with. They need to be tried on, discarded, remade, quilted together with outrageously contrasting remembrances and dreams. Our campuses these days are not too good at this sort of playfulness, with students having forgotten to set their serious purposes aside for the nonce of their collegiate interlude. Nor do administrations know how to laugh nor faculty to play the clown; nor is Puck much in demand as a guest lecturer. And yet a community of reconciliation is possible only if people learn somewhere, somehow that their worlds have alternatives as important to others as theirs is to them and that only chance and a choice still open prevents them from inhabiting those other worlds instead of their own. Colleges and classrooms need to lighten up. They need to put the overweening demands of everyone's so very serious purposes into proper perspective. What subject is worth teaching, what purpose or method, if our moral practices, their alternatives, and their limits are not learned along with it?

At the same time as they provide the leisurely reflection and encourage the playfulness prerequisite for developing citizens adept at the moral practices of social reconciliation, colleges need to be constantly redefining the shape of their leisure and the scope of their playfulness so that students will find that their best role models for reconciling practices are always being challenged by other models, and so that they will find themselves lured, pushed, and tricked into looking for a between of the reconciliation models, constantly reinventing how best to fashion a practice able to guide their pursuit of an ever-elusive e pluribus unum. This task is education's most difficult challenge: to be always putting everything into question so that what must on any given practical occasion be put to use unquestioningly will be the best purpose, method, or practice at the time achievable.

It is uncomfortable having to interact with people who do not share your beliefs and purposes, your life-style, your sense of what makes sense, who disdain your memories and are indifferent to the things for which you hope. It is more uncomfortable still to be striving to reconcile those differences by searching for and inventing some common ground in the civility by which disputes are adjudicated, opposites made into complements, differences at first tolerated, then respected, and eventually co-opted. But it is uncomfortable in the extreme to cast doubt on even these practices, to confront works of reconciliation with their failings and to toy with the very risky alternatives those failings suggest. Yet how else can a pluralistic community like America survive? So our colleges must be where students begin to learn the value of discomfort, where they discover that searching it out and manufacturing it are responsibilities they ought not and cannot shirk. The college experience must be where people learn that the communities important to them will thrive only if among the moral practices of its citizens is a way of fostering reconciliation without closure, unity without loss of plurality, ultimate meaning rooted in ultimate uncertainty. Colleges that pander to the desire we all have for closure, certainty, and like-mindedness are betraying their essence as educational environments and thereby betraying the communities of reconciliation they are supposed to make possible.

Activities that have no essential purpose include not only playing games but also the playfulness of intercourse. Concerning sexual intercourse, traditional Christian orthodoxy has argued that the activity should be engaged in only with the intent of producing offspring. Saint Paul, however, adds the pragmatic suggestion that its routine practice within marriage is a safeguard against social promiscuity and violence. Masters and Johnson claim that sexual activity promotes long life, and my local newspaper recommends it as a cure for arthritis. The foolishness of these appeals to practical results, to techniques, and even to religious mandates is patent. Sexual activity is, after all, its own justification. Its intrinsic value needs to be affirmed lest anyone take too seriously any of the various claims regarding its usefulness. Only by not being reduced to its pragmatic values is the true worth of sexual relationship retained and sustained.

What is true of sexual intercourse, and of leisure, is true most fundamentally of intercourse unqualified by any further specifying adjective. Intercourse among human beings in its most general sense is conversation. Talking together is a distinctive activity of the higher primates, the uniquely perfected activity of the symbol user and symbol maker, *Homo loquens.* The Faithful Community, preferring *Homo oratiens,* finds the value of speech in its power to persuade others to embrace a common good. But the ability to converse is persuasion's prerequisite and the source of the conditions without which it is no more than sophistry, no more than the clever ability to make the weaker case appear the stronger. The Guild of Inquirers, with its emphasis on *Homo sapiens,* finds the value of language to be its use in the symbolic representation of systems of natural relationship. But the accumulation of knowledge apart from the freewheeling inquiry for which conversation provides the necessary conditions will too easily confuse truth with adequation to a favored methodology. The Resource Center, with its celebration of *Homo faber,* insists upon the close link between communication skills and success. But unless the conditions for personal and communal integrity are learned in talk that has no relevance, high-priced goods will cease to be distinguishable from priceless goods.

The essence of a college is that it is an agora for conversation.[11] Whatever its mission, its methods, and the outcomes it might seek, it is first of all an environment where many voices can be heard conversing with each other. The conversation of a college is neither as genteel nor as vaporous an activity as it may at first seem to those who would pride themselves on not being tender-minded. For if to be human is at its most profound level to be in intercourse with others, then it is tough-mindedly appropriate that the heart and soul of a college be symbolized by its loquaciousness. Tough-minded institutional management at the turn of the millennium requires imaginative and dynamic commitment to the vision of a college as primarily a place for people to converse and only secondarily as an occasion for them to do, or learn to do, something useful. Students need to learn the skills of cultured intercourse more than they need to learn a tradition or a technique or a trade.

The conversation of a college can give fresh meaning to the proposal that it function as a Resource Center. The skills of intellectual intercourse are learned skills and not biological givens. Traditionally communities have recognized this truth and so have insisted that nothing was more important than creating an environment in which parents could raise their children on healthy doses of home and neighborhood conversational experiences. Until recently, for instance, the bourgeois family in Western culture has found table talk to be a training ground for citizenship. Reportorial description of the day's activities, interpretation of the minor triumphs and tragedies that were central to those activities, speculating about the meaning this discussion might have for the next day and for a longer future obscurely glimpsed: these activities require the same skills the wider society requires of its members. Societies work only if people are willing and able to take an active role in creating conditions for mutual benefit and for finding satisfaction not only in personal gain but in collaborative endeavors. The necessity of providing one's own home entertainment through reading aloud or telling stories or playing music was once an opportunity for self-expression and for discovering the pleasure of bringing others pleasure. In neighborhood pickup games and rivalries, children learned to accommodate to one another's differences by on-the-spot negotiations, threat and bluff, persuadings and exhortation. If matters occasionally collapsed into fisticuffs, the violence was brief and the victories recognized as ephemeral. The talking was quickly resumed.

In recent decades these resources for developing community skills have weakened or broken down. We find ourselves needing to settle for superficial and passive substitutes. Television sitcoms and videotapes replace family conversation, neighborhoods are uprooted and replaced by the isolated housing patterns of the suburbs and the isolating violence of the inner city. Even children's games are organized for them by others, Little League umpires replacing the ad hoc litigations of the sandlot. As a result, the tacit dimension of social existence is never practiced, its moral prac-

tices never caught, the potentiality of the loquacious animal never realized. Our children grow up chock-full of practical purposes to be pursued,
but they are unpracticed in articulating those purposes and so inept at
deploying interpretations that when explored creatively open avenues for
their realization. Our children grow up expecting to hold interesting and
well-paid jobs, to have trusted friends and a loving family, to live fulfilling lives. Or they worry that these goods may not be given to them and
so renew in panic their uncritical pursuit of the information, skills, and
credentials they think can guarantee them those goods. But without a
sense of their capacity to be distinctive selves, selves with a character
marked by good sense, a sense fashioned out of having to hold, defend,
and compromise a viewpoint in the give and take of play and argument,
they lack the basic prerequisite for a fulfilling life.

Where society at large has failed, there the colleges must try their best
to serve as remediation centers. Colleges should seek to rehumanize the
nation's youth by reversing their drift into passivity and inarticulateness.
Colleges should explicitly strive to create an atmosphere in which their
students might learn how to communicate, interpret, explain, and reconcile their differing points of view. They should make a place where students will come to enjoy the delights of self-expression and service, where
they will become sensitive to the limitations of self which that process can
disclose. As students develop these practices, the colleges will be preparing them to create perspectives of their own that are adequate to the full-
ness of experience, resilient and dynamic, interesting and even elegant.
There is no task more practical. It is what students should be demanding
they have an opportunity to learn while in college. It is the primary
resource for which a college should be the center.

The Guild of Inquirers model for the colleges draws strength from a
legitimate concern any society has for assuring a continuous flow of people with the expertise needed to maintain effectively the complex interactions of civilized existence. The techniques for organizing experience in
some disciplined manner are difficult to acquire and necessitate long years
of apprenticeship. The quantity of what we know and have created, its
sophistication, and the rapidity with which it must be further improved
make specialization mandatory and therefore demand that education be
tailored to the professional requirements for training specialists. To think of
the college as essentially a conversation is to contain this demand by surrounding it with another demand, to insist that what seems so obviously

a societal mandate is only half a truth. For it is as imperative that there be techniques for gaining general access to specialized information as it is imperative that there be techniques for acquiring that information in the first place.

The voices of the academic disciplines speak in many accents and dialects, but their speech involves a fourfold doing. Each discipline is engaged in constructing a view of things: a perspective on the world, a style of action that quite literally makes a world. The tasks of construction blend imperceptibly into those of description as the disciplines attempt to articulate for others the characteristics, structure, and functional relationships that compose their constituted worldviews. But what is described must also be interpreted, its meaning and its significance elucidated. Facts are not only pieces of information regarding what is now the case but also signs and symbols to be read by those who know the proper grammar and vocabulary of meanings. The facts signify other facts, suggest trends, imply general truths, and reveal hidden relevances. Interpretation shades off into explanation, the creation of global theories able to account for why things appear as they do and when they do, theories that evoke the underlying assumptions and overarching principles in virtue of which we understand our world and ourselves.

The voices of the disciplines should be busy creating, describing, interpreting, and explaining the worlds their speech authors. In general conversation, however, these voices are not allowed to settle for merely conversing each with itself, muttering in its own ear the frustrations and satisfactions of world-making. The general intercourse is among the voices, each one endeavoring to speak intelligibly to the others and in turn to hear what they might be saying. For the conversation to be mutually intelligible, the descriptions offered will need to be such that others can comprehend the dialects in which each speaks, can make sense of the way of thinking and feeling and acting each exhibits. Interpretations play a key role in this regard, providing the necessary mediating linkages. It is not enough to be able to see from another's perspective for a moment. The familiar seeing and the unfamiliar must come to be seen together as two facets of a whole, the separate voices rescored as a duet. A discipline thereby indicates the scope of its applicability, defines its logical place within the intelligible universe. The explanations each disciplinary voice in a conversation then provides must go beyond simply accounting for the world of its worldview; they must explain why such a viewpoint has arisen at all, how it sustains itself, and why it should not have long since perished or should not henceforth be included within another perspective of broader and deeper scope.

When description, interpretation, and explanation are turned outward in conversation, the differing voices are made resonant by a sounding board they share in common. The fallacy in hearing only your own voice, seeing only from your own perspective, is that it misplaces the concreteness of the process. Your perspective is taken to be the reality of which it is merely a view. The rhythm of speaking to others and hearing them speak in turn is tonic against this fallacy.

Conversation, from the perspective of an expertise, is superficial. A general approach maintains its generality only by glossing over the subtle distinctions and precisely defined relationships that are the consequence of a well-honed methodology. But a successful method can be as narrow as a general approach can be thin. There are superficialities in depth as well as in breadth. The vocabulary of general conversation, of discussion across the expertises, is especially suited to rescue depth from the dangers of narrowness by constantly opening it outward. Conversation is the way differing perspectives, each powerful in its capacities to organize experience into a specific system, are transcended by becoming voices in a common transsystemic enterprise. Because the transcendence is never final, never fully integrated into a complete and consistent system, conversation across the disciplines seeks, more modestly and more fundamentally, mutual illumination. It seeks to lead those who converse to a better understanding of the horizon and the possibilities of their own perspective through the encounter with other perspectives. Conversation is the refreshment of method and thus of the academic disciplines. It is the way by which they can be saved from their own proclivities to closure.

When a college defines itself as a Faithful Community devoted to an intellectual heritage it treasures and augments, it proclaims the saving power of its ideals. Every proximate purpose of the college is seen as serving a higher ultimate purpose, one that brings all purposings to completion. The Faithful Community is bent on realizing this ideal, reconciling the conflicting pursuits of parochial ends into a perfect universal harmony, a peaceable kingdom first to be achieved within its ivied gates but eventually to be spread throughout the globe. Conversation is the apparent enemy of such lofty purposes. Those loyal to an ideal of transcending significance find conversation to be little more than idle chatter, the discourses of classrooms and coffee hours a proof of the decadence of privilege. The leisurely contemplation of vague ideas and fanciful possibilities is always out of place in times of social unrest when political ideologies or religious beliefs struggle to control the levers of historical power. Any utopian ideal seriously pursued as a historical objective can be victorious only when it is able to close off debate about itself, to silence the incessant, interminable chattering of the voices.

Yet it is important for the voices to continue being heard. No matter how desirable it is to obtain an objective, to get over the bickering and get on with the tasks required for that objective to be realized, doing so is always premature. Fallible creatures that we are, any decision people make is based on insufficient evidence and inadequate reflection. Of course we must act despite these deficiencies, committing ourselves to a policy or outcome based on the best evidence and the most considered judgments available. Perpetually to hesitate in the realization that further study might be helpful is never to act at all. Nonetheless our hesitations are crucial. They save us from many a foolishness and they remind us that even when we risk our lives, our fortunes, and our sacred honor for a cause, other judgments and thus other commitments had also been plausible and in some cases would have proved to have been the wiser course.

Thus the meander of idle conversings about even the most important things reminds us that the ideals we seek are always only approximations of the ideal. Our conversing is how we recover an openness to fresh approximations even at the moment when we are most convinced that we have the ideal at last in hand. Conversation rescues us from confusing the Faithful Community with the Messianic Kingdom.

A typical college in the decades or centuries since its founding has probably advocated a great many purposes and in doing so drawn from all three educational models. Yet in framing their mandates of faithfulness, those institutions that put a higher value on critical reflection have never fully identified with any religious community nor with some latter day form of a civil religion. They have celebrated the virtues of academic method and the excellences of the scholarly disciplines but have never collapsed into the mere handmaiden role of providing mail and parking for a collection of departmental fiefdoms. They have offered to serve the career needs of students as these have been defined by each new generation, while all the time retaining a bemused recalcitrance toward identifying today's agreed upon meaning of relevance with relevance.

Exasperated by such a college's irrational loyalty to its traditional practices, the proteanists among its critics have grumbled at its failure to recognize economic necessities and to change with the changing times. Frustrated by that same college's demented willingness to innovate simply for the sake of innovation, its procrustean critics have fussed over its lack of principle and consistency. But perhaps, just perhaps, these seeming inadequacies are signs of strength, the college's resistance to forces that would destroy its essence as a college. Perhaps a college reveals itself as having character by a curious ineptness at defining its purposes, by its odd inability to carve out for itself a boldly distinctive educational role, by its singular failure to take itself seriously.

A crucial requisite for conversation that creates an agora where moral practices can be learned is that it be open-ended. Unlike a parliamentary debate or an election campaign, conversational discourse is not constrained by the need for a definite outcome. There is no resolution to be voted on that determines the importance of what is said and consigns some speech to the irrelevance of being out of order or beside the point. A conversation bloweth where it listeth, and no one knows nor can predict the way of it. Nor is a conversation constrained by precise rules and procedures regarding who may talk, under what conditions, in what order. The practices are looser and may vary, some styles of conversation inviting frequent noisy interruption, others expecting participants calmly to hear each voice through to the end before seeking permission to reply. There are no referees or judges who stand outside the melee to give order to the jousting that takes place. Everyone is a participant and everyone the judge. Anything goes except for actions that would have the effect of shutting off further conversation. In a land where the physical power to compel assent has been blinded, the power of an illuminating voice is one-eyed king and the struggle for domination replaced by the interdependence of mutual exploration into an unknown where domination spells disaster.

Socrates is the patron saint of the college, the exemplar of life within the agora of conversation. He talks interminably and can be tempted away from any serious task by the opportunity to strike up an inquiry with strangers or friends regarding the nature of virtue or the meaning of truth. The emblem of Socratic conversation, as recorded by Plato in the *Symposium,* is a drinking party in which the participants wile away their idleness by spinning tales of love. At the dawn Socrates is found by

Aristodemus still chattering on with two of his friends, the comic poet Aristophanes and Agathon the tragedian. They are "drinking out of an enormous bowl which they kept passing round from left to right," and Socrates has been trying all night to convince his friends "that the same man might be capable of writing both comedy and tragedy—that the tragic poet might be a comedian as well."[12] Socrates invites us to join in these endlessly exploratory actions, critiquing obvious truths, attempting to find a middle way, becoming intoxicated by a search pursued without regard for the cares of tomorrow.

In the *Meno,* a young and very talented know-it-all is stung by the "broad torpedo fish" of Socrates' questioning into recognizing that in fact he has no idea what virtue is, even though he has made "speeches about virtue before large audiences on a thousand occasions." Socrates acknowledges that he himself is also perplexed by what the answers might be to the questions he asks, as perplexed as are those to whom he asks such questions. "So now I do not know what virtue is," nor do you, Meno; "nevertheless, I want to examine and seek together with you what it may be." For "we will be better men, braver and less idle, if we believe that one must search for the things one does not know."[13]

Searching in the company of others, sharing together their perplexity, looking for a knowledge none can teach to the others but that each can learn under the sting of each other's perplexing questions: such are the moral practices of Socratic inquiry. We are invited to join in a conversation that goes on and on because it cannot ever find a satisfactory definition for virtue, much less determine whether virtue can be taught, but a conversation in which friends become better because of what they are doing. And hence precisely by failing to answer their questions, by failing to bring closure to their explorations, by remaining in unresolved conversation, they come to possess the virtue they were seeking. For virtue is an adverb and not an object; it is acquired by learning how to ask questions with a proper humility, by coming to know that you do not know. Virtue is not an answer to a question but a way of asking questions. And to engage in every sort of activity in the same way you properly ask questions is to act virtuously, to practice a moral truth you cannot preach but you can exemplify.

A conversation is good because of the texture of its contrasts, the polyphony of its voices, the complicated twists and turns that trace its meandering path. Even the best of good discussions comes to an end, however, when the practical requirements of life intervene, as they always do. Guests must get the babysitter home, the class bell rings, the mind suffers fatigue. But resolutions, solutions, refutations, and all the other acts of closure that bring a project to its completion, a purpose to its purposed end, lie outside the pale of the conversation. The conversing left to itself would go on endlessly. Socrates would still be at the banquet table debating the meaning of tragedy and comedy except that the dawn intruded and summoned him from his play to the courtroom and the hemlock.

We need resolutions to our problems; our issues need to issue in some sort of outcome. A college ought to have a purpose, a statement of mission, and some sturdy objectives worthy of its commitments. But these requisites should be subservient to its role as an agora, calling us all away from our specific tasks to a conversation in which our accomplishments and accustomed procedures can be brought into proper perspective, critiqued from outside the guild, cultivated for unsuspected nourishment, appreciated for what they are in themselves as creations of the human spirit. The character of a college, that which alone justifies its existence as an educational institution, is found in its efforts to fashion itself as a place where we can be rescued by others, and where we can rescue others, from an unthinking or too narrow pursuit of purposes. The essential task of a college is to recall us constantly to the only justification for our seriousness: the celebration of life and the endless challenge of its possibilities.

The academic agora is an inefficient institution, lacking in the proper seriousness needed to function effectively within the social order. But it is the special achievement of Western civilization to have devised an institution the inefficiency of which is the basis for its distinctive social contribution. The essence of a college is to be the critic of purposes and thereby their refreshment. Its role is to be without essential purpose so that the purposes of other institutions can be saved from their self-destructive tendencies.

Athens destroyed its gadfly and so it perished. It would be ironic were America, with the eager cooperation of its colleges, bent as they are on the pursuit of their several purposes, to do the same. Our nation's colleges, however, if they manage to retain or recover their essential integrity as places where gadflies nip playfully at our moral practices, can foster the conditions for our society once more to learn how to renew and transcend itself.

NOTES

1. From William Carlos Williams, "Asphodel, That Greeny Flower," book 1, in *Journey to Love* (New York: Random House, 1955); cf. Christopher Mac-Gowan, ed., *The Collected Poems of William Carlos Williams* (New York: New Directions, 1988), vol. 2, p. 318. These lines are quoted (without citation) by Linda Ray Pratt in "Liberal Education and the Idea of the Postmodern University," *Academe 80* (November–December 1994): 46–51. Pratt is concerned about the "nightmare vision" of an America without any shared values, any sense of itself as a people. She exhorts us to "discover the philosophical underpinnings that can reestablish our sense of belonging to a human community" (51).

2. John Dewey, *Reconstruction in Philosophy* (Boston: Beacon Press, 1948), chap. 4, "Changed Conceptions of Experience and Reason," or *Human Nature and Conduct* (New York: Henry Holt, 1922), part 3, "The Place of Intelligence in Conduct." But these references are somewhat arbitrary selections, since Dewey develops similar points in most of his major philosophical works.

3. I am aware, of course, that this characteristic does not apply to performative statements. In a wedding ceremony, "I do" is not an image of an action but the real thing: I say it and I am married. See J. L. Austin, *Philosophical Papers,* 2d ed. (Oxford: Oxford University Press, 1970). There are occasions, however, in which what the words perform is playful rather than for real. I can say "I do" to the minister's question "Do you take this woman to be your lawfully wedded wife?" and not in fact have married her if the occasion is the wedding rehearsal or if this statement is in a scene from a stage production of *Blood Wedding*.

4. Ludwig Wittgenstein, *Philosophical Investigations* (New York: Macmillan, 1953).

5. This ubiquity is more or less how Alfred North Whitehead characterizes a metaphysical statement: "We habitually observe by the method of difference. Sometimes we see an elephant, and sometimes we do not. The result is that an elephant, when present, is noticed. . . . The metaphysical first principles can never fail of exemplification. We can never catch the actual world taking a holiday from their sway. Thus, for the discovery of metaphysics, the method of pinning down thought to the strict systemization of detailed discrimination, already effected by antecedent observation, breaks down" (*Process and Reality* [New York: Free Press, 1978], p. 4).

6. Jean-François Lyotard and Jean-Loup Thébaud, *Just Gaming* (Minneapolis: University of Minnesota Press, 1985). Lyotard wants "small narratives" rather than a "great narrative," a multiplicity of language games without any one of them containing rules that are prescriptive with respect to the rules of other games. He does not want an overarching game of games, a "Jacobin game" with some new Robespierre as rule maker. Except that Lyotard needs to account for *this* pro-

scription, which he does by the notion of an "empty transcendence" to replace the Categorical Imperative and the notion of a "rule of divergence" to replace the usual "rule of convergence." I do not think the ploy works; see my *The Realizations of the Future: An Inquiry into the Authority of Praxis* (Albany: State University of New York Press, 1990), pp. 280–88.

7. Whitehead's famous phrase occurs in *Process and Reality*, p. 39.

8. As Wittgenstein states: "As if giving grounds did not come to an end sometime. But the end is not an ungrounded presupposition: it is an ungrounded way of acting" (*On Certainty* [Oxford: Basil Blackwell, 1969], p. 17).

9. One of the most convincing arguments for insisting that fundamental beliefs should not be the basis for societal unity was made some time ago by Charles Frankel, *The Case for Modern Man* (New York: Harper and Brothers, 1956); in particular, see chap. 5, "Liberal Society and Ultimate Values."

10. Josiah Royce, *The World and the Individual*, 2 vols. (New York: Macmillan, 1901). I discovered Royce's argument by reading John E. Smith's essay "Creativity in Royce's Philosophical Idealism," chap. 9 in his collection of essays, *America's Philosophical Vision* (Chicago: University of Chicago Press, 1992), which then led me both to Royce's own writings and to Smith's excellent commentary, *Royce's Social Infinite* (New York: Liberal Arts Press, 1950). For a contemporary version of this approach, see William Desmond's important and very fruitful notion of a "metaxological community," in *Philosophy and Its Others* (Albany: SUNY Press, 1990), and *Being and the Between* (Albany: SUNY Press, 1995).

11. The notion of "conversation" comes from Michael Oakeshott; the related notion of "voices" in a conversation is the topic of Oakeshott's best known essay, "The Voice of Poetry in the Conversation of Mankind," in *Rationalism in Politics* (New York: Basic Books, 1962). I have developed the notion somewhat differently than Oakeshott does.

12. Plato, *Symposium;* the Michael Joyce translation in Edith Hamilton and Huntington Cairns, eds., *The Collected Dialogues of Plato* (Princeton: Princeton University Press, 1961). The quotes are at 223c–d.

13. Plato, *Meno;* the G. M. A. Grube translation in *Plato's Meno* (Indianapolis: Hackett Publishing, 1976). The quotes are at 80b, 80d, and 86a.

6

The Standards of a College

[A QUADRIVIAL CONVERSATION]

—I simply can't understand why the federal government wants to establish national standards for what students are supposed to learn in school. It's bad enough when the local school board insists on imposing standards. It's worse when those standards come from the governor's office or the state legislature. It will be horrible if they are mandated by a national agency such as the Department of Education. I'm not objecting because I think federal intervention is a bad thing in principle. I'm all for government regulation where it serves a social good. We need standards for butchering meat and constructing bridges; we need to regulate stockbrokers and certify the competence of doctors. But educational standards imposed on teachers from the outside are inimical to education. The standards put learning in a straitjacket and so by trying to make things better only make them worse.

—I'm afraid I can't agree with you. A community needs to be assured its tax dollars are being wisely used. Maybe private schools can get away with doing anything they want, but public education at every level from kindergarten to graduate school should be answerable to the people who make it possible. The reason neighborhoods have elementary schools, towns have secondary schools, and regions have colleges is because the citizens recognize that young people need to know certain things if they are to become productive members of their community. At its most basic, this means reading, writing, and arithmetic, plus an appreciation of the history of the community and what democracy is all about. Beyond the basics, students need to prepare for a trade or a profession, which often means that they must acquire more sophisticated knowledge and skills. But the justification for providing the requisite educational resources remains the same no matter how subtle or complicated the subject. A society needs competent citizens, and schools and colleges are where people are taught what they will need to know in order to be competent. So it's obviously important to a community that its educational institutions do their job properly. Standards are merely the measuring devises for making sure this happens.

—Pretty lousy measuring devices, in my opinion. If standards were very general guidelines, I suppose I could live with them. If they said that students should study American history in eighth and eleventh grades and that colleges should require at least a semester of study in some aspect of European history, that would be fine with me. But the standards imposed on schools are always far more specific than that. When they say that an eleventh grader should be able to write an essay on the causes of the Civil War or that the college course must include a component on ethnic diversity, the standards are starting to dictate what the teacher is supposed to teach. Worse still, when the standards are about factual information and are measured by a multiple-choice examination, and that's what it usually comes down to, then the teacher is forced to teach to the exam. The American history course had better include plenty of names and dates to be memorized, because that's what the standards will test for. It makes the teachers little more than tutoring machines.

—Your attitude is blatantly self-serving, if not downright arrogant. Who are the teachers to be deciding what young people need to know these days? That's the proper task for a community to determine. Teachers are then hired to carry out its wishes. It's ridiculous to argue that this division of responsibility takes away the instructors' freedom, that it turns them into pawns of the school board or the state. Even with community-established learning standards, there's ample room for a teacher's creative imagination, pedagogical judgment, and all the other freedoms treasured by teachers.

—So you agree, at least, that teachers should be able to decide what the content of their courses will be, how the subject will be treated, and what testing devices are most appropriate for assessing what they have learned?

—All I ask is that teachers be held accountable for what they are doing. If we agree that it is important for our schools to prepare children to function in society as competent workers and good citizens, then we should agree that it's equally important for us to have some way to know whether they have in fact been properly prepared. We can't leave this up to the teachers. It's only being realistic, after all, to note the obvious temptation to do what's easy rather than to do what's needed in situations where you're allowed to be your own judge of whether you've been successful or not. More important, the problem is that each teacher will have a different sense of what is needed and whether or not it has been achieved, so there would be nothing you could be sure all students know by the time they've graduated from school. Leaving the question of standards up to each teacher's discretion is the educational equivalent of anarchy. A community has to have a common standard, and it has to have a common way to know whether that standard is being achieved.

—You two are squabbling about a false dichotomy. I'm all for evidence. There should certainly be some sort of proof that teachers are doing their job, that their students have learned the history and science and whatever else society expects them to know. But a pile of inert disconnected facts is not knowledge. An eighth grader doesn't know American history by being able to name the presidents of the United States or to locate all the state capitals on a blank map. Moreover, there's simply too much information available these days, more than anyone could be expected to remember, no matter how tough-minded we might be in separating the important from the unimportant. Besides, most of this information will be superseded or irrelevant by the time the eighth graders are adults. Students need to learn how to learn for themselves so that they can acquire information on their own on a need-to-know basis. What they should be taught first is how to ask the sorts of questions that tell them what they need to know and second, how to formulate plausible answers and determine whether those answers are any good.

—I agree; an educated person should not be someone prepared to do just one thing but rather someone able to learn whatever the situation might require. Otherwise, we will be preparing people for what the past thought important rather than for what the future will need. We have to prepare our young people for the unknown, not the known. It's a matter of a learning style, not content. What counts is how you go about doing things, not what you do. But there's no objective way to test that. It's absurd to use multiple-choice questions to determine whether a student knows French. You find that out by conversing with him. Knowledge is an activity, not an outcome.

—I think you are overstating your case. I'll grant that the process of getting there is more important than getting there, but the destination is still crucial. If the only thing we need to teach our students is how to think critically, they could just as easily end up as clever crooks than as good citizens. You are willing to advocate teaching a mode of inquiry rather than a body of results because you are confident that this method is the only way to get good results. Scientists use an experimental method because they are confident that over the long run it will yield the best information possible about the world. There's no need to focus on the results if the method warrants in advance that whatever they are, they will be correct. But this approach doesn't mean we shouldn't have standards and tests. It means we need to design standards that emphasize proper methods of inquiry, and then we need to design tests that ask for answers which can be acquired only by the right application of those methods.

—If only you would leave it at that. But I suspect that you really want to turn this relation on its head. You are more comfortable placing your confidence in a particular set of results, then gladly embracing any method that produces those results. You are all for science, but only if it doesn't conflict with religious belief. Political reform is fine with you, as long as it preserves the free enterprise system. You think the arts are celebrations of the human spirit, except when they are pornographic. That's why you insist that the effectiveness of teaching be measured by the facts a student has learned, allowing you to filter out teachers who ignore or critique the facts you think fundamental to your community's well-being or to its very existence. Critical thinking, yes; but it had better not be too critical. The gadfly can nip at the heels of the horse of state, but its sting had better not be poisonous.

—I don't think there's a dime's difference among you. The standards for learning promulgated by a religious or political community are always a not too subtle way to assure conformity, to be sure everyone is properly corralled within the fences which define that community's narrow world. No wonder the teachers are upset: they are being asked to turn free-spirited young people into docile riding ponies. But trumpeting the scientific method as the standard is just more of the same, only in this case the world to which students must conform is that of the learning community itself. You don't want the local burghers or the feds telling you what to teach, but you're happy to have the full professors tell you. Well, I don't want anyone telling me. There's simply no such thing as a definitive method, anymore than there's such a thing as a definitive body of knowledge. Everything's in flux, and trying to pin knowledge down by imposing standards on the flux is like trying to catch water in a sieve. It's convenient to believe in standards if you are a beneficiary of the stability they presume: normal science and traditional culture. But it's oppressive if your beliefs or your methods, or you yourself, are not in the societal mainstream. Knowledge and the means for acquiring it are contextual. They have a history, which means that they are functions of limited purposes and therefore not legitimately universalized. Indeed, to claim that some historically crafted truth is a general truth, some currently workable method a universal engine for obtaining truth, is a form of self-aggrandizement. Standards of any form are external impositions by those in power on the members of the community over which they exercise that power. Away with standards, I say! Learning should not be in thrall to the governing elite.

—I agree with your rejection of standards, but for a quite different reason. What's upsetting teachers is not that this belief or that method is being imposed, but that anything is being imposed. They don't like the idea of an external authority of any sort telling them what they should teach, or how they should teach, or when they should teach. And that's not because they're left-wing anarchists or right-wing libertarians who can't stand authority. Their complaint is that an imposition of educational standards by others undercuts their authority as teachers. It substitutes an external authority, thereby delegitimizing theirs. Someone from the outside, someone who isn't a teacher and probably knows very little about teaching, is telling them what they need to do. The teachers protest that they are professionals. They were trained to make decisions about what topics might be most important to cover in an American history course or an earth sciences course, given who their students are, what materials are available, and how the semester has been going. By what right do these school board members or these legislators think they can tell the teachers how to teach? Well, I don't mean to be so strident. Actually, the primary mood of teachers is not anger but discouragement. They thought that they had entered a respected profession, but they find themselves either patronized or reviled. What's education coming to when teachers are treated with the contempt that masters have for their slaves or colonizers for those they colonize?

—That's the advantage of being a college professor. The administration wouldn't dare dictate how or what they teach. Within their expertise, professors are autonomous; their authority is recognized and respected by colleagues. I can barely imagine anyone from another department raising any serious objection to a department's new course proposal.

I can't imagine at all someone from the same department raising an objection to a colleague's proposal, as long as the topic was well embedded in the proposer's area of specialization. This authority comes at a price, I admit, but it is one that college faculty are more than willing to pay. If they are to be respected as authorities in their expertise, they need the self-discipline to refrain from pontificating on topics they know nothing about. And let me be quite clear about it: this restriction includes topics on which they may hold strongly felt but merely subjective opinions, especially those topics on which only subjective opinions are possible.

—So since elementary and secondary school teachers don't have subject areas of expertise, they obviously aren't professionals. Is that what you're saying? You really know how to rub salt into a person's wounds! Your argument implies that it is appropriate for the representatives of a community, their authority validated by their election to public office, to determine what students need to learn about the basics, about the nonexpert general knowledge required by any citizen. The community representatives may need the help of experts, however, in determining those standards, so they should turn to professors whose authority in the relevant subject areas they acknowledge. But schoolteachers are neither experts nor community representatives, and so they have no legitimate say in what they are to do. When they speak out on these matters, they are seen as merely expressing subjective opinions and self-serving ones at that.

—The 1940 AAUP Statement on Academic Freedom is quite explicit in saying that a professor's speech is protected only when making assertions in areas where his or her expertise has been certified. But I don't think I'm selling the schoolteachers short; they are experts in pedagogy, after all. That's why they take all those education courses and why they have to meet standards for teacher certification. I don't think school boards should be able to tell a teacher how to teach, but I don't think the teachers are competent to decide on their own what young people need to know by the time they've completed their secondary education. Teachers should demand their autonomy as professionals in child and adolescent pedagogy, but they overstep their bounds when they think this autonomy gives them the right to decide on the community's educational goals and the outcomes by which attainment of those goals is measured.

—But overstepping the bounds is what citizenship is all about. It's an abnegation of your civic responsibility to draw a circle around your little area of specialization and limit your concerns to what is within that circle. We need all the scientific knowledge we can muster to help us understand the complexities of the natural and social environment, but scientists can't stop thinking and talking when it's time to decide if the old-growth forests are more important than the jobs created by cutting them down. You can't get away with the easy distinction between speaking ex cathedra as a scientist when the question is about the ecology of a forest and speaking as just an average everyday citizen when the question is about trees versus jobs. Political decisions need to be made by informed citizens, and a citizen informed by the relevant scientific information is a darned sight better citizen to have around than one who doesn't know anything about spotted owls or marginal utilities. We should be teaching our students to think it important that their expertise be relevant to their civic responsibilities, so that they grow up willing and able to make intelligent practical decisions.

—The problem with academe is that it's full of professors who think that in order to be objective professionals they must refrain from making value judgments. So chemists have nothing to say about the evils of pollution, political scientists are silent about the injustices of poverty, poets and philosophers abjure the role of gadfly by couching their words in ways unintelligible to a general audience. In other words, when it comes to public issues they don't have anything to say as chemists or political scientists or poets. The price they have paid for their autonomy, their respect, and their authority is that in the realm of civil discourse they lack all three. As citizens they are neither independent thinkers, respected pundits, nor authoritative voices, even though they look and sound as though they should be. This recognition of their limitations comes across as fake humility or arrogant withdrawal; neither goes over well with the general public. I don't think professors are any better off than teachers when it comes to public disdain.

—You forget the terrible consequences whenever the distinction between expert knowledge and subjective opinion breaks down. If scientists speak out on political issues without making it clear that they do so not as scientists but only as citizens, then soon nonscientists will be speaking out on scientific issues on the assumption that if the issue is of concern to citizens, then they have as much of a right as do scientists to play a role in what is decided. Creationism is a case in point. The only way genuine science can protect itself against the intrusion of religious belief is to insist on the absolute authority of scientific method and hence of the scientists who practice it. There are no nonscientific arguments relevant to the truth of the theory of evolution, so citizens pushing a nonscientific agenda must firmly be shown the door. There's no room for them in the hallways of science. The takeover of some school boards by religious fundamentalists who then pass edicts requiring that creationism be taught in the public schools proves my point. They couldn't get away with it at the college level. It's only because teachers are not scientific experts whose authority is recognized by the general public on these matters that they get pushed around by the creationists.

—Careful now! Evolution is just a scientific theory, and the authority of the scientist only extends over the procedures by which such a theory is formulated and tested. No further. Science has nothing to say about the meaning of evolution, about the relation of an understanding of natural processes to the important ethical and religious questions about how best we should live our lives. Questions of our nature and destiny have answers that draw from more fundamental truths than those found through scientific inquiry. The creationists are confused because they want faith to dictate how the processes of nature can most adequately be interpreted, but they are right to insist that science cannot dictate how the value of those natural processes for our lives is to be determined. Our schools need to teach children both about natural processes and about their value. Science is competent to do the former but not the latter, so it is quite legitimate to insist that more be taught in school about evolution than the theory of evolution. We need experts in ethics and religion teaching alongside the experts in evolutionary theory, so that the values of the community can supply the proper cultural and religious framework within which to understand science.

—That's just about as blatant an example of the fact-value split as one could imagine. All that was missing was for you to make explicit the sneer tincturing your mention of clergy as experts. The real message is that scientific method is a rational activity, self-critical and so therefore self-correcting, which results in truth. Whereas religion is a dogmatic activity, rooted in emotion and immune to rational criticism, which results in opinion. There are standards for the one but not for the other.

—No, that's not fair. The differences between facts and values, science and religion, are real and important. But for each there are truths to be learned and so standards possible for measuring whether they have been learned. With respect to science, it makes sense to devise standards that apply to every school and college, anywhere, anytime. After all, "2 + 2 = 4" is true in Madagascar as well as in Des Moines, and the theory of evolution is as fully validated by facts concerning the Jurassic period as by today's facts. Opinions, whether abstract beliefs about human nature and social good or concrete beliefs about the heroes and the turning points of a people's journey from primordial origins to eschatological endings, are local options. Any particular community has the right to impart its own opinions to each new generation. Because such truths are not universal and not open to critical scrutiny, the standards for them are appropriately set by the relevant circumferencing communities. There should be international science standards, but belief standards can only be local.

—What you're saying reeks of prejudice, my friend. Standards that are culturally localized and immune to criticism are catechisms. You can hardly contain your disdain of them, and I agree with you. But the same criticism applies to your vaunted standards for scientific knowledge as well. The community they catechize is bounded by a method of inquiry rather than a geographic border, but the dogmatism is just as rampant. The theories generated by scientists may be criticizable, but the scientific method isn't. If you take a nonidealized close look at science as it's actually practiced, you discover that there's a great hodgepodge of different methods at work, some of them more ad hoc and opportunistic than rational. And there's as much bias, prejudice, and struggle for power in the community of scientists as in any other community, the quest for truth as often as not obscured by the quest for further funding and personal advancement. This emperor has no clothes either: the science community is as naked as the political community. For both, standards are locally produced and their purpose is to legitimate and perpetuate the self-serving understandings and procedures they are designed to measure. So I think teachers should be freed from hegemonic subservience to others' standards. Maybe that would free them to do what they should be doing: teaching children how to become free, autonomous persons.

—I'm surprised that you think it legitimate for teachers to call into question the authority of the community to impose educational standards on them. The local school board attempting to ban *Huckleberry Finn* from an American literature class is on a par, in your view, with the American Chemical Society attempting to specify the minimum number of hours of organic chemistry that must be taught in a college major. You think both are self-serving ploys and so unwarranted intrusions into the classroom by outsiders. You think only the individual teacher has the right to decide what books will be read in a literature course or what topics covered in a science course. But the logic of your argument is a slippery slope. What do you say if students reject their teacher's authority to impose Huck Finn on them? Suppose they find organic chemistry boring and insist that it shouldn't be required for a chemistry major? By what authority do teachers impose their preferences on students if wider social and intellectual communities lack authority to impose their preferences on the teachers?

—You see? It's just as I warned: abandon standards and what you get is anarchy. Our schools and campuses are a confusion of conflicting voices, each demanding that what it thinks important deserves as much recognition as what anyone else thinks important. Every ethnic minority claims its rights, demands its own dormitory, its own cafeteria food, its own meeting places, its own courses and majors. How can you teach a novel by a dead white man, they say, unless you also teach novels by authors who aren't dead, aren't white, and aren't men? The point is not that the old ways are being called into question. What's troubling is that there is no possible justification which can be offered anymore in defense of whatever you end up doing. And that's because there is no longer any authority to which you can appeal. There are no criteria for what should be included and what eliminated in a course once the standards by which to assess relative importance have been thrown overboard. There is no way to decide which demands for special consideration should be supported and which rejected if there are no general expectations against which can be set the arguments for making an exception in the case at hand. Take away the authority of the community and all that's left is the power to lure or intimidate others into supporting your approach. But that's exactly how Hobbes described the state of nature. Get rid of communal standards and you no longer have the necessary conditions for civilization. Whether velvet-gloved or ironfisted, what you get is barbarism, the war of each against all.

—That's a bit hysterical, don't you think? But I'll agree that the reason why so many people hold faculty in disdain these days is because professors seem unable to resist the demands of politically correct special-interest groups. They're just like the politicians, who suffer the same inability. Everything on a college campus seems to be politicized, which is to say that every claim is judged only in terms of the power it wields. The claim will be denied if the opponent has sufficient countervailing power, or it will be granted if the claimant's power is overweening. In politics, the power equation is usually mixed and some sort of accommodation required by both sides. But college faculty and administration have few resources to resist claims put forward by groups based on ethnicity, race, or gender, or even to resist claims made by single individuals clever enough to define themselves and their aims in those terms. So no one cuts the Chinese Culture Club budget or votes against a Black Studies major or denies admission to a fifty-year-old Chicana lesbian feminist. The colleges are jerked around by these special interests all the time. It's pathetic. They complain they don't get any respect; it's obvious why.

—We're not much better when it comes to academic standards. The virtual disappearance of grades below B– is the scandal of higher education. It's said that the old grading scale with its preponderance of Cs was a victim of the Vietnam War, faculty assigning high grades to prevent students from flunking out and so becoming eligible for the draft. That statement sounds apocryphal, but it captures a deeper truth: the politicization of grades, the use of practical consequences as the appropriate measuring stick for educational advancement. Students sniffling into their handkerchiefs can make a powerfully emotional case for why they should be excused from the consequences of a low grade. But parents are a more powerful pressure group for making sure teachers do not spoil a student's chances for getting into a good school or getting a good job by assessing their work at any level less than excellent. Academic marks, like personnel assessments and letters of recommendation, now begin with excellent and then shade upward by an awkward use of relative modifiers: very excellent, outstanding, superlative, more superlative, most superlative, superlatively superlative. I once judged a colleague's work satisfactory and was told this assessment was tantamount to saying he was incompetent. Grades have become meaningless because like the children in Lake Woebegone, everyone has to be above average. Whatever grades do, they no longer measure academic achievement. Everyone knows this fact but everyone pretends otherwise, and the resulting hypocrisy is so blatant it is no wonder that the general public sneers when we boast of our school's Excellence, its Distinguished faculty, and the Great Honor earned by this year's crop of summa cum laude graduates.

—On the contrary, I think this situation is just wonderful. You complain about the breakdown in standards, but I've been arguing that those standards are stalking horses for someone's special privilege. The collapse of standards means the exposure of that privilege. The cacophony of claims for special consideration shouted by people who have been repressed and oppressed by someone's standards is the voice of justice at last being heard in this land. No standards means equality, and it's about time! We don't need the authority of those in power to sort us into first-class and second-class citizens. What we need is our own empowerment, which comes by shrugging off the deadweight of imposed standards and replacing it with individually negotiated arrangements for whatever sort of education each person wants.

—But justice is a standard. Equality is a standard. The claim that your group deserves its fair share of a community's resources, or deserves more than its fair share in recompense for past injustices, is an appeal to a standard. Even your insistence that you should be free to study whatever you want as long as you find it personally fulfilling is to make each individual's wishes the standard for decision-making. There's quite a difference between the collapse or overthrow of a traditional standard and the elimination of all standards. Changes in our standards are inevitable and even healthy, a sign of a community's capacity to respond to changing realities. But there have to be standards or there can't be communities, and without communities we are no longer human. Standards are measuring devices, and measuring things means sorting them into longer and shorter, simpler and more complex, better and worse. Standards are what we use to identify how important things are for us and to organize those things into a coherent arrangement where the more important ones are central and the less important ones peripheral. So any human community, any ordered grouping of persons, has to have authority sufficient to determine the standards by which it orders itself. That's why the present-day undermining of any kind of authority is so terrifying: it undermines the principles of order we need to create and sustain the communities by which we are human. Abolish standards and there won't be any communities of faith, no communities of inquiry, not even any communities providing support for individuals following their own star. Nor any communities of reconciliation.

—Now wait a minute. I'm no anarchist; I'm not against order. I'm just saying that we need to recognize that the way in which knowledge is organized and the way in which our society is organized are our creations, that we make up the standards we then apply to ourselves, and that if this is so then those standards need to be negotiated among the members of the community. Political standards should be by the consent of the governed, academic standards by the consent of the learners. Autonomy doesn't mean solitude and isolation; it means having willingly assented to the rules by which we conduct our common life.

—That's not going to do the job, though. If standards are the outcome of a political process, then they are functioning as instruments by which to obtain a certain outcome. But as you have just been insisting, communities are not composed of people who share any single vision of what that outcome might be. Black Americans often find themselves at odds with the majority consensus because the whites of European origin who dominate that majority are insensitive, indifferent, or even partial to the ways in which racism still constricts the chances blacks have and think they have to live the American dream. Women don't always see things the way men do and so approach issues from a different perspective. Age cohort, geographic location, and all the other differences of varying scope and importance that characterize us add their vectors to the trajectory of each person's life. And so our purposes vary, and the variances are often too fundamental simply to be ignored or papered over with vague generalities. Where outcomes are being negotiated, there will always have to be winners and losers, and even the most optimal of compromises will fall short of satisfying everyone. So if standards are determined politically and if willing consent is the criterion for granting a standard its needed authority, then our standards will always be in question. The consent will not have been all that willingly given, and for some will not have been given at all. So for a lot of people the standards, no matter what they are, to some extent will have been imposed, and hence their authority as standards will be to some extent compromised from the start. Standards determined by negotiated outcomes don't seem to be a solution very far removed from the problem they were meant to solve!

—If everyone in the community shared the same ideals, the same essential purposes, then there would be no problem with imposing standards. Teachers would be preparing students for ends they as teachers thought important and those would be the same ends everyone else in the community thought important. Disputes would arise, I'm sure, about whether this or that standard was the best measure of those ends, but such disputes would not be pernicious because compromise wouldn't involve any change in what was being measured. But if we are going to have a community that is pluralistic in its ends, that tolerates differences in the fundamental beliefs and purposes of its citizens, then it only makes sense to carry that

toleration over into the educational process and into the methods for measuring what students have learned. The community should celebrate its
differences, and that includes expecting students to know and to appreciate each of the various cultural traditions it encompasses. You don't have
to believe in something to respect it as a belief. You can understand and
even empathetically identify with another cultural perspective without
having to embrace it as your own. The myth of America as a melting pot
presumes the need to negotiate a fusion of differences, but if we think of
America as a mosaic, then our differences need not be merged. Our unity
can be the togetherness of variety: a unity in our plurality rather than a
unity that overcomes plurality.

—You know as well as I do that "separate but equal" is a recipe for
disaster. No matter how empathetic your sensibility, the plain fact is that
one way of doing things is in your opinion fundamentally meaningful and
the other ways aren't. Even-handedness is simply not possible, despite the
best of intentions. If the decision-making power in a community is vested
in a single leader, that person will probably favor his or her own subgroup
and will most certainly be perceived as doing so by any subgroup that feels
aggrieved by those decisions. Or if to remedy this problem, power in the
community is evenly distributed among the appropriate cultural subgroups, the resulting collective leadership will be unable to agree on anything important. In a pluralistic society, educational standards based on
outcomes will be an incoherent juxtaposition of numerous sets of subgroup standards. Worse still, the requirement that students be knowl-
edgeable in what the standards of other subgroups measure will be taken
as a threat to the subgroup to which each student belongs. How can you
trust a teacher who wasn't raised in your subgroup's world to present its
beliefs in a manner that conveys fully their insight into the truth of things?
A different view is an implicit critique of one's own view. A person with
a different ethnic background is an unavoidably subversive presence. But
even if this mutual suspicion is overcome, the situation remains unac-
ceptable because a policy of toleration erodes conviction. The politics of
accommodation dilutes importance until appreciation turns to indifference, including indifference concerning one's own beliefs and practices.

—A better strategy would be to neither obliterate differences nor appreciate them but to make use of them. Any cultural perspective is going to
have its strong points and its weak points, its profound insights and its
blind spots. So people need to learn to work together. They need to col-

laborate, so that the greatest possible range of perspectives will be available to the general community as resources for dealing with the problems it confronts. Educational standards shouldn't measure how much students know about another culture or ethnicity but how effective they are in cooperating, in making common cause, and doing so in such a way that the full range of viewpoints, methods, and information possessed by the community is effectively brought to bear on the problems at hand. The best way to learn to respect a different approach is to discover that without it your own approach can't attain its goals.

—You're arguing that communities are not something we have but something we build. You're saying that a community is built by people cooperating, that trusting people and working out commonly accepted educational standards are emergent qualities of communities rather than prerequisites for them. They are not presuppositions of community but consequences. But if you're correct, then it is irrelevant that a college have standards and that it measure its success or failure by their means. What's important isn't what students know when they graduate from high school or college compared with what they knew when they entered. It's not whether the school has taught students their cultural catechism, or whether they have learned the sort of critical thinking that can catch a catechism parading as self-evident truth and expose its pretensions. It's not even whether the school has equipped them with the skills they need to function effectively in the contemporary world. All of those things are measurable and so require standards. But knowing how to cooperate, trying to build communities where they didn't exist, isn't measurable because it isn't a result or a presupposition, nor is it even an activity. It's a manner of knowing and doing, and manners can't be formulated as questions for which there are right answers. Or even wrong answers.

—I've enthusiastically supported attacks on those who censure ideas and banish activities that they claim are at odds with community-wide values. Individual rights and freedoms need to be protected. The problem with a requirement that students demonstrate they know a specified list of things is that what's excluded from the list is often considered not merely inferior but irrelevant, obscene, or dangerous. So because I don't want school boards telling me that multiculturalism is great or that the United States is a Christian nation, I've done all I could to undercut the authority of lists of any sort. The tyranny of the majority in education kills a child's creative spirit and washes out the vivid colors of individual and ethnic diversity. But I have to agree that this constant criticism of community values has left us with communities that lack any moral authority whatsoever. Children disdain parental authority, the courtesies of the road are ignored wherever convenient, townspeople complain about taxes while public services decay from lack of funds, and people don't vote because they know all politicians are crooked anyway. These days it's always my rights, my needs, my inner child, and never my responsibilities to home or clan or town, to God or country. Anything goes if it contributes to fulfilling personal desire, because no goods broader than the self are acknowledged anymore, their legitimacy having long ago been pounded flat by the hammer blows of constant critique.

—My problem is the inverse of yours. I've been so set on protecting traditional values, so concerned that we not lose a sense of a shared history and a common destiny, that I've insisted individual preferences should be sharply circumscribed and errant idiosyncracies squelched. As the twig is bent, so the tree grows. Therefore I've been willing to support whatever means might be necessary to be sure our children grow up believing the right things and acting in the right ways. And so I've thought it crucial that schools, just like all the other institutions in a community, should be expected to inculcate our ways of thinking and acting, and that clearly defined tests measuring learning outcomes would assure that this process was in fact happening. You took freedom to mean liberation from the prison of imposed constraints, but I took it to mean liberation from the wilderness of a life lived without constraints. We both have been overplaying our hands. Your anarchy, my tyranny. Neither alternative makes much sense, I'm afraid.

—This dilemma certainly sounds familiar enough. It's the old chicken and egg conundrum: do individuals come first and then contract together to form civilized communities for their mutual benefit, or does the community come first and provide the conditions for the development of civilized individuals? Which is more important, the One or the Many? Either choice pays too high a price for its victory, however, and so it seems sensible to strike a compromise. The Adam Smith solution is to believe that individual desires are automatically checked and balanced in a free market. Applied to education, this approach means letting any idea into the marketplace of ideas, confident that the interplay of arguments and counterarguments will winnow out false or malicious notions. So teachers need to make sure everyone has full access to all the relevant facts, and then to regulate the processes of exchange so that arguments are not cut short by the intrusion of illegitimate threats and temptations. That's the old-time liberal confidence in a preestablished tropism toward harmony. Or, if you prefer, it's a kind of Darwinian conviction that the most fit ideas will win out in any struggle for survival, presuming that the field of battle is kept reasonably level. From Bentham to Marx, the new-time liberals differ from their old-time colleagues only by insisting that communities need to impose regulations and sanctions on individuals in order to keep that field level, that people need to be taught to find pleasure in serving others, and that mechanisms for redistributing social goods need to be introduced in order to dampen the consequences of entrepreneurial success. Educationally, this approach has meant compulsory universal education laws, state tax support for schools and state-owned university systems, head start programs, tutorial and financial aid assistance, affirmative action mandates, and all the other ways in which the free play of market forces is tweaked so that the community's interest in an educated citizenry of a certain scope and character can be assured.

—This last point is pretty close to what I believe. Communal sanctions are important because they create habits of cooperation, which then makes it unnecessary to impose rules on people. If the family values taught to preschoolers are consonant with communal values, our children will enter school having already internalized the fundamental worldview of our culture. Teachers and professors can then presume that framework and reinforce it by adding appropriate cultural and scientific information and skills. These cultural values have to be learned uncritically because children are too young to know how to handle the tools of criticism. You don't teach a person how to drive a car until they're old enough to be responsible and intelligent drivers; critical thinking, like driving, is an adult skill. So first comes the process of internalizing our cultural ways and resources, then later on it's time to develop critical habits of mind. This sequence has the important benefit of increasing the likelihood that the criticism will be constructive, that it will be aimed at improving rather than merely destroying past accomplishments. I'd argue that somewhere during the period of secondary education the transition should begin from cultural appreciation to the creative use of experimental intelligence, building skills of problem-solving and reform on the firm basis of skills of appreciation and conservation.

—I could buy that sort of a compromise. At first blush, it seems horrific. Education as a process of socialization, mandated to create social conformists. Students brainwashed to work cooperatively. Big Brother with a velvet glove. But it's not as horrible as it sounds because it's all done at an age when students are in need of absolute truths and unvarnished loyalties. Once upon a time, young people were required to memorize poems they didn't really understand. They were at a point in their lives when their powers of memorization were in full flower, even though they still lacked any ability to comprehend more than the superficial meanings in the poem. No problem; insert those birds into the birdcage of the mind when doing so is easy, then later on they can be inspected, more deeply understood, and put to good purpose. Love now, use later. British soldiers in the Great War could make sense of what was happening to them with respect to both the glorious ideals for which they fought and the stupid actions of generals and politicians by which those ideals were betrayed because they had a heritage of great poetry by which to frame their interpretations. Shakespeare, Milton, and Tennyson gave form to their enthusiasms and their despair, to lives of bright promise and joy that were turned into lives of suffering and endless carnage. In the Second World War, that poetic heritage no longer perched in the soldier's mental cages awaiting their loving use. The soldiers could find no deeper meaning in what they were experiencing than what appeared on the surface. They were rendered mute by the absence of a culture learned uncritically in childhood as a resource for making critical sense of what they were going through as adults.

—I'd add one caveat, however, and it's an important one. In a pluralistic society, you can't inculcate the heritage of the cultural mainstream and think that this effort will suffice. For many young people, that heritage may not be a repertoire of items which give content and weight to the inchoate framework of understanding and action learned from their family and neighborhood. Teaching black urban sidewalk kids who live in HUD high rises to appreciate a world of white suburban front-yarded homes is to contradict what they have learned as normative. It mounts a ravaging critique of their uncriticized cultural presumptions under the soothing guise of presenting them with something obviously good. Somehow or other, the appreciative phase of education has to include learning how to appreciate the differences among students. And not just their ethnic, religious, gender, and class differences. I'm not sure how we do that without weakening the initial cultural base we said it was important to strengthen. Besides, the comparative appreciation of different worldviews is pretty sophisticated stuff. It seems more fittingly introduced in high school along with the tools of critical appropriation than in early school or preschool contexts. But maybe there's really no problem. Is it too cynical to note that since in America we live de facto in segregated neighborhoods, elementary education can teach to cultural standards defined at the neighborhood level without having to worry much about diversity?

—I find it striking that our discussion hasn't been able to shake loose from a fixation on ends and means. You spell out certain goals: teach cultural frameworks in the home, fill those beliefs out in elementary school by appreciative appropriations of one's tradition, introduce critical reflection in secondary school, and presumably then let college be the occasion for learning job and citizenship skills that draw from this now critically appropriated cultural heritage. But the only reason to have goals is in order to achieve them. So a successful educational program is one that arrives at its goals, one that produces at the far end of its pipeline young adults with the knowledge and skills specified. We have been trying to figure out what goals were appropriate, and we've talked about the most efficient pipeline to construct, including the question of quality controls so that student movement along the pipeline will optimalize the inherent tension between how long it takes to get to the end and the adequacy of what comes out. Everything we've said has been couched in terms of measurable success rates. If I may put it this way, our discussion has been utopianist: we have made the value of anything a function of its relevance to the supreme value, which is our goal realized. Success is our god; it's our goddess too. We prize those who have sufficient vision to see what our real goals should be and the skill to manage the resources available so that those envisioned goals will in fact be achieved.

—Sounds like a job description for a college president! Someone who can work through, for us or with us, the nettlesome problem of what it means to develop adults able to love their family, job, and country but also able to express that love in a way sufficiently critical to assure the continued creative adaptation of home, workplace, and community arrangements to changing conditions. Someone who having won consensus on that goal can marshal, for us or with us, the resources and cooperative energy requisite for realizing it. Someone who can articulate all of this information to the college community and to its friends and enemies in the wider communities upon which the college depends and which it serves, in order to elicit at minimum their understanding and preferably their support.

—That's a good job description, as far as it goes. But vision and managerial skill are not enough by themselves for leading a college. Maybe they're sufficient qualities for a person to be the CEO for a business corporation or to be a mayor or a governor, but we're talking about colleges. An educational institution is a peculiar sort of institution with a special sort of mission. So college presidents need to have a vision for their campus and the requisite management abilities, but they also must be properly credentialed academically. Presidents should come from the ranks of the tenured faculty, although I suppose I could compromise with something short of that, maybe just a Ph.D. and a visible interest in and knowledgeability about important ideas. The goals of a college need to subserve knowledge and not just profit. Or maybe it would be more accurate to say that the goals need to exclude deficits and include increased financial reserves and endowment, but for the sake of supporting knowledge and not for their own sake. It takes an academic to make sure there is no slippage in this order of priorities. The transmission of old knowledge and the creation of new knowledge are the goals for which all other educational goals are the means. Too many college presidents, boards of trustees, and legislators forget this rather elemental fact.

—One more addition. Our college president should be sensitive to student needs, remembering that there is more to education than supporting scholars inquiring into how best to determine the truth of things and teachers figuring out how best to transmit what has been accumulating from the past. Students are just beginning their adult lives, and their orientation is toward the future. The vision of a college president needs to be fresh and constantly refreshed. The way a college president manages the structures and processes for realizing that vision needs to be fine-tuned to their modulations, lest the college's graduates end up having been prepared for the twentieth century instead of the twenty-first. Education is for tomorrow's world, not yesterday's nor even today's. So I'd want the presidential job description to read: candidate must have an educational vision, must have proven management skills, must have a distinguished academic record, must be sensitive to student needs and the challenges they will face in the new millennium. And, of course, must also be able to walk on water!

—Suppose, however, that we didn't want a utopianist as our president. Would that mean that we would be looking for candidates who have no vision, no managerial skills, no academic credentials, and no concern for students? Only duffers need apply! This strategy would be silly. Our intention would not be to give up a good utopianist in order to acquire a bad one. What we would want would be someone with a different kind of vision altogether: a nonutopian one. We would not be looking for someone who was farsighted enough to see over the far horizon, but instead for someone clear-sighted enough to be able to see through the opacities beclouding the present. A deep-sighted person. We would want someone who was less concerned with blazing a new trail to some future goal and more interested in improving the character of the clearing in the wilderness where we are right now.

—I don't know what you mean by a vision of the present. Isn't a visionary someone who sees something greater than the present, who grasps an ideal that is in contrast to the un-ideal present? To have a vision for a community is to call it to a higher loyalty, to ask that it be committed to what it could be rather than to what it is. A vision turns us away from the present toward the future, so it makes no more sense to have a vision of the present than to prophesy the past. We know where we are and where we came from; the tough question is figuring out where we should go and how to get there.

—You're close to understanding me when you mention a higher loyalty. I would describe a nonutopian visionary as someone who calls us as a community to be faithful to a higher authority than the satisfaction of our individual and collective desires. An authority not of ends and means but of the conditions for both. If our loyalty is to some ideal which if achieved will bring us a commonwealth able to support personal fulfillment, then wouldn't anything be justified that brought that end closer to hand? I'm reminded of the old moral dilemma about whether it would be okay for one innocent person to suffer terribly for eternity if that person's suffering permitted the eternal happiness of all other human beings. My answer would be no. The end may justify the means, but it cannot justify the conditions constraining how those means—and indeed those ends—are determined. How we go about determining our ends and pursuing them is more important that what ends we select, what means we pursue, and whether we are successful or not. There's a higher authority governing how we should act at present than the one governing what we should expect might lie over the horizon.

—This arrangement sounds like some kind of master/slave relationship: acting under the aegis of a higher governing authority. If you're not advocating conformity to a ruler, then you must at least be advising us to conform to a rule. You sound like a good bureaucrat saying that it doesn't matter what we do as long as we follow the rules. That's not a very attractive model to be trying to emulate. I have this image of a grumpy, bored, self-serving person who seems single-mindedly intent upon putting obstacles in my way, making it as difficult as possible for me to get something done. I think of the clerks in the registrar's office who are always making sure that students have jumped through all the hoops and who are always barking at the heels of faculty about getting their grades in on time. Bureaucrats don't give a damn about individuals, just the rules. Faceless, soulless clerks, making an idol of the rigid pipeline through which they insist that everything be forced. But I'm not being very fair to them, am I?

—Academic regulations are something like highways, I suppose. They smooth the way through the educational jungle for most students most of the time. The highway may not always get you to graduation by a direct route, but the winding pathway certainly is quicker and easier than trying to strike out in a straight line through hilly terrain and tangled under-growth. It would be nice to be a crow or own a helicopter, but us down-to-earth folks can at least count on the highway, whatever its idiosyncra-cies, to get us to our destination. Bureaucrats point you to the highway and make sure you keep on it. Like traffic cops. But they don't tell you where you have to go.

—Oh, but they most certainly do in the sense that you can only go where the highways go. Regulations keep you on the beaten path; they work against those who would like to be more adventurous. That's why I've argued for negotiated learning contracts in which any destination tra-versed by any pathway is acceptable. Students should beat their own path, with the help of all available resources, because they have different needs and different abilities and so should go their separate ways. But I recog-nize that this strategy is terribly time-consuming. It presumes nothing generic about our interests, no truths that apply to all students all the time or at least to most of them most of the time. But we aren't absolutely unique, are we? We are more alike, and therefore more predictable, than we'd care to admit. So I say let's negotiate the exceptions only, and let those who are content to follow the tried and true do so. Bureaucrats who don't permit any exceptions are what give rule enforcers a bad name. Flex-ible, sensitive, concerned bureaucrats I could stomach.

—Flexible bureaucrats are as oxymoronic as compassionate inquisitors or smiling Puritans. And rightly so because some things simply aren't negotiable. I'll grant that quite a bit of the time the reasons given for why the rules can't be bent have to do with convenience and efficiency. The registrar can't run the spring semester grade reports until all the grades have been turned in by faculty, and only after those reports are run can the list of graduates be compiled for approval at the faculty meeting, and the Commencement program can't be printed until the graduate list has been approved. In any system, synchronization is crucial: what "x" depends on must occur before "x" is scheduled to occur. So the registrar's office is inflexible in its demand that all grades be turned in by noon on Tuesday, no excuses please, although the justification for this stipulation is merely that any slippage makes it more difficult to pull off the commencement exercises on schedule. That's a big "merely" when people are coming from all over the country to see their friend or relative graduate, but it's a matter of convenience rather than a moral issue. Which doesn't mean it isn't important. We always have certain things we want to be sure take place when scheduled, and bureaucrats play the key role in assuring that things are coordinated so that we reach our routine goals when and in the shape we have requested. Whatever else a community is, it should be a place where the trains run on time and the television evening news comes on promptly at 6:30 P.M. rain or shine.

—It's not just efficiency, though. There's a moral justification for rules inflexibly imposed. For instance, requiring semester grades all to be due at the same time is a matter of fairness. If the purpose of a test is to measure each student's achievement relative to some standard of expectation, then it's unfair if one student is given extra time to finish up or is allowed to reschedule the exam to a less hectic day. The playing field is supposed to be level, with all variables held constant except the quality of the students' answers. If the test is designed to measure mastery without regard to the length of time required, the inflexibility would not go away. It would shift to insisting that all students be asked the same questions and that they have access to the same resources. Suppose one of the quarter-milers at the track meet was required to run only 90 percent of the distance, or suppose that for one baseball team but not the other it was four strikes before you're out. We'd hardly think the race or the ballgame fair and would not be prepared to press a laurel wreath on the brow of the advantaged runner just because that person crossed the finish line first, nor think the four-strike club a legitimate pennant winner. Demanding that everyone follow the same rules without exception is close to the notion in science of replicability. The experimenters' procedure includes specifying the conditions under which the results were obtained, so that another experimenter running the procedure under similar conditions should get the same results. It wouldn't count as the same results if the conditions were altered to the equivalent of a 90 percent or four-strike handicap. Replication means replication under the same rules.

—I understand your point, but don't forget that the conditions under which the experiment was run and is to be replicated are not ones designed in order to assure the truth of a particular hypothesis. The conditions are neutral to the results: they are required to hold whether the hypothesis is confirmed or disconfirmed. The conditions guarantee that whatever hypothesis is validated will have won the race to truth fair and square. You don't have a winning baseball team in mind and then design the rules of the game to assure that team's victory. First you make the rules, and then whichever team wins will have won because it is the better team at playing by those rules. Our judgments of success are conditioned not just by having achieved our goal but by having done so within the constraints of what is permissible or not permissible to do when trying to succeed. The political candidate who wins an election by cheating will not be certified for office, because it isn't only whether you win but also how you win that counts. The bureaucrats in the registrar's office make sure that whoever earns a college degree from that institution, however typical or strange the pathway, will have done so under conditions equivalent to those that were applied to all other graduates. Therefore the student is certified as having a degree that is a replica of those received by the student's predecessors in the graduation line.

—So you're saying that the virtue of bureaucrats is their loyalty to procedures that assure fairness rather than their loyalty to certain participants or particular outcomes. The baseball fans want the home team to win, and the sponsors want a close game in anticipation of which the fans come to the park and because of which they stay late. But the umpires want the game to be played fairly, and they will insist on this condition even if it means the score of the game is lopsided and the home team loses. Umpires are much like good scientists: they stick to the method even if it means failing to prove a cherished hypothesis and so losing a shot at the Nobel Prize. They think how you proceed is more important than where you end up.

—Having a higher loyalty to the rules than to the players may be a noble commitment but it isn't very easy. Imagine being surrounded by people clamoring for the realization of their ends, demanding that you favor them and their purposes or at least get out of their way. A faculty member asking for an extension on the grades because some big research opportunity has just come up. Parents yelling that they have already bought their airplane tickets and aren't going to be denied seeing their son graduate just because of a stupid D in his last course. It takes patience, levelheadedness, impartiality, and just plain guts to make sure the rules are followed when no one really wants to follow them. Indeed, these bureaucratic virtues sound surprisingly like the four classical virtues: prudence, temperance, justice, and fortitude. Might we say, therefore, that the registrar would have been thought a hero by the ancient Greeks?

—But temperance means more than levelheadedness. The extremes to be avoided are not only emotional and intellectual; there is also a need for temperance with respect to the application of the rules. What I'm saying is that a good bureaucrat should be willing to explore interpretations of the rules that might prevent someone from becoming impaled on those rules in their headlong drive toward some impassioned goal. We can be intemperately inflexible as well as intemperately flexible, especially since a good rule should be general and so always requires some interpretation regarding how it might be applied in any given situation.

—Even those who complain the loudest end up respecting the clerks in the registrar's office for insisting that everyone follow the rules. We want to have the regulations waived in our special case but strictly applied to everyone else. Yet at the same time we know deep down that it's really not right for us to be treated differently. Our begrudging respect for the clerk who says no is our way of tacitly acknowledging that the rules are more important than our desires. All the clerk is doing is reminding us of this fact, even though we really don't want to be reminded of it. Indeed, we feel free to push our case for exemption because we are confident the bureaucrats won't let us get our way. We trust them to act for the sake of the wider community, doing for us what we should have done ourselves. The rule enforcers thus make manifest the latent ties of mutual responsibility that knit us into a community. They reaffirm an enduring unity where otherwise there would be only the momentary intersections of individual purposes. The bureaucrats create this unity not by changing any of our purposes nor by altering the extent of our interactions but simply by imposing the same conditions on every purpose and every interaction.

—No, the clerks don't impose the conditions of our mutuality; they merely enforce them. Bureaucrats don't make the rules, they are given them. And by their commitment to the rules as goods higher than the good of any individual or collective purpose, they see to it that a community functions properly. A bunch of people may come together on a certain day to form a group in order to achieve some particular purpose: to play bridge regularly or to work for the reelection of a senator. They may draft a constitution and bylaws to govern their newly formed organization or the rules may be crafted implicitly by particular actions that eventually turn into routines and become customary. Some of these practices will be functions of the ends for which the group was formed, like making sure there are sufficient card tables or creating subcommittees for fund-raising and for publicity. But other practices will be functions of the group being a group, ways of behaving that are required for any group to hold together, for the members of any group to continue working together as a team. In creating a new group, its members tacitly accept the requirement that they subordinate their desires to the conditions of their functioning as a group. They blend their personal desires together into the collective desire constituting the group's purposes, and then pledge allegiance to it as a higher good while simultaneously taking an oath to do whatever is necessary to realize that good. But they also pledge allegiance to whatever constraints on their activities might be necessary simply because they are a group. So the rules of a voluntary organization are not imposed on anyone, or rather they are an imposition to which everyone has consented: they are self-imposed. And this self-imposition applies even for cultural communities, nation-states, and other fundamental forms of human relationship in which our membership is nonvoluntary. It's as Socrates argued in the *Crito:* although he had no choice over being born an Athenian, his remaining in Athens after he had grown to adulthood was his tacit acceptance of its laws and conventions as appropriate sources of constraint on how he should act. Having accepted its laws as his, Socrates was then bound by them and hence required to accept as legitimate the consequences of that acceptance even if he didn't like what they were.

—Even if the laws have been robbed of their impartiality and made instruments of a political faction's purposes? That's going too far, I think. I understand the argument for why a community's laws and customs take precedence over the purposes of any individual, but that's only on condition that they are impartially enforced. If rules are more important than purposes, then they are surely delegitimated as soon as they have been subordinated to some purpose, no matter how noble. Meletus wanted to get rid of a bothersome gadfly, and he used the Athenian court system as his means for doing so. Socrates should have objected to this abuse of rules by refusing to acknowledge the authority of the courts since they were no longer impartial arbiters of the clash of peoples' purposes but had become merely lackeys of a particular person's purposes.

—I disagree. Athens with distorted laws is better than Athens with no laws. Our respect for the decision Socrates made to accept the authority of the courts, including its condemning him to death, is rooted in his unqualified respect for the laws of his city. He thought his respect for a process, even when it had become diseased, might contribute to its cure. By honoring a dishonored law he brings into view those things about it that make it still worth honoring. It's like escorting the old crone through the village on your arm as a way to remind the taunting crowd that she was once a lady and deserves to be respected for what she was instead of ridiculed for what she has become. Socrates reminds his fellow citizens that this instrument of injustice and greed is, when administered fairly, the community's protection against injustice and greed. He treats the law as though it were being applied moderately, impartially, consistently, and unambiguously; the contrast to how it was actually being applied exposes its failure. Had Socrates merely rejected the law because it was at odds with his own purposes, he would have assisted Meletus in his poisoning of the city's health. By doing what he did instead, Socrates earned the right to request as his dying wish that a cock be sacrificed to Asclepius, the god of healing.

—In other words, Socrates was a good bureaucrat. He trusted in the law as a higher good that deserves an unstinting loyalty expressed in prudent, temperate, courageous, just actions on its behalf. That's an understanding of what it means to be faithful to a community that makes sense to me. Faith is a matter of loyalty and trust, but a Socratic faith is not trust and loyalty with respect to some utopian goal. It's faith in the agreed upon procedures conditioning such a utopian pursuit. The purpose of our nation, as of any political community, is to provide for the safety and prosperity of its citizens. So we should judge our statesmen and politicians by their ability to provide for such ends. But it's more important that we can trust them to follow the rules while doing so. Our secondary judgment about their effectiveness should be whether they were tough on crime, preserved the peace, lowered taxes, and reduced unemployment. Our primary judgment should be whether their actions were marked by prudence, moderation, justice, and courage; whether they were self-disciplined, willing to compromise, even-handed, and principled in how they went about doing whatever it was they did.

—So a college as a faithful community should have an academic ethos to which it is more loyal than it is to its purposes. At a college faithful to such an ethos, you would trust the faculty to judge your work by its quality and not by your beliefs, ethnicity, or gender. You would trust the curriculum to contain academic programs of the highest quality possible, given available resources and opportunities. Whether those programs might strike you as tiredly traditional or as vital fresh approaches, as tried-and-true workhorses or as faddish flashes in the pan, you would be sure they were worthwhile educational experiences because you would know the faculty had set conditions on what they will teach and how they will evaluate student work that were intended to assure uniform high quality. And these are conditions to which you would trust them to adhere at any cost.

—This sort of nonutopian, nonutilitarian faith is obviously based on the college's integrity. Because it has character, you trust it to keep faith with itself and therefore with you. It's an institution the worth of which is not based on the success of some venture it has undertaken, some over-the-horizon risk it has decided to run. If this college were a good school only because its average freshman SATs are over 600 and it places 95 percent of its seniors in professional and graduate programs of their choice, then if those achievement levels were to slip in any noticeable degree the school would no longer be any good. Those colleges that live by the expectations they kindle will perish when those expectations flicker out. But how sad for a college to have staked its reputation on something educationally unessential. Wouldn't it make more sense for the standard by which a college is evaluated to be based on the qualities it exemplifies right now, including a standard for how it goes about assessing and insisting upon those qualities?

—Being faithful to standards of educational conduct is hardly sufficient, though. There's such a thing as being loyal to what is essentially evil; there's honor even among thieves. The question is not whether the members of the community play by the rules but whether those rules are good ones. It's not enough to be committed to quality unless it is clear of what that quality consists. Procedures are good if they get you where you want to go, and for educational institutions where you want to go is to truth. What the college claims it is doing must satisfy generally accepted truth conditions. Colleges these days all announce their devotion to educational excellence but then debase its meaning to the point where anything they do they are willing to call excellent. When all the students earn an A, then A is no longer shorthand for a superior level of academic accomplishment. What's needed is a principle of falsifiability: what could possibly count as an instance of nonexcellence under your definition? What course of action could possibly not be in accord with your rules?

—You're making an argument that applies to scientific method. As you will recall, this method is a prudential practice, a set of rules that if followed is likely to prevent you from slipping into unrecognized error and thus likely to support your efforts to arrive at truth, at an adequate theoretical or practical understanding. And that's just the way it should be, but the pursuit of understanding by means of scientific method presupposes wonder, skepticism, curiosity, honesty, humility, perseverance, interpretive clarity, and logical articulateness. These are qualities that have to do with why a person should ever bother to be interested in truth. They are intellectual virtues that adhere to the pursuit of knowledge rather than to its attainment. They have to do with the love of wisdom as distinct from its possession: philosophers rather than sophists. We all aim to be sophists, to be sure, because it is important that our need to know be satisfied. But the condition of our journey from ignorance to truth is that it begin in wonder, proceed without illusion, and lay no personal claim to possess what it accomplishes.

—There's something freeing about that. If everything isn't riding on the success of my efforts, then despair or cynicism need not accompany failure. If the goal is worth striving for only if the goal is attained, then falling short of the mark renders the whole effort vain. But if the striving for that goal is what is worthwhile, then the effort will never be in vain. So I can set out optimistically, hoping for success but confident in the value of the venture whatever may come of it. Because the love of truth is more important than truth, I can hope even against all odds that I might reach it without my hope having to bear a weight too heavy for gossamer. Measure us, I say, by our hopes, by our loyalty to a quest that is its own justification, and let the consequences be damned.

—So hope doesn't have to be utopian. You aren't saying that to hope is to cross your fingers and bet that you'll succeed. Hope, rather, is the buoyant confidence born of the realization that trying to be successful is its own reward. Einstein spent the last years of his life attempting to come up with a unified field theory for the sciences and failed miserably. But I'm not prepared to say that those years were wasted. I certainly don't think the less of him for having failed. Quite the contrary. I respect him and celebrate his intellectual integrity. He had a vision he pursued hopefully and in which he persisted without falling victim to the various cheap solutions that must have been a constant temptation. It's too bad he didn't come up with an adequate theory, but it's better that because he hoped he would he was able to refuse the sirens' song.

—Okay, so a college is supposed to be faithful to a genuinely academic ethos and to nurture the hope that inquiry into the nature of things is self-justifying. But surely all of this energy, all of this conviction, can be justified only if the college manages to transmit such faith and such hope to its students. So let's not forget love. The love of wisdom and the love of our loyalties and our questings, yes. But love for our students at least as much, a love deep enough and strong enough to lead us to give ourselves unreservedly and without expectation of reward to the task of helping them become persons who love wisdom and loyalty and the quest for truth. But it's not monetary reward I'm saying we should not expect, because certainly one of the purposes of pursuing a career is to make a decent wage, and college faculty and administrators should be paid well for their efforts. It's easy, however, to earn a good salary without caring a fig about your students' moral and intellectual development and so contributing nothing toward it. Love is crucial, but it must be given like an old person planting trees: with no expectation of reaping a return. It's gratifying to receive the thank-yous of appreciative students at the end of a semester and the letters of gratitude written long years afterwards by former students only now fully grasping what your teaching and friendship had done for them. But most students will never remember to thank you, nor even realize your influence. Although if they turn out bad you'll be sure to be remembered, as Socrates was for having taught the traitor Alcibiades and for having undermined his students' faith in the gods and in the obviously better case.

—Ah, yes. Now I catch the drift of this conversation. Love completes the triad of Pauline virtues. Add in the classical ones, and we have the traditional seven cardinal virtues that characterize a good person: faith, hope, love, prudence, temperance, courage, and justice. Bureaucrats are defined by these virtues; colleges exemplify them; students learn in college environments to be good bureaucrats by acquiring them. And to adhere to the seven virtues consistently over the years, making them conditions of all one's conduct, that's character. The standard by which colleges should be judged is whether their graduates prove to be in their adult years persons of character, exemplifying in their conduct the moral practices so crucial to societal intercourse.

—Good heavens! How conformist can you be? You're saying that college is where you learn the rules of the game. It's where you pick up the interpersonal nuances and cultural subtleties you need in order to function effectively in your society, ones that will allow you to go on and succeed in life because you are so adept at how things are done. It makes college sound like a finishing school. You're saying that the standard by which a college should be judged is whether its graduates fit in. I might be tempted to argue that way, but I'm surprised you would.

—There's nothing conformist about embracing the cardinal virtues when you live in a culture like ours where those sorts of virtue are in disarray. We've lost any consensus in America regarding what general rules should govern our relationships. Anything put forward as a consensus belief or practice is immediately condemned as a masque for some special interest. And even when you merely suggest that we might explore the possibility of a consensus on something, people immediately wonder what's in it for you. What we've got in America these days is a lot of different cultures each with their own cherished moral practices, plus a wider society that is increasingly devoid of any moral practices whatsoever, an essentially anarchic society in which anything goes. So to claim that there are conditions governing intergroup relations and that people should be educated to respect those conditions and live in accord with them, that's quite radical and not conformist at all. It's like arguing for world government at a meeting chaired by Henry Kissinger.

—Colleges committed to an education in moral practices would be gadflies in our society. Because their commitment would be a subversive presence. You can imagine how upsetting it would be to reactionaries on the right if students were learning to be skeptical of the old hegemonic virtues of Puritan America and the middle-class entrepreneurial norms to which all we subsequent immigrants are to conform, into which we are to melt.

But imagine also how upsetting it would be to reactionaries on the left if students were learning to be skeptical of the new hegemonic virtues of multicultural America and the race-gender-class system of group rights by which we are all to be defined and our acceptable practices pigeonholed. And how upsetting it would be to almost all of us if students were learning to be skeptical of those who say the point in life is to get yours and to hell with rules.

—That sounds good, but it's a pious platitude. Colleges reflect their culture more than these idealistic comments are acknowledging. If American culture as a unifying reality is in disarray, so are its colleges. Look around the campus and what do you see? Fragmented academic studies and fragmented student life. Students live in residence halls segregated by race, gender, ethnicity, or special interest. Faculty work in buildings segregated by academic discipline. The campus is a vast anarchy of little groups, each with its own precious little practices, while the interconnections among them, the lifelines of the wider community, wither away.

—I don't see why the moral practices of the whole need be the traditional ones. America was probably never a monoculture even if it thought it was or at least that it ought to be. Now everyone is discovering the value of their differences and recognizing that some differences create fundamental incompatibilities which cannot be covered over by a facile rhetoric. But can't there nonetheless be a network of vital community-forming relationships among these different groups? And if people are interacting with others different from themselves, if difference doesn't mean isolation, and if isolation is impossible anyway in a world of CNN and the World Wide Web, then there must be conditions governing those interactions. The question shouldn't be whether Americans as a nation are governed by moral practices, but what those practices are and might become.

—Yes, but the moral practices of a community are only found in the actions they condition. They can't usefully be talked about in the abstract, and certainly, as we've all agreed, they can't be taught—although obviously they can be learned. By pointing out the incompatibility of anarchy and civilization, we would be calling attention to the need for unifying practices; by celebrating American pluralism, we would be rebuking the claim that conformity is the only alternative to anarchy. By respecting the moral practices already governing our technicolor world, we would be doing the Socratic thing by reminding ourselves of what we have known all along about the grounds of our unity.

—But don't forget to lighten up. An American college should be a microcosm of America, but because it is an artificial community in which the serious purposes of the nation have been dampened down, its special role is exploring ideals and other interesting alternatives playfully. Our colleges are constantly criticized for their excessive sensitivity to the clamor of special-interest groups all demanding newly invented special rights and privileges. But a campus should be a safe place to suspend our disbelief, to recognize these claims conversationally and to link and merge them experimentally, tentatively, playfully. It should also be, of course, a safe place to call those claims arbitrarily into question and to suspend our belief gratuitously in any claims to rights and privilege. The college's alleged overconcern with difference, its propensity to be politically correct, is quite fitting if it means that those on campus have a heightened awareness of the varieties of ways by which people share frameworks of understanding and action, and if it means they are involved playfully in the search for the higher loyalties appropriate to bureaucrats in a genuinely pluralistic society. It's wonderful if our students are busily at play, naively fashioning relationships in which unexpected moral practices might be disclosed as already at work.

—So we are agreeing that the essence of a college is as a learning environment for standards of conduct fitting for American twenty-first-century realities. Schools and colleges are unique in our society because they have this mediating, neutral, contextualizing character. They are places where people are supposed to learn how to function in the real world, and for us that's a world profoundly divided against itself. But exhilarating as all of this sounds, it also sounds impossible. Like trying to intervene in a fight between two angry armies by walking onto the battlefield unarmed and wearing a brightly colored shirt. We're supposed to stand for unity and civility in a world enamored by separation and animosity. So the idea, I take it, is to offer ourselves as a noble sacrifice. It doesn't sound very appealing.

—There are worse things than dying; there are worse things for a college than not surviving. But it's not obvious to me that we're talking about futile gestures. Battlefields were no place for compassion until Florence Nightingale came along, and now medics are routinely on the field of combat and the Red Cross accepted as a legitimate enforcer of conventions for the care of the wounded and prisoners. Medics get killed all the time, but so do soldiers and civilians. That even warfare might have moral practices is exhibited by the white trucks with their red cross, but the truth of these conditions is independent of whatever risk those who witness to them might happen to undergo.

—Having faith in the moral practices appropriate to a pluralistic community, hoping in their emergence as the framework for sustained communal relationships, motivated by a loving concern for people liberated by such a context to lives they can fully live, proceeding cautiously, impartially, flexibly, and courageously to implement the authority of those practices: these convictions are not things to be arrogantly brushed aside as though they were idle dreams. After all, the cardinal virtues are not inert passive facts to be arrayed on a shelf like so many collector dolls. They are adverbs that when exemplified in actions have the power to transform a world. Even our world.

—But if no one believes in these virtues, much less in the moral practices we would have them support, then what good are they? We can't make something out of nothing. I doubt that the moral practices we've lost are really recoverable anymore. Besides, colleges are too concerned with survival in these difficult times to have any time for such airy things as virtue and character.

—So where have you been all these pages? There you are once again insisting that survival is what is essential, that a college's purposes are its essence. But ends are extrinsic, remember? And the essence of a college lies elsewhere. I'd go over this point with you again, if that's what you want, but I'm afraid the pages have run out and we will have to stop. Perhaps another day. . . .

INFLUENCES

The rhetorical form for this chapter is suggested by what Jacques Derrida does in "Restitutions," the concluding section of *The Truth in Painting* (Chicago: University of Chicago Press, 1987), pp. 255–382. He writes what he calls a "polylogue": a number of different voices, not easily distinguished, engaged in a discussion about a Van Gogh painting and its interpretations. I've borrowed Derrida's literary device, but my use of it has nothing to do with his.

The four voices in this conversation, of course, are representatives of the college as Faithful Community, the college as Guild of Inquirers, the college as Resource Center, and the essentially purposeless college. Each voice in speaking reflects explicitly its appropriate framework of beliefs and practices, but I have not identified the voices by the usual convention of naming them in a bracketed identifier each time they speak. My hope is that this device will help draw the reader, wondering at times which voice might be speaking, deeper into the conversation.

I could have called this chapter a "quadrilogue" in imitation of Derrida's "polylogue." But I wanted not only to indicate the presence of four voices but also to suggest their convergence. The etymological meaning of "quadrivium" is "a place where four roads meet." This meaning survives in English only in adjectival form, and then only barely. The noun form survives only as referring to the medieval foursome of mathematical subjects—arithmetic, geometry, astronomy, and music—studied after the trivium. Of course I like this educational resonance to "quadrivial." And also the faint echo of "trivial," the etymological meaning of which, obviously, is "a place where three roads meet," hence "belonging to the crossroads," "a public place"; and therefore as an adjective, "commonplace," "ordinary," "unimportant." In this sense a college education is essentially trivial or, since it would mean the same thing, essentially quadrivial: having to do with the things that bring us together, that we have or should have in common—the moral practices conditioning our far from ordinary, uncommonly serious purposings. A quadrivial moment is when people traveling along the four ways meet. But their meeting brings no conclusion to their journeys. The roads meet, the travelers pause, conversing for a time, and then diverge. The better, I should hope, for having taken this brief respite from their important pursuits.

My continued reliance on Michael Oakeshott's *On Human Conduct* (Oxford: Oxford University Press, 1975) should be evident.

The latter part of this chapter revolves around the virtues of being a bureaucrat. I've taken my basic argument from Louis C. Gawthrop's interesting inaugural lecture as Tinbergen Professor at Erasmus University, *Ethics and Democracy: A Call for "Barefoot Bureaucrats"* (Rotterdam: Erasmus University, 1993). My use of Gawthrop's ideas is very much my own, however. Initially I dismissed Gawthrop's reasoning as an odd tour de force but then found myself returning to it again and again as its point finally began to get through to me.

My critique of the breakdown of moral practices in Western civilization draws from all the usual popular and scholarly materials, but one writer deserves to be singled out. G. M. Tamás, a Hungarian philosopher and Soviet-period dissident, contributed "A Clarity Interfered With" to Timothy Burns, ed., *After History? Francis Fukuyama and His Critics* (Lanham, Md.: Rowman and Littlefield, 1994), pp. 81–109. I have used Tamás's distinction between "utopia" and "evangel" without naming the second term. I have also benefited from Tamás's argument that both contemporary Western capitalism and socialism are forms of liberal utopianism, which in either form is drying up Western culture by draining it of any sense of public responsibility, leaving people free to an unrestrained but therefore inevitably nihilistic pursuit of their personal desires.

The point about the way poetry was used to help soldiers give sense to their World War I experiences is made by Paul Fussell, *The Great War and Modern Memory* (New York: Oxford University Press, 1975). The contrast to World War II is developed in his *Wartime: Understanding and Behavior in the Second World War* (New York: Oxford University Press, 1989).

Among recent attacks on intellectuals, faculty, and institutions of higher education, none has been more vicious than what appeared in a column by George F. Will, "Political Narcissism on Campus," *Washington Post,* 18 April 1996. Will's disdain of today's academics and liberals, who he thinks are the same, has become so strident of late that in this particular essay he irresponsibly links their inability to resist "identity politics," and thus their acceptance of "political narcissism," with their predecessors' inability to see any fault in Stalin, Mao, or Castro. I've used some of Will's examples and a bit of his rhetoric.

The Socratic references, of course, are to the *Crito* and the death scene from the *Phaedo.*

Index

AAUP 1940 Statement on Academic
    Freedom, 192
Abbott, Edwin, 84–86, 107
Academic disciplines, 178–79
    anthropology, 66, 137, 161
    biology, 66, 73
    chemistry, 66, 68–69, 73, 115, 136,
        193, 195–96
    economics, 66, 73, 161
    engineering and mechanical arts, 6,
        31, 73
    ethics, 37, 137–38, 194
    fine arts, 73, 90
    grammar, 26, 31–32, 73
    gymnastics, 25
    history, 66, 73
    humanities, 83, 166
    languages and literature, 6, 34, 73,
        195–96
    logic, 48, 55, 59, 62–65
    management, 6
    mathematics, 48, 59, 64, 73
    music, 26
    natural sciences, 26, 34, 47, 48,
        69–70, 83, 166, 194, 196
    philosophy, 25, 50, 51, 52, 66,
        78–80, 90, 193
    physics, 66, 73
    poetry, 66, 73, 90, 172, 193
    political science, 73, 193
    psychology, 66
    religion, 194
    social sciences, 73, 166
Actions, 126–33, 148–49
    adverbs of, 1, 126–28, 132, 133, 144,
        162, 182 (*see also* Practices)
    civic (*praxis*), 139–45
    means-ends structure, 114–19, 156,
        160, 169
    productive (*poiēsis*), 138, 139, 141,
        144
    purposeful, 140, 141
    sexual, 174–75
    theoretical (*theōria*), 138, 139, 141,
        144
Alcibiades, 216
Allan, George, 15n, 146, 185
Amherst College, 5
Anglicans, 17, 45
Aristophanes, 51, 182
Aristotle, 20, 27, 51, 54, 55
    on first principles, 61–62
    on practices, 10, 138–40, 146
    on women, 79, 80, 107
Athens
    and Isocrates, 19, 22–25, 24n, 28
    and Socrates, 183, 212–13
Atwater, Jeremiah, 36
Augustine, 96, 97
Austin, J. L., 184

223

Becket, Thomas, 29
Bentham, Jeremy, 117, 203
Bergson, Henri, 81, 107
Bernard of Chartes, 32
Bible
  Ecclesiastes, 118
  Genesis, 80, 107
Black Muslims, 80
Bob Jones University, 38
Boeing Aircraft Corp., 99–100
Brigham Young University, 37
Bureaucrats, 208–17, 221
Burns, Robert, 141

Central Oregon Community College,
  5
Cézanne, Paul, 157
Character. See Essence
Chartres, Cathedral at, 143
Cicero, 19, 28, 32
Citizenship, 187, 192, 199, 203,
  213–14
  and Faithful Community, 18,
    21–25, 27–28, 30–31, 33,
    34–37, 40, 44–45
  and Guild of Inquirers, 68, 72–75
  and moral practices, 121, 139–45,
    167–68, 169–74, 217–20
  and Resource Center, 81, 86–90,
    99–100, 102–3
Colleges and universities, positions
  administrators, 105, 173, 208–17,
    319
  faculty
    as guild masters, 72, 111, 117,
      120, 190, 193, 218
    as inculcating ends, 24–25,
      32–33, 71–72, 109
    at play, 165–67, 173, 203
    as resources, 91, 92, 104–6,
      196–97

and schools, 190–93
governing boards, 91–92, 109, 206
presidents, 92, 205–7
students, 196–97, 206, 208,
  216–17, 218
  in Faithful Communities, 25–26,
    32–33, 37–40
  in Guilds of Inquirers, 68–70,
    73–74
  in Resource Centers, 92–93,
    97–99, 103–104
  see also Teaching
Colleges and universities, programs
  curriculum, 25–27, 40, 72–74,
    93–94, 103–4, 106, 113, 158,
    161–62, 214
  democratic governance, 90–92
  outcomes, 81, 112–13, 114, 115,
    116, 175, 199–200, 202,
    205
Commonwealth. See Nation
Congregationalists, 45
Conrad, Joseph, 157
Conversation, 10, 153, 175–83, 185,
  219
  quadrivial, 11, 187–222
Cooper, Thomas, 36
Cromwell, Oliver, 13

Damascene, John, 54, 55
Definition, truth-functional, 63
Deighton, Len, 99–100, 108
Deontology, 117
Derrida, Jacques, 220
Descartes, René, 47–50, 54, 59
Desmond, William, 185
Dewey, John, 66, 106–7, 146,
  148–49, 184
Dickinson College, 5, 17–18, 36–37,
  38–39, 46, 79–80, 91, 107
Drew Seminary, 35

Dualism, 47, 48–49, 82–83, 84–86, 86–88
Dunne, Joseph, 146
Durban, John Price, 37

Education
    cost of, 2–3, 6
    electronic, 95–97, 103–4, 106
    models of, 8, 9–10, 113, 114, 151, 180
    liberal arts, 5, 40, 46, 74, 77–78, 82
    monastic, 9, 32–33, 53, 103
    oratorical, 9, 50
    philosophical, 9, 50
    practical, 81, 94–95, 100–103
    scholastic, 9, 50, 53, 75
Einstein, Alfred, 67, 216
Enlightenment, 8, 9, 110, 111, 132
Environmentalism, 171–72
Essence of
    a college
        no purpose of, 7–10, 114, 121–26, 134, 152, 169, 175, 177, 181, 183, 217, 219–20
        purpose of, 3, 6–7, 14–15, 17–18, 36, 40–41, 44, 68, 74–75, 99–100, 102, 114–21, 214
        modernity, 46–56
    a person, 20–21, 27, 29, 41, 75, 122–23, 124, 169–70, 177, 217
Ethnicists
    creative, 89–90
    tribal, 89
Euclid, 61–62, 65, 67

Faithful Community, 8, 10, 13–41, 71–72, 220
    ancient, 19–28, 41
    critique of, 35–38, 43–46, 51, 74,
        87, 109–10, 115–16, 119–20, 175
    medieval, 28–33
    modern, 33–39
    Puritan, 13–19
    purpose of, 13–15, 38–39, 114–15, 117, 179–80
Flatland, 84–86, 107
Frankel, Charles, 185
Fussell, Paul, 222

Gambino, Richard, 88–90, 108
Games, 130, 153–54, 156, 174, 184
    language, 154–55, 184
    rules of, 168–69, 209–10
Gates, Bill, 100
Gawthrop, Louis C., 221
Gogh, Vincent van, 220
Goshen College, 37
Great Awakening, 16
Grinnell College, 5, 79
Guild of Inquirers, 8, 10, 43–76, 220
    ancient, 50–52
    critique of, 87, 110–12, 117–18, 120, 175
    medieval, 53–56
    method, 49–50, 56–67
    modern, 46–50, 72–74
    purpose of, 114–15, 177–79
    rejecting Faithful Community, 43–46

Habits, 128, 130
Hanson, Norwood Russell, 70
Harvard University (Harvard College), 19
Hierarchy of knowledge. See Knowledge pyramid
Hobbes, Thomas, 196
Homo faber, 20, 139, 175
Homo loquens, 175

Homo ludens, 20
Homo oratiens, 20, 140, 175
Homo sapiens, 20, 139, 175
Hugh of St. Victor, 32n

IBM, 123–24, 125
Illich, Ivan, 9, 32n, 53–54, 95–97,
    103–4
Iowa State University, 77, 97–99, 108
Irving, Washington, 89
Isocrates, 13, 19–27, 19n, 30, 33, 35,
    38, 41, 50, 135

James, William, 86, 107
Jefferson, Thomas, 73
John of Salisbury, 19, 19n, 29–33, 35,
    39
Johns Hopkins University, 74
Junior-year-abroad programs, 161–62

Kant, Immanuel, 78, 79, 80, 117,
    133, 163, 185
Kimball, Bruce, 9, 19n, 40–41, 50,
    74–75
Kissinger, Henry, 217
Kneale, William/Martha, 62
Knowledge, experiential, 97–99
Knowledge pyramid, 56, 57, 61, 65,
    66, 67, 68–69, 70–71, 72, 75,
    142

Laws, Priscilla, 70
Leibniz, Gottfried Wilhelm von, 60,
    61
Leisure. *See* Playfulness
Lyotard, Jean-François, 86–88, 107,
    155, 184

McCarthy, Cameron, 90, 108
Manhattan Project, 99–100

Marx, Karl, 203
Master narratives, 86–88, 107, 184
Metaphysics, 1
Method, 175
    axiomatic, 56, 62–65, 67, 69
    Cartesian, 49–50, 56, 67
    Platonic, 52, 56
    Scholastic (Thomistic), 53, 54–56
    scientific, 49, 131–32, 190, 193,
        195, 215
        critique of, 111, 117–18, 120
        and Guild of Inquirers, 56–71,
            75, 179
    Methodists, 36–37, 45
Microsoft Corp., 99–100
Middle States Association of Colleges
    and Schools, 145
Miller, Howard, 15n
Miller, Perry, 14n
Miss Manners, 128
Mission. *See* Purposes
Modus ponens, 64
Morningside College, 5
Morrill Land-Grant Act, 74
Muhammad, Elijah, 80
Myth, ethnogenic, 44, 51

Nation, 207, 218
    Christian, 13–19, 34–36, 47, 89, 201
    democratic, 24–25, 47, 87, 90, 92,
        198–200
    pluralistic, 81–82, 88–90, 108,
        109, 167–74, 196–203,
        204–5, 218
New London Academy, 16
Newman, John Henry, 19, 33–35,
    33n, 38
Newton, Isaac, 65, 67
Nightingale, Florence, 219
Niles Register, 36

Oakeshott, Michael, 10, 146, 185, 221
Orators, 24–26, 32, 50, 51

Paradigm
  education, 68–74, 113
  knowledge, 56–67, 87
  political, 87
Parochial, critique of, 43–46, 110–14, 161
Paul, Saint, 175, 216
Phronēsis. See Practices, moral: good sense
Plato, 19, 20, 27, 50, 54, 135, 160
  Crito, 212–13
  Gorgias, 51–52
  Meno, 182–83
  Republic, 44–45
  Symposium, 181–82
  theory of Forms, 52, 157–60
Playfulness, 10, 149–56, 161, 162, 164, 165, 170, 180, 183, 219
  and leisure, 149–53, 165, 180
  uses of, 173–74
  see also Games
Poiēsis. See Actions, productive
Practices, 128–38, 212
  moral: good sense (*phronēsis*), 10, 133–83, 217–20
  prudential, 131–33, 134, 138, 144, 147, 153, 154, 165
    competence (*technē*), 139, 145
    wisdom (*sophia*), 139, 145
  reconciling, 170–74, 198–201
  see also Actions, adverbs of
Pratt, Linda Ray, 184
Praxis. See Actions, civic
Prejudice, 81
  class, 77–78, 196–97
  gender, 78–80, 196–97, 199
  race, 80–82, 196–97, 199
Presbyterians, 15–18, 37–38
Princeton University (College of New Jersey), 16, 36
Project Kaleidoscope, 70
Proof-tree, 61
Protagoras, 51
Puritans, 13–15, 17–19, 28, 35, 45, 209, 217
Purposes
  of a college, 6–7, 10, 124–25, 134–35, 175, 179, 183, 199, 205–6, 213–14
    as Faithful Community, 13–18, 34, 37–40, 44–46, 109, 114, 115–16, 119
    as Guild of Inquirers, 68, 74–75, 110–11, 114–15, 117–18, 120
    as Resource Center, 77–82, 90, 99–103, 112–13, 115, 118–19, 120, 176–77
  of a person, 158, 167, 169, 174, 162, 177, 213
  God's, 13–18, 28, 46

Quakers, 45
Quintilian, 19

Resource Center, 8, 10, 77–108, 220
  contractual, 100–106
  contrasted to other models, 77–90
  critique of, 112–13, 118–19, 120, 175
  high-tech, 95–97, 103–4, 106, 108
  holistic, 82–86, 88, 107
  open to all, 77–82, 86–92, 107, 108
  practical, 94–95, 97–100, 108
  purpose of, 115, 176–77
  student-centered, 92–94

Rilke, Rainer Maria, 142–43
Roman Catholics, 33–35, 47
Royce, Josiah, 169–71, 185
Rudolph, Frederick, 8, 9, 15n, 38, 46,
    72–73
Rush, Benjamin, 18

Scholastics, 50, 53, 54, 75
School
    board, 187, 191, 192, 201
    teachers, 188–94, 199, 200, 202–3
Smith, Adam, 202
Smith, John E., 185
Socrates, 24n, 44, 51, 181–83,
    212–13, 216, 222
Sophia (wisdom), 139, 141
Speech, persuasive, 19–27, 29–31,
    175
Standards, academic, 11, 40, 101,
    117, 187–222
Statements
    derivative, 60, 61
    protocol, 59–60, 61, 64, 65–66, 67
    tautological, 60, 61, 65
Strategic planning, 3–4
Suppe, Frederick, 70

Tamás, G. M., 221
Teaching and
    Faithful Community, 25–27, 32–35
    Guild of Inquirers, 53–54, 68–71
    moral practices, 1, 134–38, 145,
        157–60, 164–66, 200–204
    Resource Center, 92–93, 97–99,
        103–4
    standards, 188–90
Technē (competence), 139, 145
Tennyson, Alfred, 82–83, 107,
    136–37

Thébaud, Jean-Loup, 107, 184
Theōia. See Actions, theoretical
Thinking, 149
    critical, 172, 190, 203–5
    rational, 29–31, 48, 53, 75
Thomas Aquinas, 54–56
Tufte, Edward, 59

Universities. See Colleges and
    universities
University of Pennsylvania (College of
    Philadelphia), 17, 18
Updike, John, 89
Utilitarianism, 117

Vietnam War, 197
Virginia, University of, 74
Virtue
    bureaucratic, 210–17
    cardinal, 217, 220
    of a college, 121, 125, 126
    of a person, 31, 34, 37, 46, 182,
        121–23, 126, 215
Vision, 114
    nonutopianist, 206–7, 214–16
    utopianist, 205–6
Von Mises, Richard, 56

Wesleyan University, 37
Wheaton College (Illinois), 38
Whitehead, Alfred North, 107, 184,
    185
Will, George F., 222
Williams College, 8, 38
Williams, William Carlos, 147, 184
Wittgenstein, Ludwig, 60, 62, 66,
    107, 154, 185

Yale University (Yale College), 16